Taste of the Nation

Taste of the Nation

*The New Deal Search
for America's Food*

CAMILLE BÉGIN

University of Illinois Press
URBANA, CHICAGO, AND SPRINGFIELD

An earlier version of chapter 3 appeared as "Partaking of Choice Poultry Cooked à la Southern Style: Taste and Race in the New Deal Sensory Economy," in *Radical History Review* 2011, no. 110: 127–53. © 2011, MARHO: The Radical Historians' Organization, Inc. All rights reserved. Republished by permission of the present publisher, Duke University Press.

Library of Congress Cataloging-in-Publication Data
Names: Bégin, Camille, 1984– author.
Title: Taste of the nation : the New Deal search for America's food / Camille Bégin.
Description: Urbana : University of Illinois Press, [2016]
Series: Studies in sensory history
Includes bibliographical references and index.
Identifiers: LCCN 2015041915 (print)
LCCN 2015051453 (ebook)
ISBN 9780252040252 (cloth : acid-free paper)
ISBN 9780252081705 (pbk. : acid-free paper)
ISBN 9780252098512 (ebook)
Subjects: LCSH: Food—United States—History—20th century. | Diet—United States—History—20th century. | Food writing—United States—History—20th century. | Food habits—United States—History—20th century. | United States—Social life and customs—1918–1945.
Classification: LCC TX360.U6 B44 2016 (print)
LCC TX360.U6 (ebook)
DDC 641.30097309/04—dc23
LC record available at http://lccn.loc.gov/2015041915

Pour Christophe et Sylvie,
Paul et Léopold,
et grand-mère Geneviève.

Contents

Acknowledgments

It took ten years, numerous conversations around splendid meals, and count-less kilometers looking at the blue bottom of a chlorine-smelling, neon-lit swimming pool echoing with the splashes of swimmers for this book to take its present shape. In the process, I have benefited from the intellectual and affective generosity of mentors, friends, and family.

This book was once a project shaped by the intellectual rigor and kind sup-port of the University of Toronto History Department's faculty. Rick Halpern introduced a twenty-one-year-old French exchange student to U.S. histori-ography; he opened the doors of academia and facilitated my journey. His steady belief in my ability to contribute to the field arguably changed the course of my intellectual and personal life. None of these pages would have been written without Daniel Bender's mentorship. He led me through his-torical scholarship with empathy, timely dares to move through research and writing, and encouragements to explore my intellectual curiosities wherever they might lead. He backed me with friendship and institutional support during and beyond graduate school, and his vision of the historian's craft will continue to shape my work. Elspeth Brown, Steve Penfold, Alison Smith, and Franca Iacovetta read introductions, chapters, and full drafts, opening new avenues of inquiry and pushing me to sharpen my thoughts and writ-ing. Franca's feminist mentorship during the many hours (days) we worked with the organizing team of the 16th Berkshire Conference on the History of Women, Gender, and Sexuality helped me navigate the shift from graduate school to a career in academia.

Scholars of food and food history shared their expertise and welcomed me to their quite fantastic world. Jeffrey Pilcher's scholarship set a high, wonder-ful standard to emulate, and I am thankful for his help trying to get there.

Donna Gabaccia's writings and encouragements were the sparks that made this book possible. Receiving her shrewd comments (and questions) at the end of the process was a wonderful way to close the circle. Brainstorming sessions with Krishnendu Ray simultaneously grounded and refreshed my thoughts. The international network of scholars who have gathered around the Culinaria Research Centre at the University of Toronto Scarborough offered tremendous support, and I enjoyed the thoughtful camaraderie of Jean Duruz, Jo Sharma, Ken Macdonald, and Irina Mihalache. I presented parts of this book at conferences, workshops, and summer institutes. Many panelists, fellow researchers, and audience members astutely commented on the project over the years. I would particularly like to thank panel discussants Amy Bentley, Erica Peters, and David Sutton, who pushed me to further my arguments.

David Howes and Mark Smith's powerful sensory prose inspired this book. Their support made its writing not only possible but also a deeply satisfying intellectual adventure. David Howes's attention to interdisciplinary scholarship made the theoretical underpinnings of my argument much more sound than they would have been otherwise. With reading and writing advice, he cleared the path as I took my own "sensory turn." I spent two years working on this book as a Social Sciences Humanities and Research Council of Canada postdoctoral fellow at the Centre for Sensory Studies in the Sociology and Anthropology Department at Concordia University. At the Centre, conversations with Ruth Barcan, Constance Classen, Nathalie Doonan, and David Szantos widened my methodological and analytical frameworks. Mark Smith's early support for the project enabled me to keep weaving a historical narrative at the edges of food and sensory studies. As my editor, he steered the manuscript with kindness and resolve so that I can hope it stands with the other volumes in the Studies in Sensory History series at the University of Illinois Press. Tracey Deutsch provided me, twice, with the most thoughtful review an author could dream of. She understood the goals of this book to their essence, and every one of her remarks helped clarify and improve its argument and narrative. An anonymous reviewer read the manuscript with an eye to multisensory arguments while posing broad, comparative questions that opened the reach of the book. Some of these paths are left for readers to explore, and all shortcomings remain mine.

Friends, many historians, and food studies scholars themselves have sat through presentations, read drafts of various quality, scanned archival material, and shared their expertise, sometimes of a grammatical nature. Food and drinks may also have been involved. I am particularly thankful to Sarah Amato, Laurie Bertram, Nathan Cardon, Lindsay Brittan, Eugénie Denarnaud, Helen Dewar, Stéphanie Dubertret, Jennifer Evans, Susan Foster, Holly Karibo, Paul Lawrie, Nadia Jones-Gailani, Jodie Giesbrecht, Stéphane Eloïse Gras, Michael Kogan, Vanessa McCarthy, Meghan Marian, Peter Mersereau, Brad Miller, Ian Mosby, Rebecca O'Neill, Jared Toney, Natacha Postel-Vinay, Benjamin Potruff, Ian Rocksborouth-Smith, Jackie Rohel, Dan Rosenthal, Christy Spackman, and Candace Sobers. New and old friends took the loneliness and stress out of research trips and conference stays. In Washington, D.C., Nehama Babin and Sarah Rosenthal welcomed me to their home; in New York, Violetta Donini, Steven Deheeger, Clémence Bégin, and Krishnendu and Rudra Ray shared their apartments and, I am thankful, took me out. In New York and Chicago, the Deheeger family remained true to its reputation for hospitality.

Some acknowledgment truism holds true: Nick Neufeld never dreamed he would ever hear so much about the Federal Writers' Project. At least it was in a French accent. His attentive love saw me through days of writing in Toronto, Montréal, and Paris. Far or close, he makes me smile.

When asked as a child what I would want to do when I grew up, I use to invariably answer: *historienne.* I would not have become one without the love of my family. They provided me with transatlantic emotional support, flew me back home whenever was needed, and never doubted my ability to finish this project. Christophe, Paul, and Léopold Bégin kept me up to date with French cultural, political, and sports life. As for the topic of this book, it owes much to two exceptional *cuisinières*, cookbook collectors, and *parisiennes*, my mother and grandmother, Sylvie Laurent-Bégin and Geneviève Laurent-Bizos, whom I miss dearly. This book is for the five of them.

Introduction

Sensing Food in the New Deal Era

In the early spring of 1941, Bessie A. Carlock, a worker with the Arizona Federal Writers' Project (FWP), traveled from Phoenix along Black Canyon Road through the blossoming desert to reach Horse Thief Basin, where she was to eat and write about a much-anticipated "real western dinner." She was not disappointed, nor was her reader. Her host for the day, Jenny Hayes, "deep-set eyes, sun-tanned almost leathery skin and a firm determined chin," put together an enticing spread for her guest and regular boarders: "Great, round biscuits—one wondered if they could dispose of one and ended up by eating three—a bowl of fresh sweet home-made butter, green onions arranged like a bouquet in a tall spoon holder, corn-bread in squares the size and thickness of a good sized cake of laundry soap, brown and delicious as any mother used to make, a great earthen mixing bowl of navy beans, (the best [she] ever tasted), a dish of cold slaw." The "piece de resistance" was a stack of locally butchered beefsteaks cooked in a way "that would have done justice to a Waldorf-Astoria Chef." At the end of the meal, Jenny set a "yellow bowl of syrupy dried peaches" on the table. Bessie and Jenny did not know each other prior to this meal. The fledging writer was in Horse Thief Basin on an assignment for the state-sponsored FWP latest project, a book to be titled, simply and efficiently: *America Eats*.[1]

With the *America Eats* project, Bessie and dozens of others in every corner of the country launched into a search for America's regional food. She put the lean years of the Great Depression behind her as she rejoiced in the abundance of this American backcountry cornucopia. Bessie's gustatory experience harkened back to a past, dreamed rugged life of pioneer settlers while also opening up possibilities for a tastier present. A three-hour car trip unlocked a world of intense sensory experiences, from the clatter of the heavy cutlery to the screeching of the crude dining room chairs. Bessie's appreciation of the "camp chuck" meal and the bold coffee that punctuated it—"it *was* coffee, rich and black with a delicious aroma and an exhilarating flavor"—contrasted with her colleagues' repeated complaints about unsatisfactory gustatory encounters with industrial food and coffee "dripotated in contraption[s] that look[ed] like a glass urn in a museum."[2] Their collective search for America's local food explored the sensory discrepancy between bold, pleasurable flavors and industrial blandness.

The *America Eats* book would have been a novel exercise in nation building, using food, the senses, and local cuisines to reassert American identity after a decade of economic depression and in wartime mobilization. Ultimately, this search yielded more frustrations and contradictions than answers and tells us as much, if not more, about memories of repasts, dreams of feasts, and present sensory frustrations than about what Americans actually ate in the late 1930s and early 1940s.[3] This in part explains why the anticipated publication stayed on the drafting table, its material filed away at the Library of Congress. Though the FWP's search for America's regional food stalled, the culinary material collected in the process provides a unique vantage point to explore how food made sense in the New Deal era.

New Deal Food Writing

Taste of the Nation is a cultural, social, and sensory history of New Deal food writing: the multisensory culinary material produced by Bessie and her co-workers while employed by the FWP. A state-sponsored cultural agency providing relief to white-collar workers as part of the Works Progress Administration (WPA), the FWP produced, from its creation in 1935 to its end in 1942, a variety of publications and records filled with culinary remarks and sensory vignettes. The agency developed a bestselling tourist guidebooks series, the American Guide Series; successfully recorded regional and group folklore as well as oral histories, most famously ex-slave narratives; and documented working and immigrants' lives in the United States. Throughout, workers produced comforting snapshot pictures aimed at providing cultural confidence to a country in the midst of one of the worst economic depression of its history and giving legitimacy to the new political, social, and economic order of the liberal New Deal state. The agency's unabashed goal was to reconcile cultural pluralism and a potentially xenophobic romantic nationalism to present "America as a culture still in the process of becoming."[4] Food, with its simultaneously prosaic and symbolic character and its ability to conjure up the past through sensory re-enactment, was a fitting vehicle for the realization of this program. The archives of the FWP's Folklore Project and American Guide Series are rich in culinary essays while more local undertakings explicitly focused on food, such as the New York–based *Feeding the City*. Culinary notations peppered the entire FWP's production, but New Deal food writing reached its pinnacle with the groundbreaking *America Eats* project launched in the late 1930s and revived in the summer and fall of 1941.

America Eats would be the FWP's culinary crown. It was to provide "a general introduction on the development of American cookery," organized in five regional essays. The tone would be "light, with emphasis on human interest and on the ever-absorbing divisions of opinion concerning ingredients and cooking methods." Potential competitors? "None."[5] Indeed, such an exercise in narrative food writing was a novel endeavor. Cookbooks, recipe pamphlets, restaurant reviews, radio shows, scientific and pseudoscientific nutrition advices were all familiar to American audiences. A lively, ethnographic, and accessible account of food inviting readers to vicariously eat and travel was something new. *Gourmet* magazine, the first publication to be fully dedicated to this genre of food writing, only started publication as the FWP wound down after the U.S. entrance in World War II. The FWP experimented with a category of food writing that now dominates blogs, glossy magazines, and best-seller lists.[6] By the mid-1930s few had cared to record Jenny Hayes's cooking; New Deal food writing, in the vein of Bessie Carlock's prose, aimed at filling that gap. In the course of their search, the FWP's composite staff recorded, organized, and archived an expansive body of culinary knowledge, sensory information, and cultural attitudes woven around food. They initiated a new way of writing about food.

Food was a topic central to the Great Depression. The soup kitchen lines of the early 1930s, though their number decreased after the consolidation of New Deal relief in 1935, remained anchored in the nation's memory. Hunger appeared as a leitmotif of a number of Depression-era novels and photographs.[7] Dorothea Lange's iconic image *Migrant Mother*, taken after a cold snap ravaged a pea crop near Nipomo, California, and left Dust Bowl migrant workers out of work, is only the tip of the iceberg of such imagery.[8] To what extent Americans' health and diet suffered during the Great Depression is unclear, though. Unemployed workers and their families lacked food, but the majority of malnourished Americans in the decade, such as black and white southern sharecroppers, were victims of an endemic poverty predating the Crash.[9] Somewhat easier to appraise and appreciate than malnutrition are the sacrifices millions of Americans made to prevent hunger. Meridel Le Sueur, an FWP worker in Minnesota whose literary explorations of working lives in the Depression are some of the most effective testament to the period's hardships, brought these sacrifices to the forefront of her 1932 "Women on the Breadlines" short story. Her account of an employment bureau's waiting room depicts how the absence of work, hunger, and the will to protect their families led women to forfeit dreams and dignity.[10] The breadlines of the early 1930s symbolically embodied broader interrogations about the viability of the capitalist market economy and its increasing role in determining American diets and tastes. This is best seen in the outraged reactions to the New Deal Agricultural Adjustment Act (AAA) of 1933, which aimed at raising the price of agricultural commodities by inducing farmers to destroy their surplus. What was the logic that enticed a country no longer able to properly feed large parts of it population to kill six million piglets and pour milk into the gutter?[11]

Bessie Carlock and her colleagues' culinary search was part of a larger, diffuse interest from the New Deal state in documenting food. The FWP was one of the branches of the New Deal's art programs, which employed writers but also photographers, painters, and theater professionals to document the hardships of the Depression, the necessity of the federal government's relief effort, and American life in general. The photographers of the Farm Security Administration, for instance, developed an iconic documentary style and produced some of the harrowing images of poverty and malnourishment for which the period is remembered.[12] In the 1936 play *Triple-A Plowed Under*, Federal Theater Project's units from New York to Los Angeles and Chicago staged "the national drama of agriculture" and proposed, as an answer to the paradox of want amid capitalist plenty, a stronger farmer-consumer connection mediated by the federal government.[13] The art programs then also offered alternatives to the images of breadlines and hunger and proposed a more optimistic vision of the country's food production capacities, ranging the gamut from consumer empowerment to the celebration of American pastoralism and the praising of scientific agriculture. In the large murals that still adorn dozens of U.S. post offices and public buildings, the Federal Art Project spurred nationalist feelings and, using an agrarian imagery deeply rooted in U.S. political culture, showcased a land of plenty in which men's work and women's homemaking tempered the uproar of capitalist modernity. These visions of an idealized rural life represented a stable past and a hopeful future that eradicated its missing center, "the calamitous present."[14] The upholding of conservative gender roles and racial hierarchies bolstered the ideological charge of this iconography.[15] In New Deal food writing, the FWP crafted its own counternarrative to hunger as it aimed at boosting morale and nationalist sentiment during the economic downturn, and, as the project grew in the early 1940s, mobilized the senses in the war effort.

A state-sponsored project, New Deal food writing ambitioned to provide a national culinary narrative filled with reassuring images of traditional regional food. *America Eats*, the largest FWP's food-focused project, was not to be a cookbook but rather a series of five overarching regional essays entertainingly introducing readers to the taste of broadly defined regions: clambakes in the Northeast, church suppers in the Midwest, family reunions in the South, game diners in the Far West, barbecues in the Southwest. The project's regional organization was in tune with the interwar revival of regionalism, a "multi-accented slogan" that ranged from white supremacist to left-wing radical groups.[16] It also meant that New Deal food writing depended on dialectic relationships between regional and national cuisines, tradition and modernity. The field of food studies offers numerous examples of how "traditional" regional cuisines are often mobilized, and in fact elaborated, though modern nation-building projects that hold diversity as a proof of strength and unity.[17] More specific to the American case is the unmistakably Creole character of regional cuisines; cuisines that are artifacts of local encounters between the flora, fauna, and inhabitants of the "New" and "Old" Worlds and between the traditions brought with them by various immigrant groups, including forced migrants, to their new American settings.[18] However, starting in the late nineteenth century, the industrialization of the U.S. food system challenged the cultural and sensory supremacy of regional food. The perceived national standardization of taste, the disappearance of "traditional cookery," and the ever-increasing "mass production of food-stuffs and partly cooked foods" in fact triggered *America Eats*. From its inception, the project was a response to change that held regions as realms of nostalgia and hope for a better future.[19]

To counteract anxieties about the impact of industrial food and the economic downturn on American culture and senses, New Deal food writing nostalgically celebrated culinary and sensory stability. *America Eats* would, for instance, focus not so much on home kitchens, deemed overrun by the products of the food industry, but on community gathering and public eating, which purportedly upheld culinary traditions. This nostalgic culinary narrative had widespread gendered consequences. When explaining the contemporary "decline in food standards," FWP workers pointed to members of the "weaker sex" who "have seldom had as great an interest in food as men have had," but who, "when housekeeping was the only career open to them and compliments on satisfying meals were the chief rewards for service . . .

spent much of their time in shopping for choice foodstuffs, mixing, beating, paring, boiling, and baking." Once in the workforce, they abandoned their kitchens and relied on industrial foodstuffs, leading the "eating public" to be "gradually accustomed to the ready-made meal" and to lose "appreciation of the finer product."[20] In this logic, community bake-off and public meals were sites of resistance to the inroads of industrial products, where none would dare serving store-bought confections. The Depression was a decade of male anxieties, as many could not fulfill the customary role of breadwinner and as female employment increased. Nostalgically remembering meals that FWP workers' great-grandmothers would have recognized as food was an efficient way to restrict women to the domestic sphere and clearly stated the "gendered limits" of the possible.[21] Celebration and blame were two sides of the feminine ideal promoted in New Deal food writing.

In celebrating pre-industrial foodways, the FWP propelled a renewed and unresolved appraisal of the role of ethnic and raced groups in the making of American regional cuisines. An animated debate ran through the project's ranks as to what food but also whose taste would be considered "American" food. Would Jenny Hayes's Spanish-speaking neighbors be part of the FWP's celebration of southwestern culinary traditions? Responses were varied and ambiguous: while most of Bessie Carlock's co-workers in the Arizona FWP recognized Mexican food as "the taste of the Southwest," they did not unanimously open up the fold of cultural and social citizenship to Spanish speakers. If essays often foregrounded the taste and food of ethnic and race groups as regional sensory heritage, this was an unintended consequence of the push to document local pre-industrial food rather than its aim.

The FWP ambivalence toward what we would now call "ethnic food" reflected changes in the legal taxonomy of race and a new popular understanding of racial difference. Where categories of "color," "nationality," "complexion," and "race" had previously co-existed, the interwar period witnessed the polarization of race. While several groups were incorporated into definitions of whiteness (Southern and Eastern Europeans, some Near Eastern groups), others became, or were reinforced, in their role as racial "others" (African Americans, Mexican Americans, Asian Americans), thus changing each group's strategies for integration in the U.S. cultural and political landscape. Though the quota system that drastically reduced European immigration in the mid-1920s can be considered as the high point of anti-immigrant nativism, the dearth of arrivals also contributed to the whitening of Southern and Eastern European "new immigrants."[22] New Deal policies, union mobilization, and the development of a national mass market of consumer and cultural goods further converged to redraw the boundaries of race and class during the Depression.[23] The category of whiteness expanded through working-class solidarity and the emergence of the concept of ethnicity as "a new brand of difference whose basis was cultural" at the same time that racial lines hardened, for instance, in terms of residential segregation.[24] Yet, the conceptualization of two separate notions of (colored) races and (white) ethnicity only clearly occurred in the postwar era, and the student of the 1930s is left observing the "messy" process of their differentiation.[25] New Deal food writing was no exception: the anchoring of race and ethnicity at the core of the project was fraught with ambiguities, and the FWP could extol multiethnic food cultures while policing racial lines.

The FWP was a pyramidal organization with a series of administrative levels, making its daily work arduous, its legacy ambiguous, and its archive a fascinating space of debate about what constituted "American" food and taste in the 1930s. The FWP was directed first by playwright Henry G. Alsberg and then, starting in 1939, by John D. Newsom, author of a military-themed novel and a more effective, if less creative, administrator than his predecessor.[26] The director, based in Washington, worked closely with federal editors with diverse profiles, such as folklorist Benjamin Botkin, African American poet Sterling Brown, or well-traveled social worker Katharine Kellock, to outline and oversee the agency's various projects. Kellock led the team that supervised *America Eats*. Throughout her work with the FWP, her education in history, social sciences, and journalism at Columbia University after World War I shaped her sense of mission to describe a "vigorous past" that also pointed toward a "credible future."[27] Federal staffers were ethnically diverse, educated, liberal New Dealers, immersed in the cultural politics of the time. Most had been directly affected by the Depression, but they did not need to qualify for relief to become part of the FWP; in fact, Kellock left a higher-paying job with the Resettlement Administration to join the agency. They were the frontline of what Michael Denning has identified as the 1930s "Cultural Front," the alliance of a wide array of organizations and cultural participants who profoundly "labored" the national mood toward a social-democrat ethos in the wake of the Great Depression and the communist's Popular Front strategy, setting the stage for what Denning, after writer Michael Gold, called a "second American Renaissance."[28]

The federal staff collaborated with state directors and fieldworkers in the FWP's decentralized state bureaus to research and document regional folklore, histories, and cuisines. The ideal state director was, according to Kellock, "a combination of administrator, diplomat, encyclopedist, creative writer, personnel supervisor, and publicity man."[29] Few efficiently combined these roles. A minority were creative writers; most had strong local ties and political convictions.[30] Fieldworkers were an even more diverse lot; they were up-and-coming novelists and short novelists, clerks, librarians, copywriters, pulp writers, local reporters, or college graduates. As FWP scholar Christine Bold puts it, "For some . . . being labeled a writer was a familiar experience, for some a long-sought dream, for some simply a means of surviving the Depression."[31] All had experienced the breadlines, and the FWP's vocation was to provide relief work; this explains why, from the start, the guidelines for evaluating who would be considered a "writer" had been necessarily vague and inclusive. Few were talented and few cared to publicize their involvement in the FWP relief work after World War II. Only a minority continued to write and publish. This anonymity puts evident limits on writing a social history of the FWP.[32] Who was Bessie A. Carlock, the avid eater and writer behind the description of the Arizona "camp chuck" dinner? Is she the same person as Bessie Estelle Carlock who, in 1935, self-published a volume of poems, *Home-Spun Verse*, in Glendale, Arizona? Did she continue writing after the 1930s? Though such elements are often tricky to assess, the occasional mention of names provides clues as to the workers' identities, notably racial, ethnic, and gendered.[33]

Responding to the *America Eats* book proposal, a publisher ironically remarked that "one of the men in his office raised the question of why these WPA fellows should know anything about eating"; indeed, "he thought they were always supposed to be hungry." Unknowingly, this publisher pointed to one of the FWP's main assets in its quest for American food. More than their capacity as writers, the common experiences of FWP workers as impoverished white-collar workers in the Depression rendered their culinary and sensory notations a rich source for sensory historical research. Their economic situation in the Depression made them part of the working class; yet, their ambitions and education could make them aspire to a middle-class status. The recurrent use of French culinary expressions such as "à la," "en sauce" or references to haute cuisine hotels and restaurants in their culinary essays, hint at this class position. When Bessie Carlock compared Jenny Hayes's "camp chuck" to the food served at the Waldorf Astoria, she at once elevated the food and created a class distance between the cook and herself.

The social diversity of the FWP staff meant that federal editors, state directors, and field workers in each locale tended to have disparate visions of the nation and understandings of the FWP mandate, including when it came to writing about the apparently innocuous topic of food. Close attention to regional differences unveils how the New Deal's inclusive civic ideal often took on racially exclusive overtones and upheld prescriptive gender roles.[34] The elaboration of *America Eats* brought to light a series of internal dissensions. In particular, the federal editors' decision to "not give much dishes of recent foreign importation" sparked debates about who *America Eats* would and should document.[35] When was the c arrival to be considered part of "American" food traditions? Wha the space devoted to ethnic and race groups in the FWP's assessment of regional foodways? Divergences on what "American" culinary traditions might be stalled the project and ensured that the New Deal search for America's food remained an unfinished project. The FWP culinary archive is neither a recipe depository nor a comprehensive survey of all foods eaten in the United States during the Great Depression. Rather than a reified list of ingredients, this archive is a dynamic repertoire of taste and a site of debate about the evolution of American foodways. It is a repository of sensory memories, preferences, and prescriptions. Searching for America's regional cuisines, the FWP left behind a large corpus of sources on food and taste documenting the cultural and sensual worlds of the 1930s and early 1940s.

Sensory Economies

To explore New Deal food writing, I consider the FWP culinary archive as both a source and a subject and use taste as my primary category of analysis.[36] The analysis focuses not only on the content but also on the making of the archive and how the FWP search for American food produced sensory knowledge in the New Deal period. Taste can be apprehended in various ways: as a physiological attribute, a social act of distinction, or the inherent—and static—specificity of a dish. In the following pages, I consider taste as the result of a process of circulation in specific historical and textual contexts and consider taste as part of larger networks of sensory, cultural, social, affective, and economic exchange that I label "sensory economies." New Deal food writing provides a window into 1930s sensory economies, understood as, at once, sensory regimes, textual representations, social relations, and networks of value creation.

The notion of sensory economies builds on several decades of historical and anthropological research on the social and cultural life of the senses. Scholars of the "sensory turn" have powerfully demonstrated that the sensory appreciation of the world around us is not only a natural experience but that our ways of sensing are also determined by cultural, social, and political formations.[37] Investigating past regimes of sensory value requires studying changes in the organization of the human sensorium, the "economy of the senses," such as shifts in the hierarchy and meaning of the senses over time and across cultures.[38] As well, understanding past sensory experiences of food involves exploring the multisensory character of human perception and interaction between the senses. The sense of taste is, at any given historical period, part of larger sensory environments also defined by sights, sounds, smells, and touch. The taste of Bessie Carlock's country dinner cannot be dissociated from the blooming desert landscape she drove through and described emphatically, or from the sight and feel of the "rheumatic warped hands" of the cook, "cracked open" by the quotidian use of spring water.

Engaging with New Deal Food writing to compose a social and cultural history of taste in the 1930s means accounting for the political nature of the archive and "sensing in between the lines."[39] It means exploring the articulation of sensory experiences through clichés, including stigmatizing racial and gendered stereotypes; appreciating how rhetorical figures shape perceptions; and carefully contextualizing sensory notations to unveil their capacities at both policing and undermining social construction of race, gender, and class.[40] For instance, comparing "camp chuck" to a Waldorf Astoria meal, Bessie Carlock did not show a particularly inventive literary style: many of her fellow FWP workers took the New York hotel as their point of reference. But while showing off her worldliness and "good taste," she contributed to subvert cultural norms by establishing an equivalency between female backcountry boardinghouse cooking and the work of French-trained male chefs. Bessie's multisensory appraisal engaged with the cultural revaluation of local, simple food as the moral bedrock of the nation central to the New Deal search for America's food. Unearthing past ways of sensing and analyzing their textual expressions and representations allows accessing felt engagements with value systems in which sensory, material, moral, and cultural appreciation blend.

Sensory economies recover premier meanings of the word economy as "a way of exercising power and accumulating knowledge" entangled in social relations.[41] The process of documentation and celebration central to the project of New Deal food writing produced and managed multisensory and culinary knowledge about the nation's regions, their inhabitants, and their ways of sensing. Exploring the process of sensory knowledge accumulation means probing how the interaction between federal editors, state directors, local field workers, and their informants structured the collection, management, and organization of a sensory archive. In his analysis of the origins of the notion of economy, Timothy Mitchell notes that only in the mid-twentieth century did "the economy" as "a free-standing object," rather than an action, emerge. Starting in the 1930s, the economy became a "field of operation for new powers of planning, regulation, statistical enumeration and representation" of which the New Deal state's sociotechnical programs, whether building the nation's infrastructure building or recording American culture (including foodways), are an incarnation. Such programs were key to the emergence of the economy as a spatially bounded (national economy) object in which money circulates, susceptible to growth, and regulated by the state. Mitchell points out that "through these novel forms of political rationality and practice it became possible to imagine the economy as a self-contained sphere, distinct from the social, the cultural, and other spheres" such as the household.[42] Recovering economy as a way of acting, of producing knowledge and managing it, then, contributes to interdisciplinary efforts to "understand the economy as sets of entanglements," entanglements that are material and financial but also social, cultural, intimate, affective, localized, and sensory.[43]

Considering economies as actively produced sets of entanglements does not mean disengaging with contemporary understandings of economic exchanges, and I deploy the notion of sensory economies to probe not only the value of the senses but also how the senses create value. Economic relations have classically been understood as processes of production, distribution, exchange, and consumption that turn sensuous objects into valued, abstract commodities, including food commodities. Along with sensory anthropologist David Howes, I consider food commodities as "not just utilitarian articles or suprasensible items of exchange . . . but rather potent bundles of sensory symbolism and social relations."[44] Bessie Carlock's sensory pleasure, social superiority, and cultural appreciation combined to elevate Jennie Hayes's "camp chuck" cooking as an object of sensory sightseeing. But Bessie's rustic meal was not only a survival of the past narrated on a nostalgic mode, it was how Jennie made a living and would become an object of culinary tourism that *America Eats* intended to put on the nation's menu. Once imbued with sensory and moral value, it could transcend its primary function, feeding hungry miners, to become an object of consumption, a tourist commodity. An appreciation of "the ways in which the sensory signs of commodities can encode crucial social values" allows exploring the valorization of food commodities through practices of sensory differentiation along and exchange across class, race, gender, and generational lines.[45]

A detour via the world of fiction illuminates how sensory economies function. African American writer and FWP worker Richard Wright's 1940 *Native Son* is a classic, powerful fictional account of the interwar Great Migration of black southerners to the northern metropolis. The novel sheds light on the psychological impact of migration and segregation (whether dictated by Jim Crow laws or de facto) on black Americans. A short scene sees a liberal white couple ordering Bigger, the novel's African American main character and their chauffeur, to drive them to a place that serves "*real*" black food (read: fried chicken) on Chicago's South Side. Wright relates the exchange:

"Say, Bigger," asked Jan, "where can we get a good meal on the South Side?"

"Well," Bigger said, reflectively.

"We want to go to a *real* place," Mary said, turning to him gayly.

"You want to go to a night club?" Bigger asked in a tone that indicated that he was simply mentioning names and not recommending places to go.

"No; we want to eat."

"Look, Bigger. We want one of those places where colored people eat, not one of those show places."

What *did* these people want? When he answered his voice was neutral and toneless.

"Well, there's Ernie's Kitchen Shack . . ."

In this scene the couple looks forward to an exotic and authentic culinary experience; they do not want to be driven to one of the popular whites-only nightclubs. All the while, Bigger is at a loss to understand why they would want to taste such a down home southern dish as fried chicken. The only thoughts that the newly arrived black southern migrant can gather are: "What *did* these people want?"[46]

In *Native Son*, fried chicken does not taste the same for Bigger as it does for his employers. The white couple envisions fried chicken as a vehicle for culinary tourism. They want to buy into the sensory experience of blackness for the evening. For Bigger, the dish is an everyday staple for survival anchored in regional identity. The couple's desire to taste authentic black food relies on the commodification of blackness as an entertaining and familiar sensory difference available to whites on demand, be it through dancing and singing in black-and-tan cabarets or eating "*real*" black foods. Breaching the sensory racial boundary could reaffirm white superiority while generating comforting feelings.[47] By understanding that fried chicken tastes black, a skill Bigger does not possess, Mary and Jan performed their whiteness. The protecting presence of her white boyfriend enables the young woman's gay and bold adventure. Eating fried chicken, Mary will not only taste a delectably juicy, greasy chicken thigh but will also engage with sensory and ideological stereotypes woven around existing notions of race, gender, and class. When she will finally eat "*real*" black food, her white-trained ear might also hear the "noises" of the black migrants' neighborhood, while Bigger, waiting for her to finish, will listen to the emerging black modern public sphere.[48] Fried chicken is here more than a utilitarian item in a system of economic exchange; its taste is imbued with power and put to use as a potent instrument of race making—so potent that, once the food is served, Bigger, confused by the situation, will refuse to eat his favorite food, before being shamed into doing so by the white couple. So potent that the association between chicken and blackness, born in the nineteenth century and reinforced in the twentieth, is still loaded with tension and racist imagery in the twenty-first.[49]

The senses were agents in the making of the modern U.S. racial taxonomy. By offering potential for crossing, twisting, and testing racial lines, they effectively contributed to their policing. Writing about southern legal segregation, Mark Smith highlights how "the sensory justifications of segregation, in fact, would have lost legitimacy if there had been a complete separation of the races. . . . It was only through day-to-day familiarity with the sensory dimensions of blackness, as whites invented and styled them, that they could maintain the fiction of sensory inferiority."[50] Southern segregation relied on a degree of sensory intimacy that did not necessarily prohibit blacks and whites from eating the same food as long as they did not do so together. But the transfer of fried chicken from the South to the northern cities in the wake of the Great Migration changed the dish's taste and made possible Mary's risqué night out in *Native Son*. Once associated with a region, the taste of fried chicken became linked to race. This shift shows how, nationwide, the senses became an agent of segregation and a potent way of establishing a modernized, industrialized, and urbanized color line. In the North taste itself became a marker of racial difference. Bigger's ignorance of the new taste of fried chicken also highlights the degree of sensory alienation felt by migrants to the urban North: historicizing the intimate feeling of sensing food is necessary to determine to what extent an individual's perception can also be the repository of collective experience.

Mary's sensory appreciation of fried chicken in this scene deepens philosophical and sociological accounts of the role of taste in processes of class formation, distinction, and reproduction. Under the sensory and intellectual regime of modernity, taste took on a plurality of meanings. The eighteenth-century rise of philosophical works on aesthetics sublimated what had traditionally been one of the lower, animalistic senses—alongside touch and smell—to the role of "arbiter" of all senses, a tool for sensory, aesthetic, and social distinction.[51] The dissociation of intellectual aesthetic taste from bodily appetites remained, however, unstable, and looking at how one seeps into the other is an important element to understanding how taste—aesthetic and culinary—is made. French sociologist Pierre Bourdieu's seminal work on this topic frames aesthetic taste, and by extension culinary taste, as "class culture turned into nature," cultural capital resulting from social conditioning passing for a strictly biological ability.[52] Bourdieu establishes a polarity between "the tastes of necessity" of the lower classes ("the heavy, the fat, and the coarse") and the "tastes of luxury" of the middle and upper classes (the lean, the light, and the small).[53] Mary's experience brings forth a nuanced understanding of this sociological account of taste. In the early 1940s, for a woman such as Mary, showing an interest in black culture was "in good taste" and a trip to the Chicago's South Side with a white date socially acceptable.[54] It was by subverting the social hierarchy of taste and choosing to partake in and enjoy the heavy food of the black lower classes that she could most efficiently position herself as an upper-class, left-leaning, white female bourgeois eater. Being able to enjoy the taste of blackness was part of her cultural capital. Her experience was dependent on Bigger's so-far-unselfconscious appreciation of fried chicken and his familiarity with the sensory world of Ernie's Kitchen Shack. Here, taste is not only a static quality of the dish, or a physical ability that emanates from Mary's or Bigger's predefined sociological profile. It is actively produced out of contextualized experiences that blur the line between sensory appreciation, class distinction, and aesthetic enjoyment. Taste is not only embodied, but it results from the circulation of sensory, social, and cultural capital.[55]

The exploration of the sensory economy of this short passage of Wright's *Native Son* unveils the critical potential of understanding sensory experiences of food as inherently relational, situational, as well as affective. Feelings such as fear, empathy, and empowerment combined with sensory perceptions to generate contextualized food experiences. A focus on taste and the senses therefore needs to be balanced by an awareness of the "the cross-modal networks that register links between perception, affect, the senses, and emotions" and an attention to how changing social constructions of race, ethnicity, and gender can regulate how we sense.[56] Studying sensory food experiences therefore requires acknowledging the role of emotions, such as hatred, but also longing and nostalgia, and their circulation in economic and affective "sets of entanglements" in determining how we sense our food. Such networks can be "binding" and create group or national identities, but they can also work to create difference and social displacement along race and gender lines.[57] My sensory analysis of New Deal food writing explores the webs of cultural, social, political, economic, and affective networks in which food made sense in the late 1930s and, in focusing on the sensory experience of eating, participates in the development of "critical eating studies" that focus on eaters, their palates, and their guts.[58]

* * *

The first chapter of *Taste of the Nation* focuses on the *America Eats* project to delve into why and how the FWP began searching for America's regional cuisines. The narrative explores how, in New Deal food writing, food became a canvas for a sensory, emotional, felt manifestation of national identity. The chapter also explores the limits of this political project as it captures editors and local workers deliberating over which and whose regional foods would be deemed worthy of integration into the American culinary narrative. Could Ernie's Kitchen Shack, Bigger's recommendation for a *"real"* black eating place, make the cut? The analysis takes into account the prescriptive but also unstable and inconclusive nature of *America Eats* as the understanding of what American food was and who American eaters were evolved over the course of the project. In looking for the taste of the nation, the FWP often stumbled upon regional ethnic tastes that defied the aims of the project. Documenting regional foods after several decades of intense food industrialization and sensory standardization and in the midst of the overhauling of the American racial taxonomy proved challenging, and the FWP walked a fine line between recording, inventing, and prescribing regional cuisines.

The two contrasting poles of modernity and tradition shaped New Deal food writing. FWP workers alternately expressed wonder for and fear of the sensory consequences of the former while nostalgically yearning for the latter. Chapter 2 explores the FWP's sensory nostalgia for regional food as a cathartic reaction to the standardization of taste triggered by the industrialization of the U.S. food system since the late nineteenth century. Categories of race and gender interplayed in the New Deal sensory economy both to buffer sensory change and to allow its critique. Women often took the blame for the decreased sensory quality of American food, making the 1930s a significant moment in the elaboration of conservative gender roles that dominated the war and postwar period. To counter this feminine threat, New Deal food writing held "virile" and uncorrupted tastes as the pinnacle of American cuisine, which, as the analysis of racial interaction in public cooking events shows, often meant tapping into the raw sensory power of racial others.

From chapter 3, the focus increasingly expands out of *America Eats* to include food writing throughout the FWP archive (American Guide Series, Folklore Project, Social-Ethnic Studies, Negro Studies Project, *Feeding the City*). This enlarged corpus forms the basis of analytical and ethnographic narratives on three 1930s sensory economies. Chapter 3 examines how southern food, following millions of African American interwar migrants, lost some of its regional sensory anchoring and became increasingly perceived and sensed as "black food" in northern and urban sensory economies. The fried chicken available at Ernie's Kitchen Shack in *Native Son* is an example of such a shift. The narrative shows how northern culinary tourists and slummers who enjoyed visiting black neighborhoods for a dish of fried chicken with a side of greens effectively redefined the taste of southern food. It also tracks how African Americans began claiming food of southern origins as one of the sensory nexus of a modern black urban identity, thereby erasing the source of earlier tensions between newly arrived migrants and better-off northern blacks. Looking at this interwar sensory shift at the national level means analyzing northern sensory economies but also the changing role of taste in southern race relations. The chapter explores how sensory reshuffling forced white southerners to re-envision the role of the senses under Jim Crow. While spatial and temporal distance had earlier been enough to assert segregation, the new meaning of southern food in the New Deal sensory economy and in northern metropolis led southern whites to reinforce sensory segregation by invoking the idea of two parallel regional cuisines. The role of class and interracial sensory exchange in the making of the region's taste was progressively obliterated.

Chapter 4 explores how the construction of Mexican food as southwestern heritage taste in the 1930s paradoxically participated in affirming the American identity of the region. Tasting spicy Mexican food offered the opportunity to re-experience the territorial conquest. The exploration of the links between tasting place and tasting race in the Southwest details how the construction of sensory racial authenticity intertwined with economic exchanges. The commodification of Mexican food as the region's culinary heritage spurred the development of practices of sensory sightseeing that participated in the making of the modern identity and wealth of the region while curtailing Spanish speakers' participation in it as it confined them to the past and lumped together populations with vastly different immigration, social, and political histories. A potent gender dynamic animated the construction of this domestic yet exotic taste: daring to eat the fiery dishes prepared by Mexican women was a central experience of white male culinary tourists. The construction of Mexican food as sensory heritage was part of the larger wave of sensory nostalgia explored in chapter 2, which constructed the taste of pre-industrial, homemade food as realms of sensory memory. But if New Deal food writing copiously celebrated the multisensory knowledge of romanticized ethnic cooks, it also provided glimpses of everyday multiethnic culinary encounters in syncretic, local sensory economies.

Chapter 5 combines the analytical work of previous chapters with an ethnographic reading of New Deal food writing to understand the centrality of ethnic taste in 1930s sensory economies. FWP workers described ethnic food using well-known keywords such as "the melting pot" or "cosmopolitanism"—given the topic at hand and the pressing need to produce material, these were tempting tropes. They were also ambivalent ones: the "melting pot" metaphor, for instance, carried an admonition to Americanize and conform that the FWP had difficulties shunning. Still, New Deal food writing coming from midwestern and western rural and industrial areas updated the paradigmatic metaphors and described a sensory cosmopolitanism where culinary encounters and working-class solidarities combined to create a cultural pluralist version of the melting pot. The chapter focuses on nodes of sensory trade such as workplaces, grocery stores, and ethnic restaurants, from foreign-themed nightclubs to working-class establishments and multiethnic diners. Throughout, the narrative provides a comparative history of the taste of Asian Americans and Southern and Eastern European ethnics to explore the role played by race and ethnicity in determining which taste and whose taste would legitimately enter the fold of American food in New Deal food writing.

In *Taste of the Nation*, I analyze taste as a symbolic, cultural, affective, and economic currency always in circulation and that, once mobilized, allows eaters to identify and differentiate themselves along race, class, gender, and ethnic lines. The notion of sensory economies is a plural one and allows exploring sensory experiences of food as the result of social, cultural, and financial exchanges always remade. When I write about the New Deal sensory economy, I refer to the deployment and regulation of the senses *within* the textual unit of the archive—an archive that can also be the object of an ethnographic reading, to get at the workings of local sensory economies in the interwar period. The first two chapters, taken together, probe the New Deal sensory economy—the management of the senses in the *America Eats* archive—to unlock the motivations, limits, and sensory paradoxes of New Deal food writing. From this grounding in the politics of perception in the archive, the narrative of the remaining chapters look at three sensory economies, understood as fluid, open, and always remade sets of entanglements in which food provided opportunities for sensory crossover, compromise, and transgression. Along the way, we hear grievances, reminiscences, and cravings. We meet unadventurous eaters and dissatisfied appetites in an equal amount to many contented gourmands, kicking back after one more piece of pie at the open-air barbecue.

Chapter 1

America Eats

The Making of a Sensory Archive

America Eats, the Federal Writers' Project's flagship culinary enterprise, was a multisensory search for America's food. The project's goal was to document regional food traditions and "group eating as an important American social institution; its part in development of American cookery as an authentic art and in the preservation of that art."[1] The team of editors who outlined *America Eats*, led by Katherine Kellock in collaboration with the successive FWP directors Henry Alsberg and John D. Newsom as well as Louisiana director Lyle Saxon, conceived *America Eats* as a retrospective, and nationally introspective, celebratory book focused on *"cookery in the best tradition."*[2] They aimed at providing a "detailed picture of the eating habits of the Americans throughout the 48 states in as lively and as amusing a manner as possible."[3] To fulfill this mandate, the federal editors requested that "creative writers" with "a keen interest in sensory perception" be put to work on this project and be careful to "avoid effusive style and the clichés adopted by some writers in food."[4] They noted that "descriptions of food should mention color, odour, and texture, since food appeals to the four senses—sight, sound, taste and smell" while carefully underlining that "the appeal is primarily to the sense of smell for taste can distinguish only between sweet, sour, salty and bitter."[5] Following these guidelines, successful copy from Virginia described how to dress "fluffy and soft" homemade biscuits by inserting "a juicy slice of tender ham" and pouring a "generous amount of red gravy" over it, hence "lifting the magic sandwich to the epitome of palatable grandeur." The author concluded on a high note: "For some—though it is strictly a matter of taste—an even more satisfying manner of eating them is to dunk the ham biscuits into the red gravy, without restraint, inhibition, or shame."[6] Such description aligned with the federal office's vision of *America Eats* as a comforting, worriless script for American sensory pageantry ready for tourist consumption.

America Eats was a late New Deal attempt at cultural and emotional nation building that set the tone for the patriotic mobilization of American arms, hearts, and senses in the war effort. First evoked in the fall of 1937, the project lingered for a few years before being revived and taking full bloom in the late summer of 1941, only to be interrupted by the U.S. entry into World War II. The culinary narrative developed in *America Eats* reached for an emotional and sensory past able to soothe the nation in the midst of economic depression and, starting in the early 1940s, to strengthen the citizenry in preparation for war. Svetlana Boym remarks in her study of the modern historical emotion of nostalgia that "the nation-state at best is based on the social contract that is also an emotional contract, stamped by the charisma of the past."[7] The mnemonic and symbolic quality of taste and food facilitated their recruitment as part of the New Deal "emotional contract"; it would provide a visceral, felt nature to national identity. While the New Deal's administration overhaul of the U.S. agricultural food production system was the object of charged debates and protests, the FWP proposed to record rather than change food habits, indeed claimed to safeguard traditions, and could cast its project as apolitical and patriotic. At a time of renewed attacks against Franklin Roosevelt's administration and increasing tension abroad, New Deal food writing aimed at establishing the fleeting act of tasting traditional regional dishes as comforting performances of national identity.[8]

The FWP attempt at compiling regional tastes is emblematic of what historian Alan Trachtenberg identified as the 1930s "search in the everyday life and memories of 'the people' for what was distinctively American."[9] The developing academic fields of anthropology and folklore inspired this search. The federal editors' recurrent mention of the need to unearth regional "eating patterns" signals their familiarity with the innovative work of anthropologists Frank Boas, Ruth Benedict (author of the field-defining *Patterns of Culture*, 1934), or Margaret Mead, whom they referred to explicitly in the *America Eats* guidelines.[10] They set out to document a specific sensory, social, and cultural object: "American cookery and the part it has played in the national life, as exemplified in the group meals that preserve not only traditional dishes but also traditional attitudes and customs."[11] This project did not necessarily align, or for that matter aim to align, with contemporary social, cultural, and sensory practices linked to food and group meals. When Kellock proclaimed in a 1941 editorial report that the FWP's "job" was "merely to record" the nation's culinary traditions, she also limited the scope of the search: "Neither calories nor vitamins will be mentioned in the book. Geographical factors will be touched on only indirectly. . . . Transportation will not be touched on in any way."[12] Given the key roles of transportation networks, especially railroads, and nutrition science in the industrialization of American food-ways since the mid-nineteenth century, this would be a major blind spot of the project, canceling any potential claims for comprehensiveness. Similarly, the sweeping yet imprecise advice to "not give much attention to dishes of recent foreign importation" left many in a liminal space, on the threshold of tradition.[13] The search would be limited.

This chapter focuses on the correspondence and administrative material related to *America Eats* to probe the cultural and sensory potential as well as the political limits of New Deal food writing. The FWP's pyramidal power hierarchy and administrative setup provoked a dynamic sensory and political dialogue between, on the one hand, educated liberal Washington editors and, on the other, local fieldworkers often with little literary experience. State offices freely interpreted federal guidelines, sometimes mounting sensory, historical, and common-sense resistance against the romanticizing tendencies of the federal office. The northeastern states, for instance, retorted that they could hardly follow the federal guidelines since "the patterns of eating established in the Colonial period persisted until they were affected during the last fifty years by the spread of transportation facilities, improvements in food preparation, the growth of cities and in some cases by the influence of immigrant groups."[14] Scrutinizing the discrepancies between the federal office's top-down instructions and fieldworkers' bottom-up interpretations of editorial guidelines reveals how sensory misunderstandings and clashes shaped the sensory economy of the archive.

Two practical questions with widespread consequences repeatedly emerged in the *America Eats* correspondence. Who was to have the authority to determine a dish's traditional standing and regional authenticity? Whose cuisine would be deemed worthy of inclusion in the American sensory past, and how would local multiethnic, syncretic tastes be integrated into the *America Eats* project? These were not questions the federal editors had aimed to raise, but such matters quickly became the main topic of their correspondence with the state offices. The various FWP administrative units never ceased to debate what the term "American" meant, whom it encompassed, and therefore whose food *America Eats* would record, memorialize, and stamp as "American" and "regional." Several answers competed. A focus on Anglo-Saxon heritage was regularly upstaged by a "contribution school" approach, depicting the slow absorption of specific immigrants' food into the national cuisine. Underneath these narratives laid the reformist potential of the celebration of ethnic and racial sensory diversity as a tool for building "a nation that was modern and stronger *because* it was both more pluralistic and more integrated."[15] No definite editorial and ideological line was settled on, and the *America Eats* archive reveals the FWP's vexed attempts at drawing a consensual "composite picture" of American taste.[16]

The FWP's effort at documenting traditional regional food regulated U.S. past and present sensory economies and policed the sensory borders of the nation. To produce an orderly and cohesive narrative out of the aggregate of local tastes, the FWP's federal office divided the country into five culinary regions and framed each regional cuisine as contributor to a national cuisine. Once recorded and archived, regional culinary histories and taste profiles would be reproducible and consumable on demand, providing a common sensory ground in a time of domestic and international political strife. In searching for the remnant of America's pre-industrial regional tastes, the FWP simultaneously recorded, invented, and prescribed culinary traditions. To explore how editorial choices regulated sensory economies, and especially the economy of the senses within the *America Eats* archive, this chapter answers Ann Laura Stoler's call to consider archives as "both a corpus of statements and a depot of documents, both sites of the imaginary and institutions that fashioned histories as they concealed, revealed, and contradicted the investments of the state."[17] Considered as both a repository and an object of study, the *America Eats* archive makes visible some of the mechanisms behind the production of sensory knowledge by the New Deal state. Divergent views on what it meant to be sensorially American informed the archive's sensory regime and its textual representation of regional tastes, vexing the federal office's goal to infuse food with moral, cultural, and ultimately economic value. Examining the making of the *America Eats* archive sheds light on the role of food and the senses in the making of region, race, and gender in the interwar period.

Notes, Essays, Reports: A Tour of the Archive

The *America Eats* project first appeared in FWP director Henry G. Alsberg's correspondence in 1937, although under the less engrossing title "America Sits Down at Table."[18] At its inception, the project was an endeavor to comfort hungry Americans by imagining a nation of hospitable community meals. As such, it did not gain much traction. Its revival in 1941, under John D. Newsom and Katherine Kellock's leadership, was more successful, and the project became a means of celebrating American exceptionalism in the face of rising European fascist movements and, after Pearl Harbor, an attempt to "be a cultural contribution . . . important in deepening the content of patriotism."

The entrance of the United States into World War II accelerated the project as the editors felt that its documentary style would appropriately highlight "the rich abundance of . . . native foodstuffs, as well as a neglected aspect of . . . national culture."[19] The communal ideal of the early years transformed into a consensual blueprint for wartime patriotism. This reflected the evolution of the FWP itself, which, since 1939, had been under the scrutiny of the Dies Committee, precursor of the red-scare-famous House Un-American Activities Committee (HUAC), forcing its revamping. The Dies Committee suspected the project of being a leftist hotbed (which some urban units such as the New York branch were) but also of "boondoggling," a period term that combined inefficiency, incompetence, and irrelevance—the *America Eats* innovative yet unusual and, for the time, frivolous focus on food being a case in point. The new incarnation of the agency took on the name of the Writers' Program and distanced itself from its predecessor's ambitious goal of weaving together a pluralistic chronicle of the nation's history and culture. This overhauling of the agency triggered the transformation of, in historian Jerrold Hirsch's words, a "liberal and reformist view of American culture" into "the basis of a new and ultimately conservative national consensus." When the Writers' Program was eventually recast as the Office of War Information (OWI) in 1942, the *America Eats* project finally ended to "clear the way for work on Army Camp guides, which [each] State [was] asked to prepare for a national series."[20] The production of sensory knowledge taking place in the *America Eats* archive over these eventful five years propelled the advent of a patriotic culinary narrative that bridged change and consensus.

The files conserved at the Library of Congress constitute the most complete records of the *America Eats* project.[21] The collection consists of different kinds of material. First, the "administrative material" is composed of the book proposal, memos, and editorial guidelines sent by the federal editors to the state offices in order to explain the anticipated content of the volume. These instructions are authorless but were in all probability written by Katherine Kellock, who was "in charge of the undertaking" in the federal office.[22] The Columbia University–educated editor had been with the FWP for several years by the time the agency undertook the project, notably overseeing with an iron fist the "motorized tours" sections of the American Guide Series. In his memoir, former FWP staffer Jerre Mangione describes Kellock as a "small tornado of a woman whose voice seemed to alternate between the sounds of scolding and laughter," and who put an almost religious fervor in her work.[23] Throughout her tenure at the FWP, she built on her social-work training, reformist impetus, and progressive understanding of American history to make "the nation appear crowded with monuments to the efforts of ordinary Americans, contributors to their country's progress."[24] Like many in the Washington office, she proposed a democratic and inclusive view of the nation based on cultural pluralism, although this framework regularly failed to "include the oppressed," in particular southern blacks.[25] The *America Eats* guidelines were further explained and detailed in the second set of material in the *America Eats* collection: the correspondence between the federal editors and the states' offices, a correspondence that often documents misunderstandings between the two main administrative levels of the FWP. Third, the bulk of the collection consists of essays on local cuisines and traditions written by fieldworkers in each state and often left unsigned. These local essays were filed under "notes, essays, reports" and organized by state. The size of the state files varies greatly, from empty or inexistent, in the case of eight states (Illinois, Louisiana, Michigan, Missouri, Ohio, Nevada, South Dakota, and West Virginia) and two anticipated culinary regions (New York City and Northern California), to hundreds of pages, in the case of Virginia or Texas.[26] In the federal office's vision for the project, these local essays would constitute the raw data for the completion of the five regional essays ("section essays") and, ultimately, the overarching national culinary narrative. Drafts of these essays represent the fourth kind of material in the collection. A few pictures, conserved in the Prints and Photographs Department, were taken especially for the project; most are reproduced in this book.[27]

The federal editors envisioned the book as essays on the Northeast, the South, the Southwest, the Middle West, and the Far West, published under the homogenizing title *America Eats*. One state per region would serve as a regional editing unit and would pick and choose among the state essays to write a blended regional narrative. The federal office asked the director of the Louisiana office, Lyle Saxon, to take on a leading role in editing material from the South to be sent to the four other regional offices as an example of the work required for the regional essays.[28] This choice reflected the culinary reputation of Saxon's home city of New Orleans and the South in general as well as Saxon's writing abilities. Saxon's version of the American past was ambiguous, though: his romanticization of Louisiana's pre–Civil War "golden age" was balanced only by his keen interest in African American folklore.[29] He was only half successful in his attempt at a master regional narrative. Kellock remarked in a January 1942 editorial memo on his contribution that, "each of the fragments is well handled, but the total effect is that of a patternless patchwork."[30] The five section essays were at various stages of completion when the project was abandoned and its papers archived. The South proposed a piecemeal narrative opening with an account of the cross-racial taste for chitterlings but then casting "Negroes" solely as servants, slaves, and hawkers. The politics of race in the region curtailed a fully blended essay.[31] The Northeast essay stretched from New England settlers' cookery to late-nineteenth-century food fads and the introduction of fruit salad "anchored in sweet glue" (also known as Jell-O); it included descriptions of hotel banquets and New York City's multiethnic tastes.[32] The Southwest and Far West essays, authored by Arthur J. Brooks and Edward B. Reynolds, respectively, proposed masculinist accounts of culinary pioneering. Brooks highlighted the "gusto" of southwestern barbecues and "redolent" Mexican food, while Reynolds celebrated the "creative ability" of male cooks so that local diets were not, contrary to popular belief, presented as entirely composed of "fried beans, baked beans, boiled beans and just beans." They clearly set the tone: "Here you will find no lacy frills to catch the eye, or subtle nuances of taste and smell to goad the appetite of the jaded and world-weary gastronome."[33] The Middle West essay, attributed to Nelson Algren, was titled "A Short History of American Diet." "Wrong," wrote a federal editor in the margin: "This was supposed to be a study of group eating"—a study of the nation's folkloric asset, not of its dieting fads. The essay was, however, one of the most accomplished and went on to describe the Middle West as a "land of mighty breakfast" and multiple cuisines. It concluded with the grand and pluralistic but ultimately vague declaration: "Many foods, many nations. Yet one food, one nation. Many lands, one land."[34] The federal office would have ultimately been judge of the accuracy, relevance, and literary value of the regional essays.

The unfinished nature of the *America Eats* project means that, despite the goal to produce an authoritative master culinary narrative on American regional cuisines, the archive contains a plurality of voices. If the federal editors were educated and politically astute New Dealers who understood food as a topic with the power to raise the emotional content of patriotism, most of the local staff members were white-collar workers trying to make ends meet in the economic depression, and their voices and styles remained plurals. FWP workers' various social and professional backgrounds defy any generalizations about their aspirations, opinions, or politics. Some, such as Richard Wright, Nelson Algren, or Zora Neale Hurston, became famous in their own right in the years after the end of the project. Many had already established careers as folklorists or local writers, and employment by the FWP allowed them to wait out the end of the Depression and pursue their research before continuing what were sometimes prolific careers. But most of the nearly ten thousands fieldworkers left scant traces after their employment.[35] The FWP aimed at authoritativeness, and most of its publications had no personal authorship. Manuscripts could be co-authored and were almost systematically, and sometimes heavily, edited by state directors and then federal editors so that fieldworkers often did not bother to sign their preparatory or final work.

The editors' ideas about regional cuisines never quite matched fieldworkers' understandings of their local foodways—in fact, they could barely understand why the topic was of interest in the first place. Freehanded interpretation of Kellock's instructions remained the norm in the state offices. When it came to the *America Eats* project, most FWP workers were "not quite sure how to approach this subject exactly" and unclear about "what form the [federal office] wanted [the] material to take."[36] One of them judged the project singularly "uninspiring."[37] Others had more positive responses. Early on, the federal office solicited Virginia state director Eudora Ramsay Richardson for culinary material. A committed liberal, field director of the National Women Suffrage Association, former head of the English department at Greenville's Women's College, and author of books and essays on women's political rights, Richardson was enthusiastic about *America Eats*. When asked who could contribute to the project, she wrote back that she "shall have to write the piece" since "the only other person on the project who ha[d] ever written either books or magazine articles [was] Aubrey Boyd—and he [didn't] know much about foods." Yet, perhaps because Boyd was a man, Richardson added that "[she] shall ask him to touch up the description of mint juleps."[38] Her contribution to *America Eats* nicely followed the federal guidelines for lightness of tone with a hint of parochialism. She centered an account of a family reunion on a debate about the respective value of Virginian fried chicken recipes, "dipped in flour and fried in deep fat . . . just crisp on the outside," and Maryland battered fried chicken, "encased in concrete."[39]

One learns more about the federal office's vision for the book's content and style in written complaints about inaccurate state contributions than by analyzing the book proposal and outlines. In a long editorial memo on a piece from Colorado, Kellock criticized the use of "generalization and trite phrases" instead of "concrete detail," as well as "colloquialism and coy-allusions instead of human interest" in order to "give an impression of liveliness." She continued by explaining that the "addition of such abstract adjectives as 'tantalizing' and 'beautiful'" to a list of dishes "will not suffice" to fulfill the goal of providing "an account of cookery and group eating as reflecting American social life, attitudes, and customs." She then provided appetizing phrases as models, such as "watermelon pickles still pale-greenish—white and crisp as when raw and so transparent it was possible to read print through them" or "the eggnog, a fluffy, saffron beverage, delicate in fragrance and pungently persuasive." The federal office pushed workers to take poetic risks and adopt a style that "must evoke an image," such as the suggestive description of "dark red beets oozing a brighter red liquid when cut."[40] Only when local FWP workers managed to overcome their temptation to use rhetorical clichés or hastily write their essays did they achieve a level of sensory awareness and social accuracy acceptable to the federal office.

The literary qualities of *America Eats* contributions were all the more important inasmuch as the food described in the book was not to be cooked but vicariously eaten and sensed. One thing was clear in the federal editors' minds: *America Eats* would *not* be a cookbook. It would be a pleasurable read rather than a practical manual. The focus of the book was on public "group eating"—church dinners, family reunions, political barbecues, and community gathering—rather than private cooking, effectively sidelining women's paid and unpaid daily food work in home kitchens. The *America Eats* project's emphasis on the role of food as locus of identity rather than provider of nutrition, the products of the food industry, the housebound work of women, or the art of haute cuisine chefs was atypical for the time. Newsom rightly noted that the attempt at inventorying—almost salvaging—local food cultures and taste, what we would now call "foodways," would "be a pioneer[ing effort] in a neglected field."[41] If most FWP workers and their readers rejoiced in the fact that Fourth of July "square dancing and fiddling contests" were still the "bug in the hill country," they expressed little alarm about the fact that it was accompanied by the consumption of "hot dogs, hamburgers, and soda pop from dusty stands"; quite the contrary, they judged that such offerings "len[t] variety to the enormous lunches unpacked from cars and wagons."[42] *America Eats*, however, would document the "enormous lunches" and purposely sideline the commercial stands. The project's oft-repeated aim was not to produce a manual of American cookery to be used by an audience of homemakers but to craft an educational, entertaining, titillating, and patriotic read accessible to every citizen. Much like turn-of-the-century travel literature, the FWP conceived of its readers as a pool of armchair travelers and potential tourists rather than cooks trying to feed their families during the Depression.[43] Readers were to experience the taste of each region through a master narrative that, in effect, regulated the country's sensory diversity.

Interwar intellectual debates shaped the federal office's pioneering understanding of the emotional and political power of sound food writing. The *America Eats* project was particularly influenced by the evolution of the field of folklore in which the FWP's own Folklore Project assumed a leading and groundbreaking role. Under the leadership of Benjamin A. Botkin, the Folklore Project shifted the emerging discipline away from the study of the survival of European traditions in the modern United States to the exploration of American folklore, understood as an ongoing creative process grounded in ethnic traditions and life in North America, including in industrial and urban contexts. This novel understanding of folklore combined nostalgia with radical politics to propose an alternative path toward a modern and pluralist nation.[44] Some of the local workers assigned to *America Eats* also worked on the Folklore Project and were familiar with this shift. However, if the *America Eats* guidelines sent to each state to revive the project in the early 1940s implemented this redefinition of American folklore, it was with important limits. The project sought to tell the story of how "native cookery" originated in the "inventive genius of settlers," spurred on by the "lack of the limited traditional foodstuffs and abundance of new ones." New dishes broke free from European influence: they did not need "spices and sauces to make them appetizing" but rather required slow cooking in open fireplaces and sturdy Dutch ovens. Yet this origins story established that the creative process had stalled by the middle of the nineteenth century, when the invention of cooking stoves and frying pans, with their higher temperatures and faster cooking times, coupled with the rise of industrially produced food, allegedly "almost wreck[ed] America."[45] This narrative left the millions of migrants who arrived in the late nineteenth century and early twentieth century in an ideological limbo regarding their part in American culinary history. The systematic search for the perpetuation of traditional taste in the midst of the contemporary "mass production of food-stuffs" led the FWP editors to draw chronological sensory borders as to who would be part of the American sensory past and present, curtailing the cultural pluralism of the Folklore Project.

America Eats was part of a wider "emotional discovery of America" that put the anamorphous figure of "the folk" at the center of intellectual and commercial life. Historian Michael Kammen considers that, starting in the 1910s, this movement "produced a vulgate of American exceptionalism never before known."[46] This rediscovery was shaped as a response to the ever-increasing reach of consumer culture and, according to Jane Becker, "expressed an accommodation to rather than criticism of the structures and values of an industrializing nation."[47] The Depression period marked a crucial point for the incorporation of "the folk" into consumer capitalism and mass culture as this constructed ideal created the potential for a home-grown renaissance.[48] The FWP was part of this trend, and Henry Alsberg, first director of the agency, expressed this vision of a commercialized folklore in 1938 when he estimated that a book on Idaho folklore "w[ould] make the sort of book that 'the folks' will buy and pass around."[49] Following this logic, the folks' consumption of state-regulated traditions would then teach them how to be folk, therefore insuring the very maintenance of folklore. Becker considers that the "fascination" with the folk was a feature of a nation struggling "to define national culture and identity" and "sustain notions of community" in the midst of "rapid and disruptive change."[50] In the case of *America Eats*, it was the hunger and massive breadlines of the early Depression and the collective feeling of sensory endangerment triggered by the industrialization of the U.S. food system that dictated the need for a comforting and reassuring sensory account of "traditional cookery [kept] alive." If Kellock asked the Colorado office to chronicle meals at which "thick pink slabs of hickory-cured country ham" were served, it was as a reaction to the state's apparently inadequate remark that "wieners . . . and the ubiquitous hamburger" were the favorite way to "fill up the cavities existing in youthful stomach."[51] Documenting the sensory and nutritional impact of the products of the meatpacking industry on U.S. diets was not the goal here. *America Eats* straddled the ideological ambiguity inherent in recording traditions within the bounds of a consumer society, aiming to sell regional tastes back to an audience of armchair tourists.

The method adopted for *America Eats* also borrowed from interwar anthropological research that developed a renewed and enlarged understanding of the concept of culture. Central to this research was the differentiation of the anthropological meaning of culture as a way of life—"whether of a people, a period, a group, or humanity in general"—from the intellectual and artistic meanings of culture, which invoked "claims to superior knowledge."[52] Intellectual and artistic cultures had long been associated with the ideals of civilization and progress—two concepts that had been central to the nation's political, social, and cultural life in the nineteenth and early twentieth century but that came under scrutiny in the 1930s as the Depression exposed the failures of the American industrial civilization. The distinction between the various meanings of culture then crystalized in the interwar period; New Deal food writing participated in this process.[53] The federal editors understood the concept of culture as patterns of life, behaviors, and taste coming together to constitute an American way independent from not only Europe but also from economic conditions. They aimed to adopt what they tagged a "popular approach" to food, putting a new emphasis on food as part of broader cultural patterns and insisting on the role of food as a "social amalgam." They explicitly inscribed themselves in Margaret Mead's developing food and sensuous scholarship when they stipulated that local workers should pay attention to the "social anthropological aspects" of food-sharing events.[54] About a southern barbecue, for instance, editors inquired: "Who hands out the food? Is the meat eaten from a plate or is it first placed in a sandwich? Are there any conventions about who eats first, any differences between what men and women do at the meal?" Also of interest were potential disputes over the "orthodox" way to prepare traditional dishes and local variations.[55] *America Eats* would not focus on elite gastronomy but bridge social classes and document the cookery of "the people."

The federal editors, Katherine Kellock first among them, participated in the interwar development of social sciences and the search for cultural, folkloric, and, in the case of *America Eats*, sensory patterns. Reshaping this trend for patriotic purposes in the early 1940s, they proposed "native foodstuffs" as vehicles for cultural and emotional nation building. In doing so, they understood that, in food historian Jeffrey Pilcher's words, "the supreme test for any expression of national culture is neither beauty nor sophistication, but authenticity. A 'genuine' work of art, however humble, demonstrates a nation's cultural autonomy, and this distinctiveness in turn justifies its claims to political sovereignty."[56] National cuisines are more than a shared set of recipes; they are political artifacts that can be "understood as having a *textual* reality as opposed to a concrete reality—something people talk about, imagine, but do not literally *eat*."[57] The FWP cared about "good" food, but, ultimately, the quality of a dish as a trace, a remnant of the past, could overcome its taste quality so that Wyoming ranch "puddings," "which bore rather incongruous names" such as, "Lumpy Dick," "Spotted Pup," "Son-of-a-gun in a Sack," and "Homogenous Mass," became cherished and symbolic sensory morsels.[58] The invention of traditions such as regional and national cuisines is one of the devices available to the modern state to prove its legitimacy and define its citizenry. Codified and symbolic meals eaten simultaneously across the country materialize the national "imagined community" as a family at the table.[59] More than just nutrition, food became in New Deal food writing a cultural performance woven into rituals of citizenship, potentially unifying sensory experiences across the nation.

Sensing and Consuming American Regions

The premise of the *America Eats* project was the conceptualization of a systemic relationship between American regions in order to define diverse "tastes of place" before unifying them under a national banner. Colonial America historian David Hackett Fisher offers a dual definition of a region as both "a physical entity formed by terrain, soil, climate, resources and systems of production" and "a cultural phenomenon, created by common customs and experiences." Regions are "cultural landscapes."[60] This twofold feature is crucial to understanding regional cuisines in the United States since local ingredients and foodstuffs as well as the origins, social status, ingrained habits, and acquired tastes of regional cooks and consumers determined local cooking styles. Food historians have highlighted the fundamental role of local foodstuffs and local constructions of taste in the diet of the "regional Creoles" of the colonial and early republican periods. Various sets of migrants, free or enslaved, modified their Old World habits in response to New World environments and agricultural resources, resulting in localized cuisines and foodways, such as Pennsylvania Dutch cuisine or southern cooking. Geography, environment, and demographics combined to form the historical foundations of regional tastes.[61]

Starting in the mid-nineteenth century, development in food processing and scientific advances in the field of nutrition, however, diminished American regional culinary differences, triggering a "revolution at the table."[62] Food production was a leading industry of Gilded Age and Progressive Era economic expansion and drove the maturation of the capitalist political economy that crashed in 1929. The second industrial revolution triggered the emergence of new foodstuffs and eating habits that were marketed and adopted on a national scale, such as canned foods, breakfast cereals, baby food, prepared meat, and mass-produced vegetables. Developments in transportation, the emergence of a mass market of advertised and standardized consumer goods, scientific management, the employment of skilled and unskilled migrant workers, and rapid urbanization were deciding factors in the gradual streamlining and industrialization of diets in the late nineteenth and early twentieth century.[63] This revolution in food production, distribution, and preparation prompted a nationwide sensory standardization that decreased the role of physical geographies on Americans' taste. However, cultural, social, and racial determinants remained in the foreground of U.S. cultural and culinary regional politics.

The rapid changes in food production, transportation, marketing, and consumption triggered anxieties among the turn-of-the-century American public, the parents and grandparents of FWP workers. Lack of quality control and sanitary regulation as well as the decrease in palatability earned the food industry numerous detractors. The Progressive Era witnessed the rise of the modern consumer movement, which campaigned for the creation and enforcement of stricter federal regulations of the food industry. Consumer advocates, Progressive politicians, and public intellectuals all denounced the danger of the industrial processing of foodstuffs, especially the use of additives, unhygienic and unsafe labor conditions, as well as the secretive ways of the industry. A new food vocabulary entered American speech around the two poles of adulteration and wholesomeness. The efforts of this budding consumer movement culminated in 1906 with the passage of the Pure Food and Drug Act. Though the food and advertisement industries were swift in adapting the rhetoric of purity and reliability promoted by the consumer movement into a selling argument, debates on hygiene and quality continued into the interwar period.[64] A New York FWP worker, for instance, cheerfully—and ironically—remarked that "bologna is better now than in your grandmother's day. The law no longer permits manufacturers to use undesirable organs of cattle as filler for this popular edible."[65] FWP workers were not fooled by the food industry's strategy and proficiently used the vocabulary forged in the early twentieth century as an argument for the need to revert to a more traditional way of cooking. Oregon worker Claire Warner Churchill nostalgically remembered the mashed potatoes of her grandmother's day and deplored the "travesties upon a self-respecting dish of mashed, and I mean mashed, not macerated potatoes" frequently served in restaurants, before exclaiming: "But heck, they even pre-fry French fries now-a-days. What chance has a potato?"[66] The FWP celebration of regional cuisines was a demand—sometimes veiled, sometimes direct—for a decrease in the food industry's encroachment on the nation's foodways.

In this ambivalent industrial nutritional and sensory context, regional histories and cooking styles provided an image of preserved wholesomeness in the face of tasteless commercial standardization, economic depression, and the ensuing social tensions. In order to write a cohesive and engrossing culinary narrative, FWP editors decided to search for remnants of regional cuisines in the midst of American modernity, tastes on which to rebuild the American citizenry's morale, during the economic depression and later in wartime mobilization. The FWP was not alone in promoting regionalist thinking: the 1930s was an age of numerous regionalisms. Despite vastly different ideological beliefs, from rural conservatism to leftist radicalism, all tended to define regions as units "that only ma[de] sense in a common text, in competition for relative advantage and influence" and considered regional differences as distinctions rather than divisions.[67] Regionalist thinking in the 1930s paradoxically offered hopes "for restoration and preservation, for *reconstruction*, [...] of the fragmented culture of modern America."[68] The 1929 Crash and the lingering economic depression reinforced the cultural value of regional foods as comforting and soothing tastes that offered a hope for cultural regeneration and a way "[to put] together the pieces of a national culture" and history.[69] The FWP's recording of regional food traditions would provide a direct link with glorious pioneering and homesteading days, a loosely defined—and implicitly Anglo-Saxon—American spirit: a "fine tradition of freedom and a noble cuisine to back it up."[70]

The call for documentation of regional habits and folklore issued for *America Eats* was not new to the FWP state offices. The Folklore Project and the American Guide Series both followed regional and/or state frameworks to document national life, and some of the workers were involved in these projects before, and sometimes at the same time as, they contributed to *America Eats*. FWP scholar Christine Bold considers, for instance, that the American Guide Series, in which Kellock played an important role, "created evidence of regional diversity, then pulled it together into a national, unified—'balanced'—expression," therefore "producing a major icon of American national unity in these fractured years."[71] Most representative of this process was the guidebook *U.S. One: From Maine to Florida*, which incorporated a five-page list of "food specialties of the area through which U.S. 1 runs." The road united the diverse culinary regions for the convenient pleasure of the motoring tourists.[72]

The five regions mapped out for *America Eats* differed from the ones used on previous FWP projects, however. The initial motive for the rearranging of American regions arose from a rather sound sensory argument. If the *America Eats* project did "not follow the lines of the . . . administrative regions," it was because the editors aspired to organize their material into loosely defined areas of "cultural continuity and historical development and relationship," akin to sensory spheres of influence.[73] The federal editors anchored the legitimacy of their spatial decoupage in the view that states' borders did not dictate tastes. They also "recognize[d] certain objections to this grouping," such as the varying sizes of the regions or "the mixed character of the food pattern within certain states as well as within some of the regions," and took the example of Texas, where elements of the southern and Mexican cuisine overlapped with "range influences."[74] For similar reasons, California was split between the Southwest (Southern California) and the Far West (Northern California). Yet, the rationale behind the regional grouping remained evasive overall as the FWP editors' views on how to apprehend regional customs evolved over the course of the project. Ideally, the sensory mapping of the nation would emerge from fieldwork, but as the editors became pressed for time, they could impose it from the top down.

While the federal staff at first gestured toward considering FWP workers' empirical mapping and sensory knowledge as relevant, their position shifted in the early 1940s as work on *America Eats* picked up. The call for material sent to the state offices in 1937 was open ended and asked for relevant regional documentation. Eudora Ramsay Richardson responded enthusiastically to the federal call for contribution and "jot[ted] down some suggestions" about the foods and events Virginia could document, remarking that writing such stories would be "a great deal of fun." She provided glimpses of potential write-ups, considered a story on the "tragically misunderstood" dish of Brunswick stew a requirement, and insisted that "the making of corn meal battercakes is . . . an art and so is the frying—no thick aluminum and greaseless cooking but crispy edges that Smithfield bacon brings about."[75] The memos sent to the states in order to revive the project in the summer and fall of 1941 were more peremptory; Washington suggested a list of three to four "traditional gatherings" for each region to document. States in the Northeast were asked to cover a clambake, a Grange dinner, and a baked-bean dinner; the South, political barbecues, family reunions, and a cemetery-cleaning picnic; the Middle West, school picnic and, after much debate about whether the meal was "American" enough, a Scandinavian lutefisk dinner; the Southwest, a cowboy dinner and a pipeline meal; finally, the Far West was asked to document a roundup barbecue, a Mormon Ward reunion, and a game dinner. Editors favored a clear-cut grouping, even if this required "shift[ing] some material from one section to the other" in the final manuscript. For instance, a South Dakota article, "The Herder and his Muttons," was deemed to "so clearly belong" to the Far West section rather than the Middle West that it was "cut" from the state's contribution and "reworked into the regional essay" on the cattle country.[76] If need be, the federal office did not hesitate to foster regional culinary and sensory differences.

The logic behind the regional organization of *America Eats* in its early-1940s incarnation henceforth involved not only the recording of culinary traditions but also their production. At times, regional differences had to be inculcated from above in order to create a national pattern. The demi-urgic tendencies of the federal editors in their search for authentic regional tastes are most obvious in their correspondence with state offices. To John D. Newsom inquiring in September 1941 "whether buckwheat cakes and buffalo meat barbecue would be representative recipes for Nebraska," the state director, Rudolph Umland, answered that "ordinary pancakes, served with sausage, are much more representative." The federal office's unwillingness to accept his insight pushed Umland to ask for the intervention of a higher up administrator, Pearl Gimple, who wrote to Washington a few days later to "make it clear . . . that buffalo meat [was] not common food" in the state. Her letter unveils the fine line walked by Washington: "If in planning your book you are interested in unusual recipes or foods which are unique to a given state, then buffalo barbecue would be appropriate. On the other hand if you are interested in 'typical' recipes for the various states, then it's the writer's opinion that buffalo meat should not qualify." Instead, she disappointingly recommended the inclusion of "pork or some fried food, as [. . .] a great deal of fried food is consumed in Nebraska."[77] This controversy highlights one of the shortcomings of the project's editorial guidelines: the federal office never clearly stated whether it was looking to document everyday food or picturesque practices.

The editors' goal to ground local food in regional histories was regularly defeated by the contemporary dislocation of taste triggered by the industrialization of the U.S. food system. In the populated and industrial Northeast in particular, fieldworkers opened their reports noting that they did "not consider that any particular dish could be singled out" as peculiar to their state and that "regional cooking ha[d] been generally forced out by the products of the fast freight and of the canning factory." "Swift transportation and the omnipresent chain store ha[d] tended to wipe out individuality."[78] Debates between fieldworkers and federal editors unveil the extent to which regional foods and their distinctive tastes had become market commodities rather than lived experiences by the late 1930s. Wisconsin cheese is another instance of a foodstuff that became the object of a heated exchange between editors and local workers, the latter reporting being "puzzled about what [the federal editor] want[s] concerning the Monroe Cheese festival and Wisconsin cheese-eating in general." Though a Wisconsin law (in effect from June 1935 through March 1937) designed to revive the local economy made it "mandatory for all Wisconsin restaurants to serve a certain amount of Wisconsin cheese and butter" with every meal, local workers highlighted that there was "nothing about the consumption of cheese as being in any way an idiosyncrasy of local diet." Yet, given the growing national image of the state as "America's dairyland," as well as the increasing importance of local automobile tourism in the regional economy, the editors seemed ready to "strain the point."[79] A number of FWP fieldworkers and state directors resisted the federal takeover on regional authenticity to the extent that one can wonder whether their efforts at setting a truthful record of 1930s eating habits and at avoiding romanticizing their regional foodways might have been one of the reasons the book was not completed.

The federal office's propensity to generate sensory regulation and spatial unification underlines the extent to which, in the interwar period, regional tastes became commodities in the nation's memory and tourism marketplace. The late 1930s was a watershed moment for the redefinition of American citizenship, as consumption practices and *America Eats* simultaneously offered an alternative to this materialist view by drawing a sensory portrait of the nation and also participated in this shift by commodifying regional foods. Starting in the interwar period, and at an increasing pace in the war and postwar period, a variety of political and social actors came to understand active participation in consumer society and mass culture, including tourism, as the bedrock of American citizenship.[80] The rise of railroad and then automobile tourism since the mid-nineteenth century had encouraged Americans to "See America First"; the FWP wanted them to taste it too. The delineation of authentic tastes in New Deal food writing contributed to the shift in the role of regions from being "locus of identity" to "locus of consumption."[81] It elevated the selling, buying, and eating of regional foods, including as a literary act through *America Eats*, as a ritual of modern American citizenship. The ultimate goal of developing a national culinary narrative collecting the taste of American regions was a commercial one: to sell a regulated version of American folklore about food to "the people." Hopes were high for the book to be a commercial success.

The federal office was not unwavering and ultimately found ways to reconcile its search for regional tastes with reports highlighting local adaptations to industrial food. Though the editors considered ostensible signs of food "commercialization" as a cultural and sensory threat, local workers' resistance led them to pragmatically adapt their definition of tradition. For instance, they admitted that "a commercially promoted festival" might assume "the character of a harvest festival" in its social and sensory role. They would consider such a festival worthy of attention on the condition that "the commercial features," such as the "crowning of a queen," would be "subordinated" to elements deemed more traditional.[82] Following this evolution, editorial instructions emphasized the need to cover "meals served in drugstores, dining cars, etc.," since "[these kinds of meals are] the commonest public meal[s] of the industrial sections of the country and [are] now assuming traditional aspects with some people regularly eating in small groups."[83] The editorial line softened up to the idea of including "incidental eating, or munching" of industrial food in *America Eats*. The federal office noted that, in some parts of the country, the new "folk custom" of "equip[ping] oneself" with "pop corn, peanuts, candy bars, ice cream cones, Good Humor ice cream bars and the like . . . before setting out for a football game, baseball game or visit to the Zoo" was too ingrained in people's habits and taste to be ignored.[84] The changing guidelines opened the door to the documentation of how products of the food industry could be locally adopted and adapted. If the federal editors were interested in Georgia's "Coca-Cola parties," a "simple, inexpensive form of entertainment . . . particularly popular with the young matrons and young girls," it was because they wanted to know how the Atlanta drink was used for the making of "strange concoctions . . . throughout the country."[85] Regional sensory differences did exist in the New Deal era, though not the ones first anticipated by the federal office. Changing its criterion for regional authenticity, the federal office somewhat reconciled its culinary quest with 1930s regional foodways, making the *America Eats* archive an important (though not comprehensive) source for the study of 1930s food habits.

Running parallel to the question of how to define regional culinary traditions in a country with a national industrial food system, a second major tension in the *America Eats* project was the extent to which race and ethnic identities were enmeshed in the definition of regional cuisines. Who were the regional and folksy American eaters sought after by the federal editors? Whose cuisine would be deemed "regional," and therefore "American," rather than "foreign" or "exotic"? How would the syncretic taste of ethnic communities integrate the national culinary narrative?

"There Is Little Room for What Is Merely Exotic": Race and Ethnicity in the *America Eats* Archive

By the late fall of 1941, as various states had started to send in material, the federal office needed to clarify the stakes of the *America Eats* project, especially the textual space that should be devoted to what the editors termed "Nationality Group Eating," and what we would call "ethnic food," in local write-ups. An editorial report sent to regional editors read: "The amount of space that can be devoted to each region is so small that there is little room for what is merely exotic if one purpose of the book is to be fulfilled; this purpose is to increase appreciation of American traditions, and traditions brought to this country and welded into the national life." The FWP's attempt at describing "meals and dishes . . . 'American' in tradition" was problematic from the start because never did Kellock, Newsom, or any other editor in Washington clearly defined what "American" meant in this culinary context and often left the adjective between quotation marks.[86] In October 1941 Kellock, who was responsible for most of the day-to-day management of *America Eats*, got caught in a telling rhetorical debate with the state offices as she recommended that the Northeast section provide "an account of a Jewish group meal, preferably a traditional celebration," and went on to note that "this is an exception to the rule against non-American material but is justified by the number of Jews in the United States and the ancient character of the feasts." Her wording did not sit well with the local understanding of race, ethnicity, and American identity in the northeastern FWP offices, and she had to correct her memo. Two days later she explained that, "in referring to Jewish feasts as 'non-American' we merely meant that they did not originate in the United States" and added, "they are of course as American, in the broader sense, as any other feasts held in the United States by natives of the country."[87] Kellock did not, however, explicitly resolve the ideological discrepancy between the "broader" and the narrower understanding of

American identity. Her inconclusive remark left most people in a grey racial area, on the threshold of American traditions.

The fast evolution of the American racial taxonomy in the New Deal Era explains in part the FWP's rhetorical and ideological impasse when it came to determining whose food to integrate in an account of American culinary traditions. While the previous period had used categories of "race" as well as "color," "complexion," and "nationality" to categorize first- and second-generation migrants, the New Deal racial taxonomy was increasingly binary, determined by two racial categories: black and white. The dearth of new arrivals after the anti-immigrant quotas law of the mid-1920s paradoxically launched what historian Matthew Jacobson neatly dubs the "manufacture of Caucasian," and, through the Depression and the World War II years, whiteness was reconstructed and unified. The white-ethnic category became a new social currency and legal epistemology that allowed the naming of internal difference while consolidating the color line.[88] Labor politics of the 1930s and the rise of the liberal state meant that becoming white provided immigrants not only with a renewed and affirmative ethnic identity but also with a sense of civic entitlement in the welfare state.[89] Despite the culturally pluralist ideals of the New Deal state, the period was marked by the persistence of a race-based nationalism that rejected blacks' participation in the citizenry.[90] Historians have shown how the implementation of New Deal policies and reforms reinforced racial discrimination, creating what historian George Lipsitz considers a "racialized social democracy."[91]

The FWP abided by the prevailing interwar racial dichotomy and created Negro Studies projects, headed federally by poet and Howard University professor Sterling Brown and staffed by African Americans.[92] In these units, a number of black FWP workers attempted to correct the accepted American culinary narrative that celebrated the ingenuity of Anglo-Saxon settlers and pioneers. Roi Ottley, for example, a second-generation Caribbean migrant, former sportswriter, supervisor of the Harlem Negro Unit, and later an acclaimed author of books on black life in the North, opened a six-page essay titled "Cooking" with the crystal clear statement: "Negro cooking is on the whole American cooking." He further noted, "The Negro's distinctive contribution to the art of cooking . . . now finds itself part of the general stream of American culture," even though "the origin of many standard dishes . . . have been lost in the shuffle of most facts concerning the Negro generally."[93] Indeed, as chapter 3 examines, material collected in the South for the *America Eats* project gave blacks a largely stereotypical role in the American culinary narrative as "mammies" and "uncles." Ottley's demand for historical accuracy was also a cultural and political claim on American taste that, though often muted, resonated throughout New Deal food writing.

Federal editors and local fieldworkers lived and sensed on shifting racial ground, and the bureaucratic categorization of race in black and white imperfectly reflected the everyday racial vernacular in use in FWP offices. The all-black Negro Studies units were mirrored by the Social-Ethnic Studies Project, which documented the lives of Southern and Eastern Europeans, but also Asian Americans, Mexican Americans, as well as Scandinavians and, in Connecticut, "Yankees." This project, like *America Eats*, eluded the vocabulary of whiteness for categories such as "national group" and "foreign-born whites," and its archives are organized along ethnic as well as occupational and class lines.[94] Reading the Social-Ethnic Studies correspondence, one often finds it impossible to determine whether FWP workers and editors considered ethnic identities as the result of essential differences or as socially determined—or both, alternatively. Nor was it clear that they thought of race and ethnicity as two different notions. Tellingly, the heading used in the correspondence of the Social-Ethnic Studies Project regularly dropped the "social" dimension and read, for comprehension's sake, "Ethnic (Racial) Studies."[95] The American Guide Series added a level of confusion, as it documented all under the broad category of "Racial Elements." As chapters 4 and 5 explore, that Asian and Mexican Americans were included in the Social-Ethnic Studies Project did not testify to a potential whitening of these populations but rather to their racialization as raced groups separated from both white and black Americans.

How to assess the fine line between the "merely exotic" and the regionally authentic was a conundrum never fully resolved by the federal office and with extensive consequences on the management of race and ethnicity in the archive. Kellock regularly reminded fieldworkers of the need to maintain "a balance between material on customs and traditions of early American origin and those molded or contributed by more recent immigrants."[96] The question of whose food to include in an anthology of American regional eating was especially acute in the Midwestern states, where "some dishes of European origin ha[d] been locally adopted" because these states had been "settled fairly late and received large numbers of Europeans with fully developed cookery traditions." To answer this challenge, the editors developed a rule for integration in *America Eats* that was seemingly aimed at reflecting sensory interethnic relationships on the ground: "Foreign dishes or customs" would be reported on "when they have been adopted by large numbers of people outside the foreign born community."[97] This rule was deceptively flexible and in fact created clear divisions. The Middle West section could "include an account of a lutefisk dinner" since it had been adopted by the entire "American" population, but the sensory integration of "foreign groups" into regional traditions stopped there, and the federal office would not consider "an account of a Chinese Christening party."[98] Making the cut into the national culinary past and sensory present was a confused but key process, as regional racial hierarchies were central not only to regional sensory economies but also to their commodified identities within the nation. As chapter 4 explores, in the Southwest, "Spanish-Mexican" tastes were celebrated as an exotic past surviving in the midst of "American" progress. The regional tourism industry grew out of the exploitation of Mexican food as an authentic domestic exoticism and a multisensory background of hanging red-pepper garlands, spicy food, and foreign-sounding cooks. New Deal food writing framed tasting Mexican food as an American experience, a way to feel the region's romantic past and re-enact its conquest.

Overall, the federal office's prescriptive sensory narrative tightened the threshold of American traditions and offered ethnic and racial communities only a tentative place in the sensory present. That racial and ethnic communities central to the New Deal political and sensory economies, such as Chinese or Italian Americans, should not be represented was a collateral damage integral to the *America Eats* project's blended and elusive discussion of time, place, taste, and demographics. A 1941 exchange of letters and photographs between Edward B. Moulton, from the Arkansas state office, and the federal office exposes some of the sensory and ideological consequences of the FWP's ambiguity toward ethnic Americans. Moulton wrote about the Tontitown, Arkansas, Italian community Grape Festival spaghetti dinner, which "ha[d] been an annual event for the past forty years," and attached pictures of the gathering to his letter (figures 1.1 and 1.2). He added that, even though this event might be irrelevant to the project and was "of course not characteristic of Arkansas, since there [were] only a few scattered Italian communities in the State," he thought that the pictures "might conceivably be of some use."[99] Clearly, forty years of sensory presence in the southern state did not give the Italian community sensory legitimacy in the region. Although Moulton judged the photographic record inadmissible as part of the *America Eats* project, his pictures are an incomparable point of entry into the sensory economy of the Italian community in the southern states. The photographs present an ethnic community not only integrated into American industrial and sensory modernity but also familiar with the taste of southern food. Integral to the menu for the "spaghetti supper" were mushy looking slices of buttered, processed white bread (figure 1.1) and, as the caption of figure 1.2 reveals, fried chicken. Moulton could not make sense of the ethnic taste of the Italian community in rural Arkansas and chose to indifferently dismiss it instead. Neither exotic nor authentic, these modern southern consumers of Italian descent found themselves in the sensory limbo of the *America Eats* project.

Figure 1.1. Spaghetti supper at the Grape Festival, Tontitown, Arkansas, 1941. Photograph by Granger. Federal Writers' Project photographs for the *America Eats* project, Library of Congress Prints and Photographs Division Washington, D.C., LOT 13328 (F).

Despite being edited out of the American culinary and sensory traditions as defined in the *America Eats* project's guideline, the Italian festival in Tontitown is part of its archives. The community holds a liminal place in the process of sensory memorialization the FWP embarked upon. Analyzing this archival margin leads to a series of interrelated conclusions. First, that the Italian community was ruled out of the sensory past reflected longstanding

Figure 1.2. Cooking spaghetti and frying chicken for a spaghetti supper at the Grape Festival, Tontitown, Arkansas, 1941. Photograph by Granger. Federal Writers' Project photographs for the *America Eats* project, Library of Congress Prints and Photographs Division Washington, D.C., LOT 13328 (F).

prejudices against a racialized, or at least "colorized," group. Yet the fact that the local fieldworker did send a report on the festival, mentioning that it was a four-decades-old local custom, also reflects their "in-between" status and their laboring toward whiteness in the Depression decade. The shifting racial status of the Italian community was embodied in their food taste—not quite southern, not quite Italian, and not quite modern; in a nutshell, it was ethnic. Their presence in the archive is not the one of a clearly identifiable sensory other; they are depicted neither as "merely exotic," nor as "foreign," nor as authentic. The food tastes of first- and second-generation European immigrants posed a multifaceted problem to the federal editors. Not only did these populations' tastes blend regional and "Old World" influences with industrial food, but their whiteness was not soundly established and, like the taste of their food, varied across the country. Italian American food did not taste the same in Tontitown, Arkansas, as it did in New York's Lower East Side. The sensory syncretism and local grounding of ethnic Americans complicated their insertion in the culinary narrative imagined by the federal office. Yet, as chapter 5 explores, their liminal place in the archive can also be fruitfully exploited to investigate 1930s ethnic tastes and ethnic sensory economies.

The determination of which and whose tastes were to be judged traditional enough to be part of the *America Eats* book, and ultimately its archive, was a political and social act of sensory discernment. If *America Eats* dealt "primarily with the present [and] current gatherings and the dishes they celebrate," the editors were interested in documenting contemporary eating events only to the extent that they were remnants of the past in the present. The accent would be on so-called "native cookery" rather than "food of recent foreign origins."[100] With some exceptions, the rule tended to favor the inclusion of Anglo-Saxon "settlers" cookeries into the fold of American cuisine rather than the "contribution of national groups" that arrived later in the course of American history. Driving the *America Eats* project was the unstated hope to conserve the past and make it possible for it to spring back to life in all its sensory details. Tasting would activate mnemonic and symbolic links to a selective historical narrative and provide the national imagined community of eaters with opportunities to perform its identity in a sensory mode. No focused debate on the meaning of "foreign" or "native" in matters of food and taste occurred during the span of the *America Eats* project. Federal editors and local workers assumed different positions on the matter and dealt with each case on a pragmatic and local basis. The federal editors' recommendation to not "give much emphasis to the food and customs of unusual or isolated groups" then legitimized the potential exclusion from the *America Eats* culinary narrative of a large segment of the American population.[101] In searching for America's food, the FWP tended to reify racial and ethnic identities and define their supposedly authentic "foreign" tastes—Italians enjoyment of spaghetti, for instance—and therefore their irrelevance to the project. Yet, as the Tontitown Italian community exemplifies, crossover sensory experiences were essential to the formation of racial, ethnic, regional, and ultimately national sensory economies.

America Eats extended the scope of the 1930s search for, indexing of, and archiving of U.S. culture to the senses. However, taste challenges the modern regime of memory, considered by historian Pierre Nora in *Realms of Memory* as obsessed with "the specificity of the trace, the materiality of the vestige, the concreteness of the recording, the visibility of the image."[102] How can the fleeting, polysemic character of taste be preserved in the archive for future consumption? Performing a sensory reading of the archive requires to simultaneously read the archive along, across, and in-between the grain in order to "exercise historical imagination while attending to how people described past flavor experiences [to] help us approximate the nature of taste historically."[103] The "realms of memory" under scrutiny in this pages are not only the food events, the rituals of citizenship sought by the FWP editors, but also the archive itself as a site of production of a national cuisine and the memorialization of taste. New Deal food writing provides a way for the historian to get at what Ann Laura Stoler calls the period's "common sense," in other words, "those habits of heart, mind, and comportment that derive from unstated understandings of how things work in the world, the categories to which people belong, and the kind of knowledge one needs to hold unarticulated but well-rehearsed convictions and credulities."[104] In particular, as later chapters continue to explore, the *America Eats* archive constitutes a rich corpus to examine the "unstated" ways racial and gender categories interacted with taste perception in 1930s America. The editors' careful editing and management of the project determined who would integrate the archive of American taste and how they would achieve it. Reacting to the industrialization of food since the late nineteenth century, they aimed at providing an alternative version of sensory modernity. Yet the focus on undetermined "traditional" food limited the project's potential at presenting a pluralist and progressive national cuisine.

* * *

The FWP's effort to produce a national culinary narrative attentive to the senses was a novel endeavor building on recent developments in the fields of anthropology and folklore. The editors grounded their national culinary narrative in a systemic relationship between distinct regions whose identities and tastes became usable, purchasable, and eatable commodities for a nationwide audience of potential tourists, armchair travelers, and consumers. But while the topic of food and taste seemed at first fitted to the production of a patriotic and eminently entertaining book, the project stumbled upon unexpected issues, such as the weight of industrial food and the influence of ethnic taste on American regional diets. This triggered the broadening of the span of the project, which came to include contemporary habits such as "munching" at the ballgame in its assessment of traditions. The FWP culinary and sensory work in fact took place at a turning point in the making and acceptance of industrial foods as "American" food and participated in this shift. Ethnic and racial groups straddling sensory and regional borders presented a more subdued but constant challenge to the federal editors' vision of traditional food and regional eating patterns. The scope of the project then also tightened as some were explicitly excluded from the *America Eats* project. The New Deal search for America's food created a selective sensory index that painted regional food cultures with a national brush, and, by the same token, helped delineate and reify the racialized borders of American sensory identity, in the past and present.

The editors' reluctance to address clearly the meaning of "America" in the very title they choose, *America Eats*, led them to draw arbitrary and often blurry lines between traditions, "mongrel" modern tastes, and "foreign" contributions.[105] Their somewhat confused stance can be explained by the shifting meaning of race and the emergence of the concept of ethnicity in the 1930s; the culinary and sensory archive they left behind in fact testifies to how the senses participate in the elaboration of such categories. However, New Deal food writing was not only an arena for the prescription of the nation's taste from the top down, it was also a space for local workers to document the evolution of how food tasted and what food meant during the late years of the Depression. Looking for the taste of the past had a cathartic effect on local workers; it allowed them to voice ambivalent feelings of nostalgia and anxiety, often expressed in gendered and raced terms. The sensory patterns the FWP went searching for were exclusionary also because they were restorative and comforting.

Chapter 2

Romance of the Homemade

In the interwar period, the town of Bowers Beach, Delaware, annually hosted an oyster festival known as "Big Thursday." The August celebration was a joyful day centered on a sprawling picnic and "given over to the enjoyment of food, games on the beach, and to renewing acquaintances . . .—all forms of sociability that add zest and savor to the fest." Indeed, the day gave farmers a chance to "take a breathing spell" from the "hot fields" and for housewives to get away from their even "hotter kitchens." The 1941 festival was the topic of a detailed *America Eats* essay focused on two contrasting feminine portraits. First, was the lengthy description of a talkative women who, "seated before an improvised table in a farm truck . . . slice[d] fresh, crusty homemade loaves with a large carving knife, spread butter with the same knife, carve[d] tender slices from home baked ham, and, according to tastes of individuals in her family and with the same knife, add[ed] jam, mustard or pickles to complete the sandwich, select[ed] from a heaped pan a large piece of chicken with her fingers, and hand[ed] sandwich and chicken to the 'next in turn.'" On the other side of the parking lot was her "sister" who, "sitting in a new and handsome motor car open[ed] for her family improved modern food hampers, filled with daintily made and wrapped sandwiches and fried chicken in paper holders, and thermos jars of hot and iced drinks."[1] The anonymous FWP workers who authored this essay presented their readers with a sensory dilemma between tradition and modernity but did not resolve it. This two-pronged description upheld a conservative gender ideal of women as mothers and homemakers while setting up a strong sensory binary that presented two opposed—yet coexisting—ways of sensing food. While one valued home cooking, local food, taste satisfaction, and sensory intimacy, the other prized modern scientific nutrition, sanitation, and mass retailing.

These sisters represented two sides of the same coin. Whether excluded and resisting the inroads of the food industry or adapting to and adopting it, they both became enmeshed in the narrative of modernity and nostalgia central to the New Deal sensory economy. This dialectic informed how the senses would be deployed and regulated within New Deal food writing and ultimately its archive. The sensory and ideological ambiguity set up in the essay on the Big Thursday picnic encapsulates the federal and local FWP staff awareness of, and uneasiness with, the inroads of industrial foodstuffs, "factory bread," and other "food a la concentrate" in the shaping of American taste in the interwar period.[2] The warmth emanating from the farmwoman gave an ironic twist to the ideal vision represented by the up-to-date homemaker and questioned the sensory, social, and moral legitimacy of modern foods. New Deal food writing, especially the *America Eats* project, was a direct reaction to the reshuffling of American taste—triggered, since the late nineteenth century, by the industrialization of the U.S. food system.[3] Though they provided their reader with a choice, FWP workers and editors alike sided with tasty traditional dishes rather than bland and "dainty" industrial foods. They reminisced with nostalgia over the taste of "old timer's" dishes and aimed at recording and reinvigorating what they perceived to be endangered regional foodways. The despised taste of industrial foods shaped the recollection and celebration of allegedly wholesome regional culinary pasts and conditioned the FWP sensory cravings for the hefty ham sandwiches of the farmwoman. FWP workers encouraged their readers to consider whether economic progress was worth the sensory cost. But the choice between tradition and modernity was not so simple. While the portrait of the second woman reads like a science-fiction satire in which a perfect and disembodied homemaker feeds her family with generic sandwiches, she also represented a persuasive ideal of efficiency and success for her less fortunate sister who, from dawn to dusk, worked on making bread, preserving fruits and vegetables, and churning butter. In both cases, the women's labor and bodies were central to the emotional and nutritional well-beings of their families.

If the description of the Big Thursday picnic was heavily gender coded and exemplified contemporary anxieties about industrial food products, it was also racially inflected. In Delaware, segregation was strictly enforced and the Big Thursday picnic exclusively white. "Black Saturday," a parallel African American celebration, traditionally took place a couple of days after the white event. As the state's American Guide Series volume explained, on this occasion "the white community cheerfully g[ave] the celebrants the freedom of the beach and respect[ed] their privilege to enjoy their traditional frolic at the shore." Yet if socialization and "courting" occurred in a similar manner as it did at the white event, the guidebook's description adopted a disparaging tone when noting that Black Saturday sometimes resulted in "affrays of fist-fighting, cutting, or shooting," making the presence of state troopers necessary. In the midst of fast economic and sensory changes, the upholding of racial segregation and racial stereotypes offered a reassuring element of stability and continuity to the white community. But taste segregation did not necessarily mirror social and spatial segregation in the South and, like the white community a few days before, Bowers Beach's black population enjoyed its annual share of bivalves. The local "concessionaires" who supplied whites with fried fish, wieners, soft drinks, and ice cream would have also coveted the black clientele.[4]

The FWP's sensory nostalgia was not so much a yearning for the past as a blueprint for the future. The impending U.S. participation in World War II accelerated the documentation of the *America Eats* project and reinforced its gender and racial limits. FWP editors revived the *America Eats* project in 1941, and a number of state's essays tend to document not only local sensory economies in the New Deal era but also the early mobilization of American senses and psyche for the war effort. The ideal of the "Wartime Homemaker" described by historian Amy Bentley had deep roots in the gender politics of the Depression that restricted women's economic opportunities and situated men at the center of the country's aesthetic, political, cultural, and sensory life.[5] FWP workers' sensory nostalgia for homemade food in the face of food industrialization reinforced the conservative vision of women as mothers and safeguards of the nation's emotional health and sensory vigor. Traditional feminine cooking skills signaled authenticity and timelessness in the midst of modernization. The argument could backfire though, and FWP workers also painted women as irresponsible consumers seduced by the sight of advertising copy and endangering their families by feeding them industrial food. The contrasting portraits that open this chapter did not go as far but indicated the two possibilities. Wartime mobilization reinforced the importance of national sensory coherence and put masculine values at the center of the wartime food culture and sensory economy. Donna Gabaccia notes that "the confusion about what constituted regional American, as opposed to ethnic, corporate, or invented foods in the *America Eats* project resolved itself in the face of national wartime emergency."[6] The rapid resolution of the question that had stymied the project for years was only possible through the sidelining of large parts of the population—women, African Americans, and some ethnic others.

This chapter explores how New Deal food writing's sensory nostalgia put men's taste and desire at its center, kept white women in their kitchens, and subjugated black Americans to stereotyped roles as either auxiliaries to white cooking or sources of invigorating, primitive sensory experiences.[7] Sensory nostalgia became a prescriptive tool used by federal and local FWP staff alike to legitimize prescriptive gender ideals, racial segregation, and the reproduction of racial stereotypes. Only tangentially would readers get a sense of the social and economic role of food in African American communities, especially how cooking and food vending gave black women a measure of autonomy.

Sensory Populism and the Contest of the Progressive Nutritional Order

New Deal food writing grounded its nostalgic outlook in the celebration of "the people" and articulated it in the abiding American populist style. It offered a dynamic model of taste as FWP workers told "the story of what people have eaten because they liked it, not what they ought to eat, or what poor selection of food has done to them."[8] The sensory recording facilitated by *America Eats* aimed at taking stock of the food preferences of the masses. Good eating did not necessarily come from haute cuisine kitchens, professional chefs, or home economics teachers but rather from the vernacular knowledge of local cooks. An editorial memo therefore insisted that stories and recipes should be collected from "a politician, the cook of a man or a woman known for the food he provides at his table, a restaurant-keeper, a cattlemen, a prominent horse-owner . . ., a miner, a store-keeper, or a hobo" and specified that "only teachers of cooking and writers of cookbooks should be barred."[9] Federal editors had to assert their choices steadfastly, as it was a definite departure from the majority of food writing during this period, which focused on dieting, provided domestic advice, and relied on nutritional expertise.[10] That the food of a "hobo," a seminal and folkloric figure representing the disruption brought on by the Great Depression, might be the topic of an essay aimed at celebrating American eating would have seemed ludicrous to many, including fieldworkers. Yet such focus also offered the taste of a life lived authentically and beyond the pretense of civilization.[11]

The populist and sensory outlook of New Deal food writing purposely clashed with the Progressive Era nutritional order that gave authority to nutritional experts, home economists, and cookbook authors.[12] Building on an American Puritan tradition that considered sensory pleasure as inherently suspicious, late-nineteenth and early-twentieth-century understandings of food often implied that food choices should not be made out of taste preferences or appetite but should rather obey the newly established field of nutritional science. The first decades of the twentieth century witnessed the development of the calorie as a unit to measure food energy and the discovery of the role of nutrients and vitamins in human health. Works by Helen Veit and Charlotte Biltekoff have shown how this new understanding of "food as fuel" containing invisible nutrients reshaped American diets and food culture. In their efforts to "get people to spend both their money and their physical energy more efficiently," food reformers came to define a new and tenacious understanding of food in which "rational decision-making based on science trumped pleasure and tradition every time when it came to eating." The Progressive quest for methodical eating equated rational (rather than pleasurable) food choices with patriotism and moral worth.[13]

Progressive Era food reformers were not so much concerned with how food tasted as with whether it provided needed nutrients, vitamins, and calories. They found their "culinary romance" in the "well-regulated functioning of protein, carbohydrate, and fat, and in the marvelous mechanisms of the digestive process" rather than in the celebration of regional or ethnic traditions.[14] The growing food industry built on these scientific and professional discourses to shrewdly market their food within this new nutritional order and paint nonconforming foodways, such as ethnic food, as potential threats to individual health and the nation's future.[15] The Progressive scientific model of nutrition carried over into the interwar period when it animated debates over malnutrition and the health consequences of the Depression. While states of undernourishment and starvation had traditionally been linked to the feeling of hunger and the vision of deprived bodies, the growth of scientific nutrition and the discovery of vitamins and calories resulted in the definition of starvation shifting away from the feeling of hunger—"hollow hunger"—and toward the idea that bodily deprivation could not be felt by the eaters but only diagnosed by doctors—"hidden hunger." The updating of the Food and Drug Act in 1938 enacted this evolution. It encouraged food companies to further research and advertise the ways vitamins could be, tastelessly and innocuously, reinserted into industrial food products.[16] The FWP sought to contest this shift in American understanding of "food as fuel" and food choices as scientific and moral decisions rather than hedonistic preferences triggered by vernacular culinary art and wetted appetites.

New Deal food writing intentionally displaced the focus of its study of 1930s eating culture away from scientific nutrition and toward a revaluation of taste. "Public taste," FWP workers estimated, was threatened by "sedentary loss of appetite, disguised advertising in women's magazines, broadening work-field of women, [and] lack of sound criticism of cookery."[17] From Del-

aware to California, they lamented the sensory loss caused by the rise of
scientific nutrition and complained about "the all-pervasiveness of modern
etiquette books and the equally pervasive educational propaganda towards
an adequate and balanced diet" that had turned "the fine art of eating" in a
"pseudo-scientific search for a lost vitality hidden in the juice of a raw car-
rot."[18] The link between the food industry and perceived sensory loss became
increasingly apparent in the aftermath of the economic crash. The Depression
in fact tightened the food industry's grip on American taste. Most industrial
food companies managed to maintain relatively low prices by drastically and
singlehandedly cutting their suppliers' prices, attracting more and more customers to their products.[19] By the same token, the Depression launched the
creation of a new type of retail space: the supermarket. Businesses came to
appreciate the savings to be made in mass buying and mass retailing of foodstuffs in interchangeable spaces and realized that, "when people had little
money to spend they were willing to forgo the conveniences of time, location,
and service to reap substantial savings on food purchases."[20] Local FWP
workers, such as Donald McCormick in Maine, reported that "despite the
laudatory, nostalgic description . . . the super-market type of grocery store
is the most important factor in . . . eating today."[21] New distribution systems
and retailing spaces made industrial foods available for low prices throughout the country, changing consumption habits as well as tastes and leading
Americans to shift their allegiance away from local, often ethnic, grocers. [22]

The FWP's culinary search aimed at re-centering taste and at reorganizing
the sensory regime of modernity by claiming back smell and touch as part
of the modern sensorium. The evolution of the American model of nutrition since the late nineteenth century increasingly called on the visual and,
through radio advertising, listening capacities of the U.S. public. Modern
nutrition science reproduced an older sensory hierarchy to disjoint food
from the senses of taste and smell, casting them as lower, irrational, and
threatening, in particular to health and morality.[23] A project like *America
Eats* provided federal editors and local workers with an arena to voice their
uneasiness with the sensory consequences of the powerful "creed of progress,"
a creed unhinged by the Great Depression. They seized the *America Eats*
project to express feelings of sensory deprivation and alienation from their
food and to contest the wisdom of rational eating. Describing an incarnated
and sensually imagined nation of eaters offered an alternative narrative to
the scientific and disembodied understanding of food prominent in the Progressive Era and into the interwar period. To inscribe taste at the center of
the New Deal sensory economy, editors and fieldworkers heavily recruited
nostalgic feelings. Their project was a distinct departure from contemporary

understanding of the value of food along scientific measures, but this sensual-ist narrative also shaped a potentially reactionary and conservative version of culinary modernity.

America Eats, the most extensive New Deal culinary project, was an en-deavor to record so-called "traditions" surviving despite the rise of modern consumerism rather than to document Depression cooking or to show how scientific cookery could enhance diets during the economic slump. The edi-tors clearly indicated that they were not interested in documenting either "the story of what has happened to diet during catastrophes" (such as, presumably, the Great Depression) or "commercialized feasts" but rather "social meals attended by friendly groups."[24] They insisted in several missives on the "light" tone of the book and required local workers to put the "emphasis on human interest and the pleasurable aspect of eating" and to write in "as lively and amusing a manner as possible."[25] The narrative the federal editors wished for was timeless—or at least not directly referential. Fieldworkers welcomed the opportunity to express their scorn for the pseudo-scientific discourse of the food industries' advertisement pitch. They went looking for the sensory vitality and common sense of the folks who "forget diets and waistlines."[26] In doing so, they contributed to the codification of a set list of traditional events as the backdrop against which to consider, weigh, and judge contemporary industrial foods and tastes. New Deal food writing is filled with quilting bees, hog-killing parties, sugar pullings, family reunions, Harvest Home dinners, Grange suppers, barbecues, rodeos, pie contests, church dinners, and box suppers.[27] The coverage of these events offers variations on a common theme of commensality, community, and abundance. The narrative composed by the aggregated *America Eats* essays represented the nation as an imagined community of gluttons, experts at "dramatizing food" and looking for any "plausible reason and social gathering" to "ma[ke] stuffed pigs of themselves and la[y] up nightmares for the coming evening."[28]

"Pitch-in picnics" and potluck dinners formed reassuring islands of sen-sory stability and comfort, quasi-utopian community events taking place in an apparently Depression-free, and mostly white, United States. During neighborly outings, church picnics, Fourth of July picnics, school box dinners, and religious all-day singing, "infinite" assortments of pies, cakes, custards, fried chicken, and potato salads that "would literally tempt an epicure" were "drawn" from trunks, "baskets, boxes and large dishpans, . . . and spread with a lavish hand," as if by enchantment. When describing these, fieldworkers constantly underlined the copiousness, tastiness, and steady quality of the home-cooked fare. Men set up boards as tables for the women to cover with hearty salads, homemade pickles, cold cuts, biscuits, pies, and cakes. Dinner was then "eaten very leisurely, as necessary with a meal of such variety and volume; people move[d] from table to table, sampling a dish here, another there, and all the time being urged to 'eat something.'"[29] Potluck gatherings were gender-coded occasions for housewives to pool their resources, and these events triggered culinary competition resulting in the offering of "almost barbarian" amounts of food.[30] Attendees of a North Carolina religious "camp meeting" could choose from fried chicken, roast beef, roast pork, boiled ham, biscuits, sweet potato custard, pumpkin custards, apple pie, lemon pies, chocolate pies, cocoanut pies, chocolate cakes, pound cake, cocoanut cakes, lemon cake, ham sandwiches, tomato sandwiches, pimento-cheese sandwiches, pineapple sandwiches, chicken salad sandwiched, relishes. "Women of the community" started planning the event "for weeks prior," cooking the dishes on "open fireplace or on wood-burning stoves."[31]

FWP workers described food events that were not inevitably unchanging but were nevertheless sensorially suspicious and conservative. Cypress Ridge, Arkansas, may, for instance, have adopted "what seemed good" from the twentieth century (such as radio, the automobile, a university education) but certainly retained "what pleased it" from older times: potato salad made with local spuds, freshly skimmed cream, and "slices of last year's best cucumber pickles"; hams cured with "a mixture of sugar-syrup and red-pepper sauce, and smoked by hickory ambers"; allspice pickled peaches; "shiny" and "deep green" "poke salad"; "ginger bread made with sorghum molasses pressed from home-grown sugar cane"; and ambrosia, a dessert consisting of layers of oranges, coconut, and sugar left aside overnight to "juice itself."[32]

As a consequence of editorial choices that favored sensory descriptions of traditional public repasts over the documentation of contemporary daily meals, the Great Depression is singularly absent from New Deal food writing. Within *America Eats* state files and the five regional essays, the word "Depression" is a rare occurrence. It appears most often in newspaper clippings from the early years of the decade collected for research.[33] FWP workers usually wrote about the Depression in the past tense; indeed, by the early 1940s the rapid development of the military industrial complex accelerated the end of the economic crisis.[34] Thriftiness and food preservation, though keywords of the 1930s and later the war period, were not qualities put forward in *America Eats*. Only one recipe, for eggless "Depression cake," directly referred to want and the need for housewives to adapt their cooking skills.[35] The main discussion of thrift appeared in a New Hampshire essay and did not discuss the Depression but aimed at debunking stereotypes about "Yankee penny-pinchers."[36] Fieldworkers underlined abundance and generous use of rich ingredients rather than frugality. Traditional foods and their taste, because of their nurturing, symbolic, and mnemonic character, provided a sense of stability amid economic and social disruption as well as an adequate sensory vehicle for a broader cultural search and longing for America.

Describing community dinners organized by church and benevolent associations in church basements or community halls was the closest New Deal food writing ever got to evoking the Great Depression. The promise of homemade food, most typically chicken pie, mashed potatoes, and apple pie, was the primary sensory appeal of these events. All were welcomed to these dinners, though the fundraising character of such meals required the purchase of a low-priced ticket; 15 to 35 cents would buy a filling "family style" dinner.[37] According to FWP workers, the regularity of such dinners increased in the 1930s. Courting customers, "church ladies" advertised fundraising community dinners as meals that would provide not only tasty, old-style dishes but also entertaining evenings. These dinners were dual charity events: they brought money to the organizers and helped provide good food and fun to participants on a restricted budget. The "silver that tinkle[d] into the church's cash box" went "to pay the church debts" or to finance the local Ladies' Aid and church relief associations.[38] The "Penny Supper" in Cheyenne, Wyoming, was an evocative variation on the community supper in which the entire meal was donated by church members and served "cafeteria style" in the church basement. "Every helping, whether it is a cube of butter or a small square of meat loaf [sold] for one penny," so that, "a hungry person [could] acquire enough to satisfy" a hearty appetite for very little pocket change.[39] The cause of hunger in this essay can only be inferred: was this the healthy hunger of a hardworking farmhand or the looming hunger of malnourished, unemployed laborer?

"Taste-Sensations That Have Withstood the Test of Time": Sensory Nostalgia in New Deal Food Writing

The sentiment of sensory loss and the populist rhetoric present throughout the *America Eats* archive resulted in an aesthetic of sensory nostalgia. The goal of the *America Eats* project was to document contemporary eating events "of the nostalgic variety [such as] family and pioneer re-unions" in which "the art of cooking" was preserved, "since preparation of fine food remains a creative activity that cannot be duplicated by factory methods."[40] Following Svetlana Boym, I consider nostalgia as an "historical emotion" dependent on the advent of a perceived change—in the first half of the twentieth century, changes brought on by "modernity" and "progress"—and a powerful tool in establishing "national awareness." New Deal food writing was part of a broader ideological reaction to the displacements of modernity that, in Boym's words, built "on the sense of loss of community and cohesion and offer[ed] a comforting collective script for individual longing."[41] A project like *America Eats*, with its focus on culinary traditions and remembered tastes, aimed at crafting a shared script of sensory identity grounded in symbiotic relations between diverse culinary regions. Regional cuisines became "discursive constructs" to answer to the displacement of modernity, recreating a sense of stability and mapping out moral and social norms.[42] Nostalgically remembered regional pasts were held as prescriptive models for individuals in the present. The sensuality and materiality of food allowed for these regional culinary pasts to be not simply imagined but potentially actualized, bitten into, in the form of newly prepared dishes. Fieldworkers dived into this collective sensualist narrative of loss, longing, and celebration.

Sensory nostalgia was a cathartic means for FWP workers to express their anxieties about the industrial food system and accept its ascending grip on American taste. Their emotional response to perceived sensory change is reminiscent of anthropologist Renato Rosaldo's notion of "imperialist nostalgia." Like agents of colonialism that mourn the "natural" or "primitive" states of the cultures that they are contributing to disrupt, FWP workers "valorize[d] innovation and then yearn[ed] for more stable worlds."[43] Longing for tastes of the past, editors and local workers alike established themselves as passive and powerless "onlookers" in the face of the "devastating effects . . . of labor-saving devices and mass production" and the industrial streamlining of their food taste.[44] Those who daily partook in the industrial diet remembered a mythic and wholesome "golden age of eating" during which the method of "cooking and flavoring" relied on "liberality in the use of eggs" and "home-tried lard and home-made butter" rather than "baking powders, soda and cream of tartar [as well as] inexpensive shortenings." Feelings of sensory deprivation and loss, coupled with disdainful mention of "store-bought" food and "confectionaries" were a leitmotif of fieldworkers' reports. Indeed, pointing to a "golden age of eating" only made sense by comparison with a later sensory fall caused by the "commercialization" of food.[45]

The FWP's culinary narrative was a romance of the homemade. More important, then, the FWP archive's nostalgic tone shared key features with the feeling that food anthropologist David Sutton labels "nostalgia for the real." Sutton uses this notion to interpret the late-twentieth-century industry of heritage cookbooks and its celebration of "authentic" tastes perceived as more "real" than the products of the food industry.[46] This nostalgia and longing for the "taste of the homemade" in face of the mass production of food was already noticeable in the late 1930s, and New Deal food writing dovetailed here with a subcategory of cookbooks published in the period that explored America's culinary heritage.[47] Tastes that had slowly complied with the dictates of the food industries and their "commercial imitation of good cooking" rebelled and now longed for home-cooked meals.[48] FWP workers rebelled against bland industrial hams, "decorated with elaborate scorings or cloves, or pineapples, or any artificial doodads" and reminisced "the real thing born and bred in the peanut section of Virginia," its meat "the color of a Cuban mahogany, not anemic pink, and the fat the deep gold transparency of amber beads."[49] They rebelled against the regulatory rhetoric of nutrition relayed by "home economist[s'] college dietetics training" as well as the "dulcet-voiced radio broadcasters and jokester [who] advertise[d] dishes made of pastel hued Jell-O and [were] paid in figures that resemble the United States public debt."[50] As an answer to the bland taste of industrial food, federal editors and local workers alike wished to document "taste-sensations that have withstood the test of time."[51] Beyond taste, it was a way of life, a sense of etiquette, a communal insularity and stability that they imagined, missed, and remembered. As a Vermont writer succinctly put it, they longed for the "world of meaning" that comes with the "home style" after the chicken pie.[52]

FWP workers related an accomplished reshuffling of the "national gastronomic economy" rather than a wholesale change. Though they might still be able to "differentiate between the genuine honest-to-goodness Johnny Cakes and the palate-insulting commercial substitutes," they were resigned. When reporting on the effects of the "hefty swings of that inevitable leveller, Progress" and how it "toppled [hallowed traditions] from [their] throne," they often adopted an ironic tone that allowed them to voice their uneasiness with their own streamlined tastes. Thus, when searching for the American national dish, a Wisconsin fieldworker arbitrated in favor of the hotdog, an "unfortunate . . . gastronomic delight [that] you've either got to take or leave alone."[53] New Deal food writing gave FWP workers the opportunity to come to terms with what one might call a double taste consciousness: while longing for the flavor of homemade foods, they showed their sensory acclimatization to the products of the food industry. Some abandoned irony to opt for a lyrical tone. A fieldworker named Thige, for instance, wrote an elegy to soup after a Pennsylvania-German dinner during which "spoons dip[ped] noisily" not into mere broth but into "rich, brown pools of liquid poetry." "This was not one of your pale, watery concoctions out of a can. This was SOUP as it was meant to be—SOUP as dreamed of by soup makers throughout the ages—a soup that is food to the soul as well as the body. It is an epic composed of butter, soup stock, seasoning and grated cheese."[54] Others combined nostalgia with humor to express regret that the accumulated changes had "relieved [them] from the pleasant past time of digging [their] graves with [their] teeth."[55]

Although the FWP's nostalgic sensory rummage for American eating ascribed prescriptive taste borders to the nation and could be used as a justification for the omission, even exclusion, of contemporary eaters from the pool of national traditions, this nostalgic ethos also led FWP workers to celebrate select ethnic meals. In regions occupied by large, cohesive, and securely white ethnic groups such as Pennsylvania Dutch or Scandinavian populations, community dinners encouraged cross-ethnic eating. The best documentation of this type of ethnic meal in the *America Eats* archive can be found in the essays describing lutefisk, "codfish soaked first in lye, then in water, then cooked, then served with melted butter or cream sauce," and smorgasbord dinners organized by Swedish churches in the Midwest.[56] These dinners were a popular sensory feature of midwestern states, drawing thousand-strong multiethnic crowds of eaters to church basements. The habit of having a public lutefisk dinner was considered by FWP workers to be a "comparatively recent innovation" in the late 1930s, suggesting that the increased taste appeal of ethnic food went hand in hand with the nostalgic sensory cravings of Americans from every ethnic group. Norwegians in Wisconsin had to set a up a "lutefisk Protective Association" to "guard the supper from the invasion of [German and Irish] epicures."[57] Ethnic food offered enhanced taste sensations and slowly became the most evident reservoir of sensory authenticity in the United States.[58] New Deal food writing's sensory nostalgia for "real" food came to embrace ethnic food as exotic but, above all, as uncorrupted by modern nutrition and the food industries.

"Light Tone, but Not Tea Shoppe, Masculine Rather Than Feminine": Tasting Virile Food, Making the Feminine Home Front

In the early 1940s, North Dakota's church basements regularly hosted Lutefisk dinners, prepared according to traditional recipes by mothers and daughters, yet a more "hilarious affair" was the Methodist's church all-you-can-eat pancake breakfast organized by an all-male kitchen crew. For a full morning, the "pancake gang" ensured that hot sausages came "off the skillet as fast as clips from a machine gun, and that in the operating room, pie would go under the knife with mathematical precision."[59] The search for tastiness also opened up to a militaristic future. The nostalgia seeping through New Deal food writing valorized perceived virile foods and tastes as a way to mitigate the sensory and social disruption brought by the Depression and enroll men and women into the war effort. For all its inconstancies, contradictions, and sheer oddities, the *America Eats* material proved systematic on one point: clear gender lines run throughout the archive, separating women's work from men's culinary undertakings. Women could be unpaid cooks for their families, but not professional chefs. An *America Eats* essay from Indiana clearly demarcated the two sides of the embattled contemporary gender front on which "expert amateur chefs, men with years of experience" had a "firm scorn for mere woman 'cooks.'"[60]

New Deal food writing linked the nation's culinary and sensory deterioration to the food industry's increasing role in determining American diet but also held women responsible for indulging in these new foods and serving them to their families. The FWP's nostalgic culinary narrative suggested that women's surrender to standardized food had corrupted their families' diets and tastes and thus weakened the nation's force. Blame for the depreciation of taste fell on women who, "in taking their rightful place in the world affairs . . . ha[d], to a large extent, deserted their pots and pans, and turned over their culinary responsibilities to the manufacturers of prepared foods." Fortunately, "there still [was] the occasional male chef, usually an artist in his line, and well able to maintain the traditions of the past."[61] The rationale that blamed women for the encroachment of industrial foods on Americans' diet and taste played on the anxieties created by women's employment and their increased autonomy during the Depression. The normative ideals of the female homemaker and the male breadwinner proved an effective way to temper women's increased role in public and economic life and were central to the political, legal, and cultural framing of New Deal liberalism.[62] In the context of the FWP culinary projects, this meant that men would have not only to earn the family's bread but also to bake it in order to mitigate their wives' and daughters' alleged shortcomings. Yet although women's failure to properly feed their families was a recurrent theme of New Deal food writing, the explicit focus on public events of a project like *America Eats* effectively forestalled any comprehensive documentation of the solitary and daily work of legions of housewives and working mothers.

Blame and celebration could go hand in hand. While FWP workers recurrently underlined women's failure to properly feed their families, they also celebrated their culinary knowledge, cooking skills, and canning abilities. Avoiding any exploration of women's actual labor, they described them as "kitchen magician[s]" whose "chocolate cakes, with the creamy, milkful

fillings that cover all the golden layers have been praised by hundreds of
preachers and laymen alike." But even homemade food could constitute a
risk, as it flattered men's senses to the point of bringing out childish behaviors
and sinful gluttony. Men, "hard put to choose between apple pie and devil's
food cake with cocoanut icing," became animal-like eaters, "straining at the
leash" before the meal.[63] The feminine original sin could take on a modern
twist when even the "pleasantly-faced" Pennsylvania Dutch girls included,
as part of "country style" meals, an egg salad composed of "chopped eggs in
mayonnaise and vinegar, a regrettable reminiscence of soda-fountain sandwiches, one in which one seems to detect a Liggett's serpent in this Eden."[64]
Women were Eves in the Garden of Eden, encouraging a dangerous gluttony
or weakly giving in to the "corrupting inroads of the dainty recipes of the
ladies' magazines."[65]

The anticipated U.S. involvement in the European conflict made the resolution of the sensory anxieties of Depression America even more pressing.
The last archival entries take the *America Eats* project into the first months
of direct involvement in World War II, a period that reoriented the project
toward overtly nationalist goals. As one editor put it a few days before Pearl
Harbor, "if we can make Americans realize that they have the best table in
the world, we shall have helped to deepen national patriotism."[66] National
wartime mobilization directly recruited Americans' senses. The "gusto" and
verve of *America Eats* now explicitly aimed at re-invigorating American
interest in "traditional dishes" to provoke an emotional and patriotic investment in the nation. By 1941 the disdain for industrial food was not so much
a nostalgic matter anymore but a concrete challenge for the mobilized nation. A Kansas fieldworker filed away a local journalist's tirade that made the
point emphatically clear: "No race will spring to man the barricades with its
stomach stuffed with Waldorf salad nestled in a leaf of lettuce plus a dab of
store-bought mayonnaise on top."[67] The need for sensory vigor and bodily
fitness provided a fitting argument against bland, allegedly feminizing, industrial food.

Recovering the anxieties and ambiguities of gendered experiences of cooking, eating, and tasting in the late 1930s unveils the roots of wartime food
propaganda and the postwar domestic ideology. Situated at a turning point
between the Depression and the economic recovery induced by the wartime
industrial mobilization, New Deal food writing announces the Wartime
Homemaker at the center of Amy Bentley's analysis of World War II food
rationing, *Eating for Victory*. Sensory nostalgia provided FWP workers with
a cathartic mean simultaneously to express and resolve gendered anxieties
through the rhetorical and sensory upholding of conservative, prescriptive

gender roles. In doing so, they paved the way for the World War II governmental and corporate food campaigns, which "perpetuated stereotypical notions of gender by maintaining segregated 'gendered spaces' and portraying women as subordinates whose primary duty was to cook and serve food." The wartime use of "images of women and food . . . to portray American society as ordered, calm, and stable, particularly with regard to established hierarchies of race and gender," built on responses to crisis and change established during the Depression.[68] The same imagined stability was later put to use in the postwar era domestic revival that curtailed women's Depression-era and wartime social advances. Disparaging assessments of women's role in the encroachment of industrial food on American taste carried on in Cold War "narratives of women's embrace of processed foods, the consequent decline in work around food provisioning, and the (welcome) divisions between the realms of politics and consumption."[69] New Deal food writing planted the seeds of this ideology as it portrayed women as eager to adopt timesaving industrial food at the cost of their families' sensory vitality.

New Deal food writing's upholding of restrictive gender roles prefigured the postwar "domestic containment" of women, especially if we understand containment in terms not only of spatial and cultural limits but also of sensory confinement.[70] Contributors to *America Eats*, for instance, considered gender difference as not only a social distinction but also a naturalized difference: the result of an essential sensory disparity. This essentialist argument held women's taste as fundamentally different from, and, because of their supposed acceptance of industrial food, inferior to men's. *America Eats* essays recurrently scorned the "delicate" foods prepared by women under the influence of food manufacturers to praise "lusty and vigorous" dishes: while women had succumbed to the sirens of radio pitches and the sight of glossy advertisements, men kept a steadfast belief in the rightfulness of their taste in directing their food choices.[71] Colorado FWP worker Gladys Gregg opted for an ironic style to express her views on the matter. She addressed her reader, assumed to be male, after a long day of work: "You can hasten to the kitchen . . . to greet the little wife who is 'dead tired' from lighting the gas stove, turning the handle of the can opener, and emptying that can of well advertised, beautifully pictured wax beans in the last home makers magazine." The "little wife" might try to conclude this sorry dinner with "elaborate, gaudily colored cuts of a variety of puddings and pastries and cakes made from especially prepared flour. But just ask any typical American man what he wants for dessert and he will (if he isn't under orders from the family physician to 'protect his stomach') almost invariably answer, 'pie.'"[72] Gregg's own role in this essay is ambiguous. She positioned herself as sensually superior to the average housewife, disparagingly assessed women's work and sensing bodies, all the while scorning scientific nutrition and turning established sensory hierarchy upside down by equating rationality with taste rather than with vision and the modern sound of radio broadcasts. Although Gregg still implied rationality to be a manly pursuit, she introduced an original twist by putting men in charge of safeguarding culinary traditions and sensory authenticity, a role usually devoted to women.

If the continuity between the late Depression and the war/postwar periods needs to be highlighted, important contrasts also exist. The *America Eats* editors chose to emphasize the public sphere and public group eating as sites of sensory stability and tradition when wartime food propaganda and later the postwar feminine mystique—despite offering "glimpses" of communitarian cooking—elevated white private households as "islands of serenity" in need of sensory and social safeguarding.[73] Indeed, according to the editors in Washington, if the private life of American families had been unhinged throughout the decade and their taste remade by the encroachment of industrial food, public eating still upheld reassuring gender roles, promising "traditional" taste experiences. The editors justified their focus on group meals by explaining that women, "even though they . . . feed their families on canned foods and factory breads at home . . . revert to traditional cooking methods when preparing their contributions" to public meals. The rationale was a sensory one but also slid into a moral and patriarchal argument. To their satisfaction, southern "women who contribute to the family income by working in the cotton mill do not expect men to share in the preparation of the group meal or in the washing of the dishes, even if they do at home."[74]

While the iconic 1943 Norman Rockwell *Freedom from Want* illustration would soon depict the white middle-class family Thanksgiving dinner as a metonymic representation of the nation, the populist aesthetic of New Deal food writing held public eating as the prevalent image of the nation's democratic ideal. Though *America Eats* strove to imagine the white domestic sphere as a nonproblematic space, a comforting buffer of tradition in the midst of economic and sensory changes, domestic life was not part of the sensory landscape the federal editors wished to document. The FWP grounded its culinary narrative in the idea that only when eaten in public could the comfort foods baked in the white home become a sensory axiom in the description of the United States as a strong and united family around the dinner table. To increase the patriotic and emotional investment in the nation, New Deal food writing attempted to disjoint food and cooking from its association with women's work and in doing so inscribed it within a masculine narrative.

Focusing on public eating put men at the center of the New Deal sensory economy, and the federal editors explicitly instructed fieldworkers to adopt a "light tone, but not tea shoppe, masculine rather than feminine."[75] Masculine cooking was public, massive, and traditional, or it was not. The federal guidelines encouraged FWP workers to focus on public performances of masculine cooking and established meat, especially barbecued meat, at the top of a symbolic food hierarchy ruled by manly, uncompromising appetites. A barbecue cook would "spur any modern method of cookery" and would always feed a crowd, since "your real barbecuer is unable to think in terms of less than a hundred guests and from that into the thousands."[76] FWP workers protested against the taste of industrial foods but also resented the alienating and feminizing character of modern cooking devices and magazines' etiquette advice. The masculine character of the meat feasts was therefore reasserted in the momentary but compulsory abandonment of table manners; indeed, "tableware [was] considered definitely effeminate" and "greasy fingers, greasy chins" were the sure signs of a successful roast. "If the fingers get too greasy suck them or use paper napkins."[77] Contributors to *America Eats* relished the opportunity to celebrate men such as Buck Lee of Utah, the "best damned artist in the San Juan [county]," whose steak was "no dainty mignon."[78]

The revaluation of taste central to the project of New Deal food writing was, at its core, a masculinist endeavor, and male public cooking was a favorite site for symbolic and sensory performances of citizenship. Fieldworkers from the West responded particularly positively to this framework, using their regions' "gusto" as a leitmotif for their essays.[79] Reynolds, who composed the Far West regional essay, played on this virile cultural mood when he presented his region's food culture as "robust," one using "few condiments . . . pastries, whipped or fluffed desserts and delicate dishes." He offered the range and outdoor cookeries of the mythified cowboys as an alternative to feminine, urban, and modern foods; the West was the land of "foods to satisfy the hunger of a virile people, adventurous, and hardy." As a result of this "tradition of masculine cookery," he explained, "a man who dons an apron . . . is not looked upon with scorn in the West. Instead, the sight conjures visions of robust food, savory, and with aroma lusty enough to banish all such anemic things as lettuce, sandwiches and frail tidbits." [80]

The *America Eats* photographic record reinforced this gendered sensory economy, offering us glimpses of bare-chested men cooking meat for the crowds. All would not put on aprons after all (figures 2.1 and 2.2). Sights, smells, and tastes worked to affirm the virile image of the soon-to-be GIs. As a Kansas journalist declared, to the delight of a local worker who copied the article word for word: "'The Old West' ha[d] a fine tradition of freedom and a noble cuisine to back it up" and on which American values could rely in wartime.[81] The Depression was a time of reconfiguration of American manhood, and New Deal food writing reflected the "re-masculinization" of American culture. The ideal manliness of the period was constraining, taking the figure of the muscular white heterosexual male as model.[82] New Deal food writing's focus on masculine public meat feasts was then no less normative than the ideal feminine cookery it called for (plentiful, tasty, and respectful of "traditions"). But it effectively relegated everyday, somewhat routine, female cooking and the documentation of food during hard times, including the Depression, to the margins of its narrative.

Direct involvement in the war slightly changed the project's emphasis. In a letter sent to all state offices a few days after Pearl Harbor, FWP director John D. Newsom indicated that, as the agency's place "in the national emergency had not yet been determined, no change had been made in plans for the [*America Eats*] book." He added, "We believe, however, that it may be desirable to increase emphasis on the way settlers and also people in later periods managed to provide themselves with very palatable meals even

Figure 2.1. Weighing the beef, Los Angeles Sheriff's Barbecue, 1941. Federal Writers' Project photographs for the *America Eats* project, Library of Congress Prints and Photographs Division Washington, D.C., LOT 13328 (F).

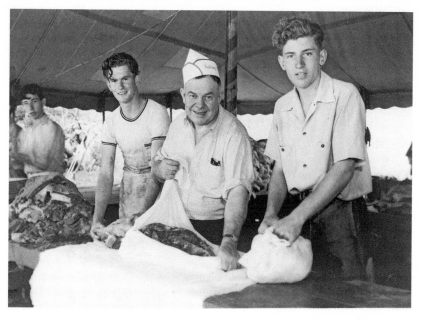

Figure 2.2. Wrapping the meat in cheesecloth, Los Angeles Sheriff's Barbecue, 1941. Federal Writers' Project photographs for the *America Eats* project, Library of Congress Prints and Photographs Division Washington, D.C., LOT 13328 (F).

though they lacked the foods and cooking facilities now considered necessities." After Pearl Harbor, material goals dominated over the sensory and emotional nation-building efforts of the earlier era. Rather than inquiring about the social customs of public meals, Newsom now required the state offices to send in "account of local gatherings of the simpler sort," which he thought "may have a stimulating effect as food supply and distribution difficulties develop."[83] This new stance retained taste as part of the project but also integrated a practical standpoint as it aimed at increasing consumption of selected products and foreshadowed the state's wartime food rationing and food propaganda.[84] The new editorial line adopted relatively flexible rules for inclusion in the *America Eats* project. If Anglo-Saxon "settlers" were still squarely situated at the center of the imagined and remembered sensory past, then the relatively open-ended meaning of "people in later periods" gestured toward the inclusion of "Nationality Group Eating" (German, Scandinavian, as well as Southern and Eastern Europeans) in the book. Yet the project still functioned according to a rigid black-and-white racial boundary.

Cooking Up Race and Gender

America Eats, to fulfill its "socio-anthropological" goal, covered a number of black public events and their food. But despite the existence of "Negro Units" throughout the country, the establishment of the Negro Studies Project in Washington, and the employment of African American men and women as FWP fieldworkers in some states, few, if any, black writers seem to have been assigned to the project.[85] As a result, when the essays collected offered glimpses of African American foodways, they often did so while relying on sensory stereotypes. Dialogues were transcribed in dialect, the written text making the "sonic color-line" visible to the reader.[86] John W. Thomas, from the Virginia FWP, interviewing an anonymous "Negro man" and Baptist preacher about the various ways his congregation prepared chicken for church picnics, quoted him calling out his congregation: "Now we come to another important part of de services, a greater time-amen! I see de sisters got a heap lot of baskets out on de yard, I jest knows 'tis chicken in dem—amen!" Building on widespread stereotypes associating blacks and chicken, Thomas added that "the very nature of the services demands chicken": "chicken baked, fried, stewed, stuffed, and broiled."[87] In another instance, from Mississippi this time, a copy included a series of recipes provided by William Wheeler, a black man from Leflore County. The essay hinted at the power dynamic between fieldworker and informant; a paragraph on "peppergrass" concluded with the comment, "Dis is fine, Miss."[88] The classed origins of black food preferences were not a primary concern for the FWP, and African Americans' food taste were described as an unproblematic racial attribute, along with the sounds of their voices, the sight and smells of their bodies. References to smell, whether the "unmistakable" and "obnoxious" scent of the chitterlings that "most of the country Negro of the South relish," or the odor of the cook's "perspiration," regularly reinforced the construction of African Americans' sensorium as intrinsically different.[89]

Black community events, when they appeared in New Deal food writing, were picturesque, multisensory, and ultimately grotesque. Audition and touch reinforced taste and smell to define a multisensory color line. FWP workers seemed more interested in describing the singing, drinking, dancing, and "all-night dice game" or the religious fervor that, in their view, accompanied or followed black communal meals than the meals themselves.[90] Most of the black public meals and events documented in New Deal food writing were religious in nature, amped-up versions of white revival meetings. Food was central to all religious events documented in *America Eats*, but in depictions of black events, the food and worldly appetites threatened to upstage the faith, the participants "mak[ing] constructive effort to infuse the spiritual meaning of the celebration, without spoiling the feasting." The largest of these events, the Wilmington, Delaware, "Big Quarterly," a yearly August conference of the African Union Methodist Church was amply documented by various FWP projects. An *America Eats* essay explained: "Feasting begins almost at dawn and lasts until dusk, the faithful making their selections and eating as they march, listen, or sing. They conscientiously bark to the preacher's words while munching a pig's feet, or chewing a cold roast-pork sandwich. They study the speakers with wide round eyes over the neck of pop bottle, and between bites on a chicken leg they would cry, 'Yes, brother!' and 'Glory, Hallelujah!'"[91] The 1938 Delaware American Guide Series volume had already put the bar low, describing a "million throngs of primitive folks . . . gathered to worship their God." The anonymous author(s) presented sensory satisfaction as the main activity of the meeting, rather than faith. In streets "phalanxed with tables," passers-by could choose from "fried chicken, chicken potpie, ham and cabbage, hot corn pone, greens and side meat, frankfurters, watermelons, soft drinks, vari-colored 'ades,' pig's feet, and dishes of unknown origin." Eating, sensing, and sensed black bodies were at the center of the FWP's assessment of the event: "To the casual observer, 'Big Quarterly' presents a kaleidoscopic mass of humanity, vari-colored in dress and hue of skin—sleek, slender, buxom, and fat."[92]

At both black and white events, cooking activities tended to be homosocial affairs. Rarely were men and women of any races described cooking together. The preparation of stewed dishes, such as Brunswick stew or chicken pileau, two southern traditions, was a social event in itself. The cooking process of the latter required boiling chickens before picking the meat from the bones and adding it to a mixture of rice, tomatoes, and salted pork (figure 2.3). Similarly, in the case of Brunswick stew, FWP workers relayed the widespread opinion that "getting ready [was] the hardest part of stew doings."[93] Women but also men cooked these demanding dishes, though not together. In fact, Brunswick stew could take a masculine overtone, and in Richmond, Virginia, the City Sergeant's recipe attracted thousands when he and his "assistants" decided to put together their "truly colossal feat of outdoor cookery" for all sorts of charities. The mayor himself served up the stew.[94] In South Carolina, men prepared "Chicken Bog," a dish that "might be called the masculine version of chicken pilau."[95] The difference here was rhetorical rather than sensory: the very name of the dish embodied the gender segregation of cooking activities. However, gender segregation did not always follow race lines: essays and photographs about pileau and Brunswick stew commonly described black men as white women's cooking help.

The assertion of prescriptive gender roles in New Deal food writing was orchestrated along race lines. Tangled culinary and sensory relationships between race and gender fundamentally shaped 1930s sensory economies. If gender hierarchies were primordial, they were trumped regularly by classed and raced logics so that black men could cook under the command of white women. When white women cooked pileaus and stews for the community, black men watched the fire, stirred the pot, made the coffee, and fetched the diverse ingredients necessary to complete the meal. Descriptions of black men's work alongside white women relied on a stereotype that food scholar Psyche Williams-Forson identifies, in her analysis of black men's relationship with food in American visual culture, as the "image of the happy-go-lucky black man . . . needed to reassure both northerners and southerners that the South remained 'in control.'" At the end of a long day of cooking, these men were compensated by either a small wage or a heaping serving of food and a slice of watermelon, "black face peering happily above a crimson slice."[96]

Racial segregation hinged on gendered interactions. Analyzing the role of black men as cooking auxiliaries to white women helps explore the interconnected construction of racial and gender categories in New Deal food writing. In a 1941 essay titled "A Ton of Rice and Three Red Roosters," FWP worker Stetson Kennedy described a peanut festival in Florida as "typically American and Southern," by which he meant that, "in spite of the area's large Negro population, the only ones in attendance were those who assisted in the preparation of the chicken pilau."[97] This was not a casual remark, as so often in New Deal food writing, but a denunciation of racial segregation and a sharp unveiling of its incoherencies. In the 1930s Kennedy worked alongside African American writer Zora Neale Hurston to collect folklore and folksong for the Florida FWP; he rose to national fame as an advocate against segregation and racial hatred in the 1940s and 1950s.[98] Kennedy's 1941 essay documented the peanut festival while exposing the interwar state of race relations to the potentially national audience of *America Eats*. He explained that, when he arrived, "preparation for the dinner had been under way since early morning, by a group of towns women who had volunteered their services. About 29 three-legged iron kettles were assembled in the park and two Negro men kindled fires under them and got them boiling." Then, "when the rice was done, the chicken meat was mixed with it, and stirred by a Negro man with a board. A woman with a spoon and boxes of salt and pepper went from kettle to kettle" while "nearby, a Negro man boiled coffee in large metal drum" (figure 2.4).[99] Kennedy also documented his visit to the festival with a photographic reportage that illustrated his condemnation of the ideology of white supremacy that enabled at-will ordering of black bodies (figures 2.3, 2.4, and 2.5).

Figure 2.3. Picking the meat from the chicken bones is one of the big jobs in preparing the pilau, Florida Peanut Festival, 1941. Photograph by Stetson Kennedy. Federal Writers' Project photographs for the *America Eats* project, Library of Congress Prints and Photographs Division Washington, D.C., LOT 13328 (F).

Figure 2.4. Coffee is made by boiling it in this large metal barrel, Florida Peanut Festival, 1941. Photograph by Stetson Kennedy. Federal Writers' Project photographs for the *America Eats* project, Library of Congress Prints and Photographs Division Washington, D.C., LOT 13328 (F).

Figure 2.5. The rice and chicken is boiled together in iron kettles, Florida Peanut Festival, 1941. Photograph by Stetson Kennedy. Federal Writers' Project photographs for the *America Eats* project, Library of Congress Prints and Photographs Division Washington, D.C., LOT 13328 (F).

Kennedy's photographs unveil a world of racialized gender relations usually considered uncritically throughout New Deal food writing. The photograph with the caption "The rice and chicken is boiled together in iron kettles" looks especially inappropriate for illustrating an assignment aimed at glorifying American foodways (figure 2.5). None of the characters are looking at the camera; the food is evidently present but not in sight. Yet it is a telling visual snapshot of the interaction of race and gender in shaping 1930s sensory economies. The white woman, with her back to the viewer, embodies a generic white housewife ideal; dressed in a humble and proper flowery cotton dress, her maternal and stout body wears the apron as an essential accessory. She is too absorbed in her cooking duties and in giving orders to the two black men to have time to face the camera, smile, or pose. She occupies the center of the scene and, with the tip of her spoon, directs the actions of the two black men. One of them is vigorously stirring a pot, the other holding a heavy tub of food. She is clearly positioned as the master of operations in the middle of the open-air kitchen. In the background, wood fences enclose the cooking area, creating a public yet privatized space in which white men—on the right corner—can only peek into. Allowed into the white feminine cooking area, the two black men are made obedient to the will of one white woman and compelled to accomplished menial tasks, bending over the cooking pots. The mixing of the hierarchies of gender and race worked to reinforce the assertion of white supremacy.

Black men were paradoxical figures in the gendered set-up of America's public meals on the eve of World War II. If white women could subjugate them, widespread stereotypes also held them as symbols of untamed masculinity and sensory primitivism.[100] In particular, black men were major actors in the extensive homosocial 1930s barbecue culture, which, in the words of literature scholar Andrew Warnes, rested on a deep-seated "mythology of savagery and freedom, of pleasure, masculinity and strength."[101] For this very reason, it was one of the favorite topics of *America Eats* contributors. Both white and black men could be barbecue cooks, but FWP workers took a particular relish in sensual descriptions of black men's cooking. In an essay on "Rodeo with Barbecue," Alabama's Luther Clark offered a multisensory description of the overnight preparation necessary to a successful barbecue. At sundown, the black men's bodies, moving through "long rows of half-hidden fires glow[ing] in the humid summer night," blended with the animal world as "a happy murmur of Negro voices formed a deep toned accompaniment to the thrills of insects and the occasional drowsy call of some bird." "An aroma, indescribable but most pleasing, weighted the gentle stirring air" and promised a satisfying meal. The author further celebrated the "black men with big buckets of barbecue sauce" who "watch[ed] with trained eyes each spitted portion of meat and pick[ed] just the right moment to swab it with the sauce and turn it to a new position."[102] According to such narrative, it was black men's closeness with the natural world and their retention of traditional knowledge anchored in the senses that made them particularly well fitted to the preparation of barbecued meat.

New Deal food writing curtailed black sensory knowledge by linking it to intellectual inferiority. Lauding black men's trained sensory apparatus and appreciating their craft at barbecuing meat did not foreclose *America Eats* contributors to adopt a condescending tone and highlight the primitive nature of the "pit artists" senses. In the regional essay for the South, Lyle Saxon built on a Mississippi write-up to describe barbecue cook Bluebill Yancey as "blood brother of the Ugly Man" before noting that he followed instinct rather than recipes and cooked "according to the stages of the moon, and [had] been known to call off entire barbecues at the slightest sound of thunder on cooking night." His superstitions did not stop there, as he required that "no women must come within smelling distance of the pit, for the meat can't 'breathe freely' with a woman cook around." Though his craft was celebrated, Yancey was also the object of ridicule, and his satisfaction upon seeing the "brown hunks of meat approach perfection" was compared to the proudness of "a monkey with a tin tail."[103] Such disparaging portraits deflated threats to white masculinity (or femininity) to cast black men's sensory superiority as, more than anything, hope for the sensory invigoration of the white race. The original Mississippi essay on Yancey described how he "dab[bed] on more hot stuff" in synchronization with political speeches, dressing the meat with his secret "mopping sauce" to energize the assembled democratic crowd of white eaters and voters.[104] Controlled and tamed by the gendered power structure of white America, the black sensory force could reverberate on the white citizenry.

The dish of chitterlings was another key site of masculine cross-racial sensory exchanges. Consisting of "hog innards chopped, well condimented and boiled" or rolled in meal and fried, the dish originated in the South and was, according to a Kentucky fieldworker, "peculiar to the old-time Negro 'mammy.'"[105] A low-cost source of animal protein, it was one of the main dishes prepared by black women to raise money; throughout the country "chitlin' struts," "chitterling feasts," and "Saturday night suppers, featuring the delicacy known as chitterlings, [were] among the most popular forms of entertainment" for "Negroes."[106] Now a classic of soul food, chitterlings was not solely associated with African Americans; white, rural southerners also adopted it as "cultural emblem and nourishment" in the interwar period.[107] Some of the *America Eats* essays on chitterlings were racially ambivalent, and the same Kentucky fieldworker who identified black women as skilled chitterlings cooks specified that even though "chitlin' suppers [were] an important event in almost any Negro settlement during hog killing time, fondness for the chitterlings [was] not confined to Negroes." In Mississippi, a group of "enthusiastic" white men formed the "Mississippi Chitlin Association," which met for the "sole object" of eating chitterlings and "waste[d] no time getting to the business at hand." Class similarities and local identities in part explain this shared taste for a cheap, tasty protein.[108]

Tellingly, chitterlings are one of the few dishes, along with barbecue, that led *America Eats* fieldworkers to regularly name race, rather than letting readers assume it from the context or style of the dialogue, and make gender apparent. The dish's overtones of untidiness and fearlessness combined to satisfy manly appetites: chitterlings were allegedly only "enjoyed by white *men* and Negroes." A Kentucky essay indicated that "one Congressman annually made a special trip from Washington to his home State for a good 'mess of chitlin's.'"[109] Crossing class, race, and gender boundaries of taste was central to the enjoyment of the meal. For white men, symbolically and practically weakened in their breadwinner status during the Depression, confidently eating the black specialty dish of offal was a source of sensory regeneration and empowerment on the eve of World War II. But as a response to the increasing association of chitterlings with blackness, the dish became taboo in a number of white communities where it caused "dismay to some, hilarity to others, and satisfaction to a few."[110] Chitterlings could trigger potent, unusual, contradictory, and in any cases emotional gustatory reactions. All were linked by "the intricate interplay of proximity and touch, desire and revulsion" inherent to feelings of disgust. Recent works on disgust have shown how pleasure and disgust, palatability and inedibility, are not opposite but categories tethered together. As Elspeth Probyn puts it, it is the "spectre of closeness that provokes disgust."[111] Here, the possibility that blacks and whites, in particular white women, enjoyed the same strong, smelly food endangered the core ideological tenets of white supremacy and racial sensory difference. The dish had to be pushed out of the edible category.

Chitterlings' association with African Americans also made the dish an early vehicle for the expression of black pride and could be reclaimed by the ones who prepared the majority of chitterlings: black women. The Louisiana American Guide Series volume, for instance, noted that Madame C. J. Walker, "the Louisiana Negress who amassed a fortune with a hair-straightening preparation" and became an early figure of black women entrepreneurship, "served chitterlings and mustard greens, as well as caviar and champagne" at her daughter's wedding.[112] She showed an acute understanding of 1930s sensory economies and was able to manipulate the sensory clichés associated with chitterlings to blur boundaries of taste, class, place, and race.

The nostalgia that contributed to the depiction of white women as either kitchen magician turning out tasty homemade food or neglecting cooks feeding their families industrial foodstuffs also encompassed African American women, though not for the same reasons. Black women's employment as domestics decreased during the Great Depression, a trend that accelerated in the early 1940s as they found work in defense plants.[113] But if black women's presence in white American kitchens declined, they stayed anchored in its food culture. The period marked the heyday of the mammy stereotype, a faithful cook dedicating her life to the white family she served and most famously represented by the commercial figure of Aunt Jemima. Through upheaval and changes, depression and war, one could always buy into the ideal of idle southern femininity and black kitchen work that the trademarked mammy made available to all consumers.[114] New Deal food writing did not depart from this imagery and depicted black women as nurturing and comforting images inscribed in the white domestic sphere and harking back to a simpler, pre-industrial past. This nostalgia in part relied on a sensory argument: black women's closeness with the "lower" senses of smell and taste and their lack of intellect meant that, despite the encroachment of industrial food, they had kept alive "traditional" foodways at the heart of the white home.

Beyond racist comments and prescriptive gender rhetoric, New Deal food writing also provides glimpses of how African Americans, especially women, used food and cooking as means of economic survival in the Depression. The *America Eats* material occasionally presents African American women's entrepreneurial strategies to make do in hard times. If the white kitchens where black women toiled were part of a private sphere infrequently documented in *America Eats*, eaters-turned-customers regularly infringed on black women's domestic spaces. Black women turned their homes into public and commercial spaces by regularly transforming them into provisional restaurants. These events, now public, came under the purview of the *America Eats* project. Harlem "rent parties" and the southern "chitlin' strut" were all "given for the same purpose as the well-known fish fries of most southern towns—to collect money for any reason, for paying someone's funeral expenses, to buying a winter coat."[115] When reporting on African American communal meals, fieldworkers put little emphasis on commensality, openly evoking poverty and the community's dire need for cash, whether endemic or triggered by the Depression. *America Eats* for the most part portrayed African American women as cooking "purely and solely for profit," either as domestic workers in white households or community entrepreneurs. Given the meager wages that the former activity provided, they often did both. In the South, cooks regularly "supplement[ed]" their salary by "pitching frequent Saturday night fish suppers, as they are elegantly termed along the [Mississippi] levee."[116] Depicting black women's entrepreneurial relationship to food in the Depression, *America Eats* presents them, although unintentionally, as agents in their own lives.[117] Despite its limits, New Deal food writing bears witness to how black women navigated local sensory economies to satisfy customers, feed their families, and find employment.

*   *   *

By the late 1930s the taste of industrial food had become a key element of regional sensory economies. Reacting to this evolution, and paying little attention to the nutritional consequences of the Depression, FWP workers yearned for the taste of remembered and imagined "real" food, they longed for the sensory comfort of homemade dishes. At the heart of the culinary narrative collectively produced by fieldworkers in all corners of the country under the leadership of the federal staff was a sensory rebellion against industrial food. They expressed this nostalgic rebellion in a populist tone and focused on public performances of eating rather than private family meals but kept conservative gender ideals and racial stereotypes at its heart. The expanding wartime rhetoric of the early 1940s, however, redirected American cultural energies away from the 1930s search for American folklore and toward military and home-front mobilization. FWP workers then assuaged national anxieties about the industrial future through the nostalgic description of an imagined sensory past but also through the celebration of white men's renewed vigor after a decade of economic Depression.

While most food histories have considered World War II and the postwar advances in food processing as key factors in the making of contemporary American taste, New Deal food writing invites us to shift back the origins of the postwar nutritional order and gendered domestic ideology to the last years of the Depression.[118] This chronological shift enables shedding light on the role of entangled histories of race, taste, and gender in the making of U.S. sensory economies. The FWP critique of the industrial sensory regime had the potential to spur a bold rethinking of the interwar food system. However, it realized this potential through the entrenchment of prescriptive gender roles and the exploitation of ethnic and racial others' sensing bodies. The two feminine portraits that opened this chapter presented a strong sensory and culinary contrast between crusty homemade ham sandwiches dripping with mustard and cellophane-wrapped white bread collations. Yet, in both cases, women remained circumscribed to their kitchen and to their role of providing mothers. Similarly, black cooks of both sexes most prominently appeared in New Deal food writing as sensory and cooking auxiliaries to white performances of gender, in the past as in the present. This was not secondary to the FWP's vexed discussion of the "taste of place" in the five American regions selected by the federal office: the impasse in delineating regional cuisines attested to the process of nationalization and industrialization of American taste but also established sensory constructions of race as central to definitions of regional cuisines. Keeping the politics of the *America Eats* project in its background, the following chapters build on food writing throughout the FWP archive, New Deal food writing in its full span, to explore the links between taste, race, and place in three sensory economies.

Chapter 3

Tasting Place, Sensing Race

At noon, on January 31, 1939, a white South Carolina superintendent on a Works Progress Administration (WPA) building project yelled to the thirty-nine black laborers under his command: "All right, boys. Knock off for lunch." Having worked all morning digging a roadside ditch and leveling the roadbed, the men put down their shovels, "scramble[d] out of the ditch," and walked toward tin buckets "dress[ed] off" by their wives the night before. While the three white supervisors "assemble[d] at a fire of their own" to partake in "cheese sandwiches," coffee, and the "treat" of a shared peck of roasted oysters, the "Negroes," in quantitative advantage, claimed the main fire. There, in a "quick motion," they "stuck" their tablespoons into "masses of hominy grits soaked with bacon grease" and "those who didn't bring fried fish produce[d] butts meat fried to a turn, or fat pork," all of which "disappear[ed] into wide open mouths." There was "much smacking of lips and licking of spoons," and the men scorned cups to drink coffee from the bottle.[1] The author of this essay, Chalmers S. Murray, was a white FWP worker in South Carolina who grew up on the Edisto Islands and became fascinated with the local Creole culture. His most successful novel, *Here Come Joe Mungin*, appeared in 1942 and mostly cast African American characters. Its eponymous hero engaged in stereotyped activities: the back cover presented him fighting, drinking, and preying on his sleeping wife. Murray's roadside essay provides a snapshot of a segregated southern sensory economy in which the color line is neatly reproduced in matters of food and taste.[2]

Murray's description of segregated eating habits in the U.S. South was a rather unoriginal work, as it used worn clichés about African Americans. Details, such as the men's lack of manners and the underscored greasiness and heaviness of the food, built on pervasive stereotypes about the coarse quality of black appetites in need of strong, sharp taste to be satisfied.[3] But while white southern FWP workers often portrayed black sensory apparatus as crude, numb, or unrefined, they were also quick to realize that, given African American cooks role in shaping southern cuisine, the argument could not hold for long and had to be amended. An undated scrap note addressed to Lyle Saxon, the director of the Louisiana FWP in charge of editing the first *America Eats* regional essay to serve as model nationwide, spelled out the sensory stereotypes that animated often-paternalist descriptions of blacks' eating and cooking habits in New Deal food writing. The note read: "Several people have raised the question of why Negroes have a special talent for cooking. Might the answer lie in the keenness of sense of perception among more primitive people: cookery makes it appeal to sight, touch, taste, and smell—above all the sense of smell, the sense of taste distinguishing only between sweet, sour, salt, and bitter."[4] From a gustatory point of view, then, African Americans were superior, more in touch with their senses. There was a twist: smell and taste have always ranked low on the established sensory hierarchy, and classical theory linked these with animalistic, "primitive" needs such as the need to feed one's body.[5] Blacks' sensory supremacy was directly linked to their alleged debased nature. This paradoxical sensory logic was a means for both the justification of segregation and the celebration of black cooks' role in creating and maintaining, somewhat unbeknownst to them, regional culinary traditions.

New Deal writing about food in the South and southern food in general unveils the central role of the senses in shaping the color line in the interwar period. It sheds light on the "historically conditioned, visceral, emotional aspect of racial construction and racism" and on the sensual and lived experience of race in interwar America.[6] Despite the inclusive civic ideal promoted by the New Deal state, a deep current of racial exclusion remained strong throughout the Great Depression, and the New Deal did not question the southern regime of legal segregation.[7] Moreover, segregation was not confined to the South, and de facto segregation remained central to the lives of the millions of African Americans who moved to northern cities as part of the Great Migration of southerners, black and white, during the interwar period.[8] This chapter considers how the national gaze promoted by the FWP prompted a reappraisal of the taste of southern food by following this regional cuisine through its spatial, social, cultural, racial, and sensual journey in 1930s America. Southern food and its taste, moving with millions of African American migrants to the northern metropolis, slipped from being mainly associated with a region to being linked to race, allowing for its later political and cultural reconceptualization as "soul food" in the midst of the civil rights movement.[9] Following the evolution of the taste of southern food, this chapter highlights how the taste of a regional cuisine became the national taste of race.

In its journey through U.S. sensory economies, the taste of southern food evolved and differently participated in making race and place. In the Jim Crow South, the judicial system forcefully backed racial segregation, which paradoxically made "sensory intimacy" not only possible but also necessary to the workings of local sensory economies. Mark Smith's work on race and the senses shows how southern racial differences were more assertively established not through absolute separation but because of white southerners' constant control of when sensory interaction could and would happen.[10] White households were a space of heightened sensory contact as African Americans' "primitive" closeness to their senses also made them valued cooks. As an Alabama essay argued, only "uncle Nat" and his fellow "specialists" knew how to prepare a proper Christmas eggnog, "a fluffy, saffron-colored beverage, delicate in fragrance, daintily blended, and pungently persuasive." The eggnog was a sensory remnant of the lavish holiday parties in the big house during the "glittery years that immediately preceded the war between the states."[11] White southerners deployed sensory relationships around food as proof of social and racial power: the food eaten by blacks and whites could be the same, but the white South would decide when and how it would be enjoyed. Questions of etiquette, taboos about certain ingredients and animal parts, and the separation of eating utensils in homes where blacks worked and in commercial spaces such as soda fountains were favorite topics in the white South's rhetorical justification of segregation.[12] Southerners recruited the senses as evidence of innate racial difference but did so within a shared food culture where class was as important as race in determining one's diet. However, in other parts of the country, what Mark Smith calls the "awkward, perverse compromises" of southern sensory economies were unsustainable.[13] The absence of a legal framework for segregation meant that race making rested not only on spatial or temporal separation but also on "visceral" means and that the senses much more explicitly demarcated racial lines. This did not mean that white New Yorkers and Chicagoans did not enjoy southern fried chicken but that, like the two middle-class eaters in the excerpt of Richard Wright's *Native Son* analyzed in the introduction to this book, by tasting place they were also sensing race.

New Deal food writing reified American regions, making them internally homogeneous and legitimizing their local social orders by describing them as natural and unchanging states. In the case of the South, food customs and eating habits were significant themes available to FWP workers in order to express local pride and reach out to the rest of the nation. FWP workers considered the "velvety gentleness" with which southern foods and drinks "caress the palate" as not only tasty but also nurturing and soothing. Southern cooking kept the "flavor of the past . . . vitally alive" and allowed for the nostalgic celebration of the antebellum slavery regime while providing a mythic sensory canvas for the contemporary expression of regional identity on the national stage.[14] In volumes of the American Guide Series that integrated essays on eating and drinking, FWP workers often pointed to the "old plantation kitchen" as the origins of southern food. The South gastronomic reputation was already well established and branded for tourist consumption by the 1930s, especially that of New Orleans, explaining the leading editorial role initially given to Louisiana director Lyle Saxon in the *America Eats* project.[15] The *New Orleans City Guide* reproduced a conventional narrative based on sensory stereotyping, to which it added a nuanced appreciation of demographic, environmental, and economic factors in the making of local cuisine. Readers learnt that "New Orleans Creole cuisine, evolved many years ago, had as its basis French delicacy piquantly modified by the Spaniard's love of pungent seasoning, the Indian's use of Native herbs, and the Negro's ability to mix and bake. Into its evolution, too, went a singularly abundant and diverse food supply, with not only a wide variety of fish, game, and vegetables at the very door and exotic products available from the nearby tropics, but a steady flow of delicacies imported from the old country."[16]

The sensory and cultural richness of southern food, rooted in a deep sense of place, provided FWP workers with a convenient contrast to Yankee puritanism and industrial blandness. New Deal food writing simultaneously cast southern food as a homely alternative to processed foods and the sumptuous feasts of the planter elite. But taste also complicated how southerners would come to promote their local customs to the nation as it represented a regional, cultural terrain not only shared by blacks and whites but also shaped by interracial sensory interactions and intimacies. This chapter therefore also explores the influence of new urban and northern mode of sensing on southern sensory economies, how it changed the way the senses were recruited to justify and explain legal segregation, and its role in shaping the Depression-era image of the region.

Black voices were not absent from New Deal food writing. The ethnic and racial composition of the FWP staff varied greatly in each state, and, if it was mainly white and American born, northern FWP state offices employed a minority of African American writers, especially in New York, where the FWP Harlem unit thrived. Some southern branches set up segregated

"Negro Units." Virginia, Louisiana, and Florida did so most successfully, although in his account of his directorship of the Florida Folklore Program, Stetson Kennedy noted: "I do not recall there ever being editorial conferences in which blacks participated. Manuscripts from the Negro Unit came to us by mail or messenger, and every two weeks they sent someone for their paychecks."[17] Sterling Brown, poet and Harvard-educated professor of English at Howard University, acted as national Negro Affairs editor and had, if not a veto, at least a say on a number of FWP projects, notably the American Guide Series volumes. The Negro Studies Project, staffed by African Americans and studying African Americans' role in American history, culture, and contemporary society, worked on a series of local folklore studies and a larger, never-published monograph to be titled "Portrait of the Negro as American." Overall, historian Lauren Sklaroff deems the inclusion of African Americans in the FWP, and the WPA art programs in general, "ambivalent," noting that if these programs offered "creativity, ambition, and unprecedented possibilities," theirs was also "a history of limitations, bigotry, and political machinations."[18] Parts of this chapter draws on sources from the Negro Studies Project and the FWP Harlem unit to explore African American resistance to the New Deal sensory logic and black FWP workers' perseverance in framing their taste experiences squarely and proudly within the American culinary narrative.[19]

Keeping "The Light of Tradition Burning": Race and Taste in Southern Sensory Economies

Southern New Deal food writing recorded the enforcement of Jim Crow laws, especially the segregation of public eating spaces, in texts and images. The FWP southern staff, composed mainly of low-paid (white) white-collar workers, set an uncritical eye on their region and described segregation as the traditional, natural, and peaceful relationship between the races. But what their work also highlighted was that segregation at the southern table was spatial, visual, and social rather than linked to taste. At a dinner in Alabama given by a black congregation but open to whites, blacks and whites were served the same food: "Fried chicken, baked beef, stewed rice with dumplings, light bread, cakes, pies, potato salad, and home made pickles." In accordance with the law, the community set up a whites-only table for their guests. This was not enough for some, and the white supremacist ideal took a wry turn: "As a general rule, the white people [were] given a plate and [could] go sit in their cars to eat if they desire."[20] The purity of the whites'

food was determined not by the content of the meal but rather by the obser-
vance of a precise racial etiquette that underlined spatial and social distance
rather than sensory difference. In homes, this distance was also material, and
black cooks and domestics used different utensils than the white family for
their meals.[21] In public settings, African Americans would often be served
the same food as whites, but their meal would take place later and consist
of leftovers. An Alabama essay on barbecue carefully noted, as if to debunk
accusations of unequal treatment, that "the Negroes are served immediately
after the white families, [and] enjoy an exact duplicate of the feast set before
their employers." The *America Eats* regional essay provides a more straightforward account, noting that when the servants' time comes, "the chicken
will be mostly backs and wings, and ham only the outside slices. . . . [O]ften
as not, some of the best food has been hidden away for them."[22] In theory at
least, the internal logic of southern segregation did not proscribe that blacks
and whites partake of the same food.

Space and time were primary markers of racial difference in matters of
food in the Jim Crow South. In southern Alabama, for instance, the FWP
documented barbecues organized every year by planters "for white and negro
tenants." These events were "second in importance . . . only to Christmas
and Thanksgiving celebrations." Enjoyment of the "beef, pork, lamb, kid, or
chicken" slowly cooked overnight on wood ambers crossed race lines.[23] A
photographer working for the *America Eats* project recorded such an event,
and the picture that survived in the archive is a typical, if spectacular, instance
of racial segregation (figure 3.1). Slices of bread neatly separate black and
white eaters. The barbecued meat is out of sight, but the bread necessary for
soaking up the juices has already been laid out. The square slices of white
bread appear to be the products of an industrial bakery, offered maybe as a
treat as well as a potentially morally and physically uplifting alternative to
corn bread by the plantation owner, F. M. Gay.[24] All dressed up for the event,
men wear ties and suspenders. Most, including children, wear hats; a woman
ornamented hers with a feather, while another holds a fan. All blacks mingle
together and outnumber white participants, who are segregated by gender
(men in the back, women and children in the front). The one exception to
this visual racial segregation is the presence of two white men on the edge
of the black group, probably the plantation owner himself and/or overseers.
The numerical difference between blacks and whites might be explained by
the racial make up of the plantation workforce and the heightened lack of
food among black sharecroppers' families during the Depression. Such a free
meal was a rare occasion.

Figure 3.1. F. M. Gay's Annual Barbecue, given on his plantation every year, Alabama, 1936. Federal Writers' Project photographs for the *America Eats* project, Library of Congress Prints and Photographs Division Washington, D.C., LOT 13328 (F).

This image of a benevolent barbecue captures white paternalism along with the social and sensory control imposed by legal segregation. The black attendees are kept in check by a row of women blocking premature access to the food. A net seems to separate the white crowd from the bread. What this photograph reveals is more ambiguous than the stark visual contrast presumes and helps flesh out a multifaceted, layered story of sensory segregation. Tellingly, while all the whites look at the camera, the black group's attention is divided between gazing at the food and defiantly, hungrily looking toward the photographer. The whites' food must have been set up separately; maybe they had already eaten by the time the picture was taken. They are then posing for the picture while African American sharecroppers wait for their food; their senses tingled by the aroma that emanated from the white tables over the past couple of hours. Assuredly, segregation here is spatial, visual, and social, but taste and enjoyment of barbecued meat also cuts across racial lines in ways that had to be hidden from the camera and controlled by the set up of the meal.

Tangled relationships between racial segregation, gender relations, and sensory intimacy structured southern sensory economies. In his powerful *How Race Is Made: Slavery, Segregation and the Senses*, Mark Smith notes that the southern racial hierarchy under segregation rested on the fact that, "white tongues tasted food prepared by black hands; white noses smelled black maids who washed white clothes and tidied white houses."[25] Daily intimate contacts with black domesticity, far from being in contradiction with the principles of segregation, were needed by whites in order to affirm sensory difference, to "maintain the fiction of sensory inferiority," and assert that they were "sufficiently powerful to suspend their own protocol." Smith concludes by noting, "The point about segregation is not that it was a system of complete separation; the point is that whites derived their authority by defining when and where sensory intimacy was permitted."[26] White households and kitchens were sites of largely black labor, to the extent that black cooking often appears as a precondition to white eating in New Deal food writing. Black women cooking the daily fare of the white households and black men barbecuing for white social events, such as religious dinners and political meetings, were quintessential to the workings of southern sensory economies. If blacks and whites did not eat at the same tables, they shared tastes and techniques.

Southerners fully participated in the New Deal sensory nostalgia for "real" food and offered southern food as a set of traditions and comfort food for a nation of industrial eaters. Events such as religious dinners-on-the-ground, political barbecues, and family reunions fulfilled New Deal food writing's goal to circumscribe the anxieties of Depression-era eaters by focusing on the superiority of homemade dishes and preserves. During the Depression years, beaten biscuits—"feathery knob, fluffy and soft, and just the right shade of brown"—, Brunswick stew, and sweet potato pies offered a heightened sensory comfort rooted in the region's racial and gendered past.[27] Recollections of mythologized dinners at the plantation's Big House, prepared by black "mammies" and eaten by white families, were cathartic means to express contemporary anxieties about the sensory alienation of modern eaters in a depressed industrial capitalist economy. The taste of a mint julep was not only "refreshing" but, above all, "carri[ed] with it all the charm of the Old South when life was less strenuous than it is today, when brave men and beautiful women loved and laughed and danced the hours away."[28] Southern FWP workers highlighted the role of their region in maintaining traditions; as one of them noted, "If the tourist does not find the Virginian foods along the highway, he should knock at some farmhouse door, register his complaint against American standardization, and be served after a manner that conforms to the ancient rules of hospitality."[29] The role of black domesticity in establishing these "ancient rules" was crucial.

Black participation in the preparation of meals was central to making certain foods and social events not only "white" but also southern and traditional. A Virginian thus thoughtfully warned the potential tourist: "To the northerners, inexperienced in so much, and especially in the preparation of delicacies. Don't try to hold a real oyster roast unless you have a son of old Virginia to supervise the work and at least one burly Negro to tell you how things should be run."[30] Scholars working on the history of the post-Reconstruction "New South" have shown how an idealized version of the "Old South" in which race relations were depicted as serene and unproblematic could work as a national meeting ground for (white) national reunion.[31] Southern cooking offered an opportunity to literally bite into this accepted version of the past and the gender and racial roles it prescribed: "Smiling white-aproned high-turbaned mammies" and "stooped and grey-bearded" uncles offered direct links to a romanticized plantation life.[32]

By the 1930s the image of the faithful slave cook was a long-running national stereotype used to sell tradition through the circuit of industrial consumption. The figure of the southern black mammy, developed since the late nineteenth century, had acquired a broad national currency through, for instance, the Aunt Jemima trademark or the character of "mammy" in the bestselling book and following 1939 Hollywood adaptation of *Gone with the Wind*. FWP essays were, for that matter, akin to palimpsests rather than original pieces, echoes of radio jingles and covered-up regional clichés that conjured stereotyped representations of race. As historians Micki McElya, Maurice Manring, and Grace Hale, among others, have demonstrated, one was not supposed to attempt to "be" Aunt Jemima but to "have" her and her food in order to perform whiteness in the national marketplace of tastes and ideas.[33] McElya explains in her study of the cultural history and legacy of Aunt Jemima that "the trademark told a story of the post-Reconstruction reunification of North and South brought about through the loving labors of a black woman and made available to all through modern capitalism."[34] The racist cliché offered a comforting and stable trope in the midst of economic depression; it was a reassuring and nostalgic figure that buffered, while bolstering, the increasing encroachment of industrial foods on U.S. diets and tastes.

The historical culinary narrative developed by southern FWP workers implied that if slave cooks "invented" southern cooking, they did so accidentally, following their senses rather than using their intellect. Black cooks, "good old-timers (and new-timers, too, for that matter)" cooked "by ear" and "taught by word of mouth" the recipes they carried "in their crinkly old heads."[35] FWP workers justified segregation by not only establishing a sensory difference between whites and blacks but also anchoring black bodies in a stage of naïve nature. The argument built on the Enlightenment promotion of rationality, intellect, and sight over the allegedly "lower" senses of smell, touch, and taste.[36] This sensory logic efficiently denied black cooks agency in their own culinary creation: they invented a new cuisine without knowing what they were doing and by merely trying to satisfy base appetites. Yet this argument also put their labor at the center of southern sensory economies, as not only were the food preferences of white southerners shaped by the food cooked by black domestics, but their sensory satisfaction also depended on the perpetuation of this racialized domestic sphere.

To circumscribe the role of black cooks in the emergence of southern cuisine, New Deal food writing insisted on white women's stewardship in directing them. Feminist scholars have highlighted the role of recipes and cooking in the creation of networks of female solidarity and resistance, as well as intergenerational binding.[37] In the case of southern cooking, the interracial relationships potentially created by domestic intimacy endangered the social and racial order. The repeated assertion of the white mistresses' intellectual superiority over black cooks' sensory apparatus eased this tension. The rationale was rather self-explanatory: if the South "developed many excellent slave cooks among the slave population," it was because "the Negro girl that showed an aptitude for domestic work was trained by her mistress, and then spent the rest of her days preparing the family's food under the direction of the same mistress."[38] This was not a novel argument but harked back to a nineteenth-century conceptualization of running a home as civilizing, missionary work.[39] McElya has shown how this "racialization of the domestic sphere as the appropriate place for black labor and white women's authority" in return offered "tremendous potential for white women to recast their own citizenship" and to demonstrate their crucial role in the nurturing of the nation while respecting the established gender roles of female housewives and male breadwinners.[40]

The construction of a racialized and gendered sensory/intellect divide between white and black women in New Deal food writing worked to reassure readers about the potentially threatening feminine intimacy in the kitchen and facilitated the portrayal of black cooks as anachronistic yet cherished remnants of the past in the middle of modernity. White women, knowledgeable about modern domestic science and normative measurements, no longer depended on black women's traditional and sensory know-how. They had the "knack of interpreting" into "cupful" the "handful," "pinch," and "dash" of an ingredient called for in black recipes, while the black cooks, of their own alleged account, didn't "know nuthin' 'bout dis messin' science."[41] That these evasive explanations and lack of written recipes could be daily acts of resistance against white supremacy in the kitchen was an option rarely explored in New Deal food writing. One essay by African American writer Eudora Welty, one of the few to become famous through her writing after employment by the FWP, tentatively did so. She told the story of a "proud and lovely lady" who had forgotten a recipe and whose Creole cook "whom she had herself taught . . . wouldn't give it back," and judged, maybe tongue-in-cheekily, that such episode was unlikely to happen again: "Generosity [had] touched the art of cooking." "Southern ladies" would now exchange their favorite recipes, "down to that magical little touch that makes all the difference." This was all the constricts of the Southern racial regime would allow for and what had become of the Creole cook and her knowledge would not be further explored in the pages of New Deal food writing.[42] If black cooks prepared food that pleased white (male) appetites, New Deal food writing explained, it was only because the feminine white mind had served as a mediator for the dish.

Southern sensory nostalgia for the traditional food cooked by turbaned "mammies" offered a path for the assertion of modern whiteness. Middle-class white southerners grounded their modern identities in traditions passed down generations through black domestic workers. While recognizing black cooks' role in shaping southern cooking, the plantation-school-inspired rhetoric present throughout New Deal food writing kept them firmly anchored in the past. FWP workers described "mammies and uncles" as "betraying a little weariness under the weight of years, but very proud in a quiet dignity of their roles in keeping burning this light of tradition." The taste of southern food and the sensory satisfaction of southerners depended on the preparation of "old fashioned southern meals" by "colored cooks" in white "up-to-date" kitchens.[43] The temporal paradox that pointed to blacks' contemporary labor yet denied them full agency in the southern sensory past and present was constitutive of an empowered white modernity. The coming together of half a century of white supremacist propaganda, mass-media national circulation, and the state apparatus in the southern branches of the FWP facilitated the elaboration of a definitively white, though at times alienating, version of modernity.

Southerners were able to bypass the contradictions of black and white sensory intimacy because legal segregation upheld the sight of orderly segregated dinner tables. But in the North, the comparative lack of legal segregation rendered this "suspension of the protocol" of racial segregation problematic.

Bringing Mark Smith's insights on the role of the senses in the culture of segregation in the South to their full conclusion, we can postulate that, in the rest of the country, the very absence of legal segregation and the relative lack of white control over everyday interracial sensory contacts (in public transportation, on the shop floor) reinforced the role of the senses as markers of racial difference. In the absence of a legal protocol to be momentarily suspended, the senses themselves became the protocol, thus shaping even more prominently and efficiently the process of race making.[44]

"Partaking of Choice Poultry Cooked à la Southern Style": Southern Food Moves North

The Great Migration of millions of blacks and whites out of the South between the World Wars (and beyond) gave southern cooking a national scope, propelling it from a mostly rural region ruled by Jim Crow laws to an urban and theoretically nonsegregated environment. Leaving the South, southerners took their recipes and habits with them, causing a recasting of black and white southern rural folks' diet into "down home" dishes. In the North, the increased association of southern food with African Americans dissociated the taste of this distinct cooking style from its regional grounding and reframed it as black food. In the new racial landscapes and sensory economies of the northern metropolis, the taste of southern food slipped from a taste of place to a sense of race. The delineation of a racialized taste line accelerated in the interwar period as an answer to the challenge of industrial modernity, economic depression, and changes in the U.S. taxonomy of race and ethnicity.

The evolution of the taste of southern food from a taste of place to a sense of race is best seen at the borderlands between North and South. Midwestern states were transitional spaces symptomatic of the gradual redefinition of gustatory taste along a racialized line. In Missouri, for instance, an FWP worker considered southern influences evident in the counties "closer to Dixieland," which were "endowed with more of the glories thereof, even in culinary matters." If we follow this culinary sketch, southern culinary glory was rooted in interracial taste, since "Negro cooks and white ones, too, . . . go in for succotash, cracklin' bread, and drop dumplings in a big way."[45] The appending of the qualification "too" provides an interesting clue on the state of sensory racial relation in this southern borderland. The FWP worker who penned this remark proved knowledgeable of the role of race in sensory economies in the Jim Crow South and outside of it; he (or she) served as a cultural interpreter informing his northern readership on quaint southern ways that differed from theirs, and whose interracial nature might surprise them. Doing so, the Missourian FWP worker involuntarily exposed the South's sensory contradictions. The fieldworker depicted the region as a society where race served as the primary element of personal and group identity, thus determining its social and political economies; but also portrayed the South as a culture that had managed to cultivate a paternalist interracial sensory intimacy that potentially weakened the whole structure. A mere adverb then unveils what Smith identifies as the "intellectual hiccupping and contradictions" at the core of southern sensory economies.[46]

As we move outside the South, New Deal food writing provides fewer and fewer mentions of interracial eating habits and taste. Fish proves a prime example. In Mississippi, mullet was described as "not usually prized as food" for the simple reason that it was "commonly eaten by Negroes"; yet a basic linguistic change was enough to reclassify it as "in the coast region . . . many white people eat it and have come to call it Biloxi bacon." In Indiana, however, "the average local white fisherman would not for a moment consider eating a dogfish he had caught," as it was "eaten only by the colored people who have come into this region as the result of industrial development." The FWP worker then concluded his essay on "eating prejudices" and "dogfish" by noting that "presently [he] would go hungry before [he] would eat one."[47] In the context of the Depression, a time when some Americans indeed went hungry, this was no inconsequential remark. In the new spatial and social context of the northern metropolis and industry towns, the social proximity of African Americans, impoverished whites, and recently arrived immigrants was too close to be satisfied with a verbal affirmation of racial difference. Since segregation had no legal backing, the incorporation (or non-incorporation) of food demarcated racial difference. Sensory performances fleshed out the color line.

The sensory slippage of southern food from the taste of place to a sense of race occurred through a series of sensory reactions and interactions on the color line and in interplay with the myth of the "Old South" foregrounded in southern New Deal food writing. The romanticized southern ideal of untouched, idle white femininity was a regional myth with powerful influence on sensory economies nationwide, especially through the newly developed mass market of standardized foodstuffs. The figure of the southern "mammy," especially as incarnated by the Aunt Jemima trademark, regularly conjured up by the FWP everywhere was one of the central characters of this national narrative. The pancake-making mammy was efficient both in the realm of symbolism and as a moneymaker, generating imitations. In New York, an adventurous tourist could travel to Harlem to find "small holes-in-the-wall, neat and shiningly clean, where hot griddle cakes are fried, in full view of the window, by a colored 'mammy' in bright plantation garb."[48] This profitable New York–based entrepreneurial venture shows the cultural grip of the mythic southern domesticity on the national mind through the commodification of blackness. While millions of black men and women were moving out of the South and its kitchen and into the northern industrial economy as part of the first waves of the Great Migration, pancake-making mammies, imagined and real, guaranteed middle-class white consumers nationally that they could still taste the food of faithful and maternal southern black cooks respectful of traditions.

Cultural and economic exchange on the color line destabilized the taste of a regional cuisine by imbuing it with blackness. In New York, FWP writers noted that "southern-style cooking [was] featured in the cosier tea-rooms specializing in fried chicken" but clearly focused their research on the black ghetto of Harlem, "the home of many southern restaurants, catering to both white and Negro patrons." Many African American migrant women, who considered cooking a respectable activity, opened up eating places in the interwar period, from modest street stands to restaurants and "shacks."[49] These were all the more successful given that interwar Harlem was a fashionable nightlife spot, home to the black artists and biracial audience of the Harlem Renaissance. This clientele partook of southern food, but the entertainment also came from watching celebrated Harlem restaurateurs "cook the dish and the yams, turnip greens, biscuits, and cornbread, and lowly but tasty black-eyed peas and pig's tails."[50] The mythical figure of the faithful mammy informed how FWP workers described female restaurateurs. A well-known figure of the Harlem restaurant scene, for instance, was an "ample Florida woman" named Tillie who owned a famed fried-chicken eatery, described by several New York fieldworkers. Sarah Chavez, a probably non–African American worker, described Tillie as the "embodiment of motherhood in its utmost simplicity. Her soft southern voice, brimming with emotion, the lines of the face revealing years of struggle; her smile so full of warmth and plump arms that seemed capable of drawing the whole world within their scope."[51] This raced and gendered description of bodily difference was the needed prelude to a satisfying meal. If national clichés about the Old South animated the ways northern FWP workers tasted southern foods, the inner workings of northern and urban sensory economies also contributed to circumscribe blackness to a familiar, recognizable, and commodified multisensory experience that combined taste and smell with sight, sound, and bodily performances.

Bestowing the taste of blackness to dishes such as fried chicken did not mean that whites were not consuming it. Rather, when they ate the dish, they did not simply taste a regional cuisine but deliberately crossed the color line and did so not as armchair travelers but as blackface actors.[52] White sensory satisfaction was grounded in the knowledge that one was crossing the line and indulging in a racial pleasure. Tillie's restaurant, for instance, became somewhat of a racial battleground in the late 1930s when it followed the path of some of the neighborhoods' most successful nightclubs by going "high brow" and trying to attract a white clientele looking for "authentic" entertainment and grew reluctant to serve black patrons. Frank Byrd, and African American writer in the Harlem unit, was riled up by Tillie's evolution and missed the times when she "used to stand in her kitchen sweating but good-naturally cracking jokes with her Negro comrades surrounded by her luscious fried chicken and sweet potatoes." But between the lines of his irritated essay, Tillie also appears as a skilled entrepreneur with an astute understanding of the workings of race and gender in northern sensory economies. She "had mural painted on the basement walls, got herself a couple of assistants, assumed the sorts of great lady in reduced circumstances and played hostess to her ofay followers who had practically taken over the place."[53] She understood that purchasing and tasting southern food in black urban neighborhoods was a means for northern urbanites to prove that their palates were able to recognize and navigate the racialized taste line. It was "in good taste."

Circumscribing the taste of blackness participated in delineating whiteness. This sensory interplay was all the more important in cities where the Great Migration encountered the "new immigration" composed of Southern and Eastern Europeans arriving en masse from the 1880s to 1924. Historians highlight new immigrants' ambiguous racial status during the interwar period as legal and vernacular systems appraised them via a series of changing categories linked to color, complexion, nationality, ethnicity, and race.[54] One of the most effective ways available for "in-between" European migrants to buttress their claim to whiteness was to differentiate themselves from African Americans through bodily performances of race. New Deal food writing recorded this process. In another essay on night life in Harlem and the "wholesale Caucasian invasion" of some of its clubs, Byrd, decidedly annoyed by the phenomenon, noted that "the majority of Lindy-Hopping whites [were] Jewish or Italian boys and girls from the Bronx and upper East Side" and complained about "their exaggerated interpretations of the Lindy, Shrug and Boogie-Woogie," judging them to be "more Negroes than some Negroes." Ethnic youth mixed enjoyment and mockery to position themselves as spectators and consumers of the black Harlem spectacle.[55] After the show, they could visit "small tea-rooms" opened in the "basements of private dwellings" by "many enterprising housewife" vying to take "advantage of the opportunity to cash in" on the popularity of Harlem nightlife among New Yorkers in the interwar period.[56] Along with the kinesthetic, auditory, and bodily experience of "black" music and dance, eating southern food and identifying it is as black was a way to circumscribe blackness, therefore to paradoxically and "viscerally" perform whiteness.

The making of a national definition of sensory racial difference allowed for sensory performances on the color line but also increasingly hampered interracial sensory exchange. Wilbur Young, an African American worker and Byrd's colleague in the Harlem office, recorded the accomplished relocation of taste from region to race. Continuing the unit reporting on Tillie's Chicken Shack, he penned ironic, advertisement-like advice to readers interested in "partaking of choice poultry cooked a la southern style." He described the well-known Harlem fried chicken "joint" in these terms: "If you like to go to a place where no one will ever think of finding you, and at the same time you can tackle your vittles with your fingers, drop in at Tillie's!"[57] The implied audience was white and middle class, looking for a way to spice up its diet and safely prove its cosmopolitanism while reenacting racial difference.[58] By the same token, this remark evokes a feeling of social shame on the part of the white culinary slummers and illustrates a changing sensory economy in which whites with a taste for fried chicken increasingly did not make sense anymore: being out of place, they would also be out of their senses. The snobbish tone hints at Young's amusement at seeing whites guiltily relishing fried chicken. Young's ironic tone and Chavez's commodification of Tillie's body contrasted with the description of the restaurant provided by Baxter Leach, a black FWP employee working on the Harlem-based "Negroes of New York" project, which assumed that its main audience was black rather than white. Leach noted that the restaurant was one of many "owned and operated by Negroes that are doing good business. Their places are clean, well kept, and their foods are the best."[59] But this subdued account would not contain the emerging sensory line. Overlooking geographical and social differences, seeing and tasting only a uniform blackness, northern whites made southern food just plain "Negro" food. African American FWP workers showed an acute awareness of this sensory slippage and were far from passive onlookers.

"Got Any Greens Left?": Black Culinary Pride in the Pre-Soul Food Era.

The reconstruction of the taste of southern foods as "black food" took place in the northern and midwestern black metropolises, themselves crucial sites of cultural and sensory identity building for the modern and urban black diaspora.[60] African Americans also participated in the remaking of the taste of southern food. In the crowded black metropolises southern rural migrants and their foods entered in contact with and often in opposition to both an estranged white world and an earlier black urban culture. From the onset of the Great Migration, food had been a subject of heated debate within the black community between, on the one hand, southern migrants longing for familiar tastes and, on the other hand, the older, and often wealthier, northern black communities whose leaders put forward the "politics of respectability" as a strategy to "uplift" the race. The image of the Southern migrants "gnawing on the chicken bone" became a derogatory stereotype shared by the northern black middle-class and white urbanites.[61] The economic hardship of the Depression hit northern black communities across class and regional lines, though, paradoxically giving more leverage to working-class southern blacks than they previously had had. This in turn triggered a unification and politicization of the community that historians have identified as the seeds of the postwar civil rights movement.[62] Ultimately, the black northern metropolis became a nexus of identity formation for a community new to all. The meaning of southern cooking then evolved rapidly in the 1930s and 1940s as the entire community increasingly and proudly claimed its taste as its own. In the cauldron of the northern metropolis a new cuisine emerged that built on iconic southern dishes, added industrial food products, and (in cities attracting transnational migrants such as New York City) featured Caribbean and Latin American influences.[63]

The ongoing reappraisal of southern food by black urbanites can be seen in many of the essays and life histories recorded by African American FWP workers in New York. Remembering a cocktail party attended by the "Negro Society," the "crème de la crème of Black Manhattan" that made up the Harlem Renaissance, the Boston-born African American writer Dorothy West reported her exchange with an inebriated southern man and his wife. Made hungry by the drinks and surveying "with distaste" the "dainty sandwiches" and "box of crackers and bottle of olives" served by the northern hostess, the man asked his wife, "Got any greens left?" He then nostalgically reminisced about the black-eyed peas and hogsheads his mother cooked for New Year "down South." He consciously reversed the qualitative and sensory opposition between northern and southern food as usually played out in the black community since the onset of the Great Migration by derogatorily casting northern ways while celebrating southern foodways as comforting to the soul and body. Fortunately, his wife recalled having some greens and spareribs left over, and she offered for West to share it with them. A polite refusal fired up a "belligerent" look from the man and this inquiry: "You don't like colored folks cooking?" To which West quickly and apologetically answered that she "love[d] greens and spare ribs" before naming "all the other southern dishes" she could think of and affirming that "[she] love[d] them, too."[64] In this casual exchange, West effectively interpreted "southern" as the sensory equivalent of "colored" in order to prove racial solidarity. Not doing so would have put her own racial belonging at risk: could she be a black woman if she did not like southern dishes? By the end of the Depression this possibility seemed to have vanished. Both participants to the scene were aware of the past meaning of southern food in the urban North and of its new prideful cultural and political status as race food. West depicted a complex relationship between race and place before equating one with the other.

By the end of the 1930s, African American FWP workers reclaimed racially denigrated foods and deployed them as sources and vehicles of black urban identity and pride in order to present a united sensory front. Historian Tracy Poe, working on Chicago, estimates that this slow yet steady acceptance of southern foodways as representative of the foods of the community showed "the integration of rural southern culture into urban African American consciousness and the acceptance of migrants not as backwards, unclean, and in need of modernization, but as brothers and sisters with common traditions and heritage."[65] Roi Ottley, the supervisor of the FWP's Harlem unit who would go on to publish a successful series of books on black life in the North, registered the accomplishment of this integration when he described one of Harlem's wealthiest neighborhood, Sugar Hill, in sensory terms: "Rents are high and only the more prosperous can afford to reside here without lodgers; nevertheless, the odors of barbecuing ribs, frying pork chops, boiling greens, and chitterlings are as characteristic of the Hill as they are of the poorer sections of the community down in what is called the valley."[66] For Ottley, neither social division nor geographic origin ought to determine African Americans' food preference; instead, he proudly held taste as a factor of sensory, cultural, and political unity and identity. When partaking of southern food, northerners on both sides of the color line not only tasted place but also felt and performed race.

If black FWP workers celebrated southern food as the taste of the race, they also aimed at setting the historical and sensory record straight. In a six-page essay titled "Cooking," Ottley debunked white stereotypes about African Americans' food and its taste by reclaiming the role of black cooks in the "origins of many standard dishes." His was a class argument; he noted that "economic and social forces which affect and determine [Negroes'] status" had forced "slaves and freedman" to be cooks and caterers. Migration had further pushed the "inventiveness of the Negro," and "a typical Harlem menu may include fried chicken, gumbo, turnips, greens, barbecue, pig feet, ears and tails, chitterlings, corn bread and hopping johns." However, he rejected the equation of this menu simply with race and class and linked it to place instead, adding that "these foods had their origins in the south and now heavily influence[d] the white culture of that section." He continued by noting: "Conspicuous among the dishes common to the white South, the Negro South, and the country at large is chicken. In fact, the Negro's supposed fancy for chicken has become proverbial. In fact, it was a standard joke for the old minstrel shows. But in actual fact, his white brother has probably outstripped him in all but story telling."[67] Ottley was treading a fine line in his various FWP essays, between the celebration of blackness and its food and the denunciation of the fallacy of sensory difference.

Unrelenting descriptions of urban poverty and ethnographic notations accompanied the Negro Studies Project's efforts at unveiling the class origins of African American foods and the hypocrisy behind the racialization of taste. In Chicago, Richard Wright surveyed the "dingy" taverns and "dingier" restaurants that offered "unique dishes, mostly of southern origin" in the "solidly lumpen-proletariat" South Side, along State Street. Most of them were "but shacks held together by rusty pieces of tin and old boards," and, in a district plagued with unemployment, "dank places where the neighborhood drunks hang out night and day." He highlighted, along others, the lack of black ownership of many of the businesses operating in black neighborhoods.[68] The Negro Studies Project also collected lore from cooks, waiters, and eaters that give us insight into the culinary politics of race and class. Jack Smith from the Iowa project, for instance, recorded the use of the term "roast beef," which meant "any dish, victuals, pastry or salad—in short—anything people eat that Negroes prepare and serve in a professional sense." He explained: "In a private home you might hear a cook remark that her white folks sure can truck (eat or do away with) a lot of her roast beef. She means that they like her cooking and 'roast beef' is the food which she happened to serve. On this particular occasion it might have been duck, or filet of mignon."[69] The New York office documented a variety of food influences: a "kosher lunch" was sardines on toast, "Virginia special" oyster fritters, "Sous C'lina" okra, and a "chaser stew," a West Indian boiled fish—"chaser" because "American Negroes often refer to west Indian Negroes as 'monkey chasers.'"[70] Despite the derogatory undertone of this last dish, the list testifies to the growing northern repertoire of "black" dishes borrowed from a host of cuisines and efficiently integrated with Southern specialties.

"They Have Their Own Preferences When They Cook for Themselves": Reconstructing Southern Taste in Black and White

National and transnational circuits of sensory and cultural exchanges determined the taste of southern food in 1930s sensory economies, shoring it up to blackness. This process triggered a re-evaluation of the southern politics of sensation. The workings of southern sensory economies oscillated between racial segregation and sensory intimacy. Even if smoothed out by the white supremacist ideology perceptible in much of southern New Deal food writing, a core issue remained at the heart of the southern culinary narrative: If the main outcome of blacks' sensory-driven past culinary creation was the contemporary sensual pleasing and psychological ease of white tongues, then could it also be pleasing to black tongues? What happened when black hands cooked for black tongues? Broadcast on the national stage through the Great Migration and by New Deal food writing, the sensory inconsistencies of the southern regime of racial segregation became even more striking and, by the end of the 1930s, untenable. Southerners reacted to the new racial reorganization of taste in black and white in the urban centers of the North. In part, they engaged in the construction of southern food as a psychologically and physically soothing heritage taste for a white modernity endangered by the industrialization of food and the economic crisis. But southern interracial taste hindered the ideological efficacy of the construction of southern cuisine as nostalgic comfort food for the (white) nation as it highlighted the sensory inconsistencies of the southern regime of racial segregation. The southern sensory ambiguity was in increasing tension with northern racially segregated sensory economies and the national scope of the FWP readership—the national imagined community of eaters it aimed to address in a project like *America Eats*—asked southern FWP workers to account for taste intimacy across race lines.

To defuse northern unease with the sensory intimacy tolerated by and, indeed, essential to the southern regime of legal segregation, New Deal food writing offered a straightforward explanation: black cooks simply did not prepare the same dishes at work and at home. In a grossly racist piece titled "Negro Restaurant in Charleston," Laura Middleton, for instance, noted that, "Negroes in the South Carolina Low-Country are well-known good cooks; and the business of meal preparing and serving plays a prominent part in the occupational life of these people, in quaint old Charleston." She then reproachfully added: "But with all the knowledge of balanced diet and proper preparation of food, it is practiced by these employees only in the kitchen of the employers—not even in their own restaurants."[71] Indeed, the content of the black family meal was closely related to its economic purchasing power—they could not afford "roast beef"—and, save for the food the cook would be allowed to tote, consisted of cheaper cuts of meat and stronger flavorings.[72] When looking at blacks' food preferences, southern FWP workers subsumed the role of class and economics under their analysis of racial difference. Their writings presented black cooks as living embodiments of the color line's path in matters of taste and considered the result of food choices made of economic necessity as a timeless natural truth. To better ground their ideological and rhetorical construction of a racially bifurcated taste, FWP writers recognized African Americans' full sensorial agency in their food choices. As the Louisiana American Guide Series essay on cooking explains, "Although Negroes contribute much to the excellency of Louisiana food, acting as cooks in many restaurants and in private families, they have their own preferences when they cook for themselves."[73] The South Carolina guidebook offered a very similar remark but let slip another explanation for this taste divergence: "The Negro cook who is an artist in preparing food for a white family will often follow quite different methods in her own kitchen. 'White folks' vittles ain't got no suption,' she will say, meaning that they have no flavor."[74] Sensory stereotypes could backfire. Overall, southern FWP workers used taste differences resulting from social disparities as, in Mark Smith's words, "authenticator of truth and generator of reliable knowledge" about racial difference and justification for segregation.[75]

New Deal food writing described southern taste as the coexistence of two layered, racialized ways of tasting, linked by the seminal yet liminal figure of the black cook. Enumerations of black food were a recurrent and crucial feature of what we may call the "bifurcated cook" rhetoric and gave this sensory set-up textual legitimacy. American Guide Series volumes on southern states regularly included detailed lists of the dishes prepared in black communities. For instance, we learn that in Louisiana, "their principal foods are sweet potatoes, fried, boiled, or baked; chitterlings, boiled, stewed, or in salads; cabbage, collards, mustard greens, and turnip greens smothered in lard with salt meat or pig tails, and eaten with corn dumplings (meal, water, and salt) cooked in the greens; pork in all forms, the year round; 'possum baked with sweet potatoes; fish; and corn bread and sweet bread (a large flat biscuit with sugar added)."[76] In South Carolina, "Negroes relish more fat in their food and sharper flavoring." They enjoyed "okra and tomato pilaus, catfish stews, 'possum and 'taters' (yam)." These enumerations often adopted a judgmental tone; the closing remark of the South Carolina guidebook literary segregated essay on "cookery" for instance noted that "even 'coon are rated as great delicacies."[77] The use of the adverb "even" proved an efficient instrument of distancing and blaming. These inventories delineated the foods eaten by African Americans, establishing a clear line between "we" and "them" and implying a detrimental judgment about "their food."

The taste line was blurry and harder to enforce than the visual color line, however. At the intersection of race and class stood the "poor whites," "white trash," "hillbillies," and other "crackers" who toiled as sharecroppers beside African Americans.[78] The two groups shared occupations, a similar kind of destitute housing, and a set of regional beliefs, folklore, and foodways. "The three Ms" had dominated the diets of poor southerners of all races since Reconstruction: Meal (innutritious sifted cornmeal and bleached white flour), Meat (pork, salted pork and pork fat of the lowest quality and grade), and Molasses.[79] When Floridians talked about "good old cracker eating" they meant "chitterlings, grits, sowbelly, side meat, corn bread, hog jowls, turnip greens, and cane syrup—all washed down with pot likker—the savory liquid created by the stewing together of greens and pork."[80] The similarity of such foodways with black southerners' diet was evident, so much so that the South Carolina guidebook had to concede that "a definite line [could] hardly be drawn between Negro cookery and white cookery" and that cooking greens with "a chunk of fat back or side meat" was a "predilection shared by many white folk."[81] If the South rooted its cultural identity in race difference and its public order in segregation, underlying class divisions were as crucial to the social and sensory making of the region. A more subdued dialogue, then, accompanied the enumerations of the foods supposedly eaten only by African Americans, one determined by class relationships within white southern society. Could one of the goals of these lists have been to point out to whites what foods *not* to eat?

Tensions and confusion over dietetic, racial, social, and sensory issues had always been a regional reality and remained so in the New Deal period. Attempts at reforming poor white southerners' diets according to prevailing ideas about class, race, and gender had recurred in the region since the late 1890s. In her analysis of race, class, and gender in the politics of baking bread in the Appalachians, Elizabeth Engelhardt analyzes how early-twentieth-century white reformers depicted beaten biscuits—demanding time, specific appliances, and economic as well as geographic access to white flour—as morally and racially superior to the humble, quick-to-rise, traditional cornbread. Biscuit baking was linked to a gender and economic system in which women would not need to work outside the home and could focus on homemaking and in which reformed dietary habits would purportedly

contribute to preserving the moral standing and refining the aesthetic taste
of the white family. In contrast, reformers attached to cornbread a negative
image of black, and unreformed white, female sharecroppers toiling in the
fields and unable to take care of their houses. Reform programs, emanating
from both benevolent and government organizations, aimed at severing the
link between taste and class habitus and reinforcing the links between food
taste, aesthetic appreciation, racial identity, and moral values. These efforts
primarily targeted white but also black southerners, although throughout
the period racial theories and sensory stereotypes remained central to both
vernacular and scientific explanations about the underlying causes of poor
nutrition and dietary choices.[82]

Life Histories interviews conducted by the FWP among poor white southern families reveal the importance of dietary issues as sites of power and
class relations within white society. The interviews aimed at documenting
the region's exploitative economic system, which was based on tenant farm-
ing, sharecropping, and low-paid work in cotton mills. They were part of the
New Deal state response to anxieties about racial and cultural degeneracy
that preceded, and accelerated with, the Depression. Interviewers did not
so much listen to as report on the lives of the interviewees, but their voices
occasionally came through.[83] Alice Fairweather, a Florida "squatter farmer"
mother of thirteen children, explained in 1938: "When we was on the Relief
a lady came out here and talked with me about food and the vegetables 'spe-
cially and she got me to promise to try carrots and beans and other things
besides collards and turnip greens." Alice, and others, resisted such programs,
and she concluded her recollection by declaring, "Collard greens cooked up
done with lots of side meat is best though, I don't care what anybody says
about hit."[84] The resistance offered by poor whites to attempts to change
and improve their diets, and distinguish it from that of African Americans,
was grounded in economic constraints that often preceded the Depression.
As one of them explained, "I ain't got the money to cook thata way . . . we
kaint afford no milk tho, only canned milk."[85] But financial limitation and
gustatory pleasures did not contradict, and respondents most often voiced
their alimentary choices as matters of taste preference. The state's meddling
with their eating habits made one "cracker" family "mighty mad": "How
did that woman know what we wanted to eat? Jus give us plenty grease, salt
pork, a little cabbage, stewed apples, and flour dough fried bread and we is
satisfied."[86] Food was a contested terrain in southern society on which poor
whites steadfastly resisted dietary and sensory reform.

Despite the repeated rhetorical affirmation of sensory segregation, southern FWP writers needed to account for the taste intimacy between "Negroes

and trashy whites" to their national audience.[87] New Deal food writing needs to be understood within a larger cultural context that elevated poor white southerners as paradigmatic victims of the Depression and put them at the center of the (white) national consciousness. The documentary aesthetic of the Depression era adopted the South as one of its major themes and produced literary and photographic exposés on the region that contributed to elevate the "barefoot South" as a national icon.[88] This renewed attention created, according to historian Jack Kirby, "a weird bifurcation of Dixies, with the Old mellowing and becoming even more entrenched in legend, the New wallowing in misery and yankee pity."[89] FWP workers adeptly journeyed back and forth between this dual image of the region, between two different sensory economies. The taste of the "Old mellowing," white supremacist, and patriarchal South rooted its sensual and ideological legitimacy in the work, knowledge, and bodies of women such as "Aunt Mary," who knew how to "knead," "pat," and "flatten" her buttermilk and hog lard biscuits dough "just right."[90] The food of the "New" pitiful South was the unfulfilling meals cooked in the one-room wooden shack of black and white sharecroppers documented by New Deal photographers.

While southern FWP workers romanticized the ideological taste of white supremacy and racial sensory intimacy, they also understood its incompatibility with racialized, northern, and urban sensory economies. Reacting to "yankee pity," southern FWP workers acknowledged the national definition of the racial taste line and endeavored to downplay its entanglement with southern foods, race relations, and class construction. Leading a fictional tourist ("Mr. Smith") through a plantation barbecue, an FWP worker in Georgia proudly flaunted a southern taste shaped by the paradoxical sensory logic of segregation and white supremacy yet also understood its increasing incongruity. He paternalistically introduced the visitor to the all-black cooking staff—in particular Sam, "whose fat, ebony-colored face breaks into a wide smile when [he gives] him a cigar" before reportedly exclaiming, "Yes suh Boss! Dese are chickens. . . . See how brown and shiny dey are? Sho' make good eatin' too, Boss. Hopes you like 'em!" Yet the FWP worker concluded with a remark that exposed Mr. Smith's differing interest as, he asked, "It's noon my boy, are you ready for dinner? After walking over that ploughed ground and miles of dirt roads you should be ready to eat. I can't for the life of me see why you Yankees want to see Tobacco Road."[91] The life and taste of poor whites, described by Erskine Caldwell in *Tobacco Road*, his 1932 novel on poor white sharecroppers, was not for the nation to witness.

The southern awareness of the national gaze and taste did not launch a direct and evident change in diet. Given the economic constraints of the

Depression, the ingrained habits of poor whites, and their sensory inclination
for the foods deemed to be preferred by blacks, such large-scale change was
highly improbable. But the new understanding of racial difference nurtured
in northern metropolises did alter how their food tasted on southerners' palates and forced them to layer and enforce a naturalized sensory difference
upon spatial and temporal segregation. Taste, then, increasingly functioned
as a marker of racial difference both inside and outside the Jim Crow South.
We therefore need to revisit the spatially and sensory segregated lunch of
the ditch-digging WPA road workers in the scene that opened this chapter.
After a long morning of physical toil, the black workers gathered around the
main fire to eat a variety of hearty southern dishes, while the white managers
assembled around the other fire. We will never know whether this description
is truthful to what actually was on the menu around the segregated fires on
that January day. What we do know is that the sensory racial assumptions
of the nation made it impossible for whites to partake in hominy grits and
fried fish. The reshuffling of the taste of southern food within northern urban
sensory economies, carried south by means of the New Deal cultural policies
embodied by the FWP, had cornered the taste of white southerners and left
them with the rather insipid alternative of "cheese sandwiches."

*   *   *

In framing the nation as a united community of regional eaters, New Deal
food writing contributed to mystifying as well as legitimizing the South's
culinary past and "perverse [sensory] compromises."[92] The culinary wonders
emerging from past and present southern kitchens served to boost and sell
an idealized image of the region's past in a time of economic depression
and search for culinary traditions. With no apparent sense of contradiction,
southern FWP workers could simultaneously laud black cooks for their culinary ingenuity, disparage their food preferences, and negate their knowledge.
All the while, the imposition of legal segregation and its domestic ironies
downplayed the ambiguity of sensory intimacy between blacks and whites.
But, following African Americans in their spatial relocation across the country, the taste of southern cooking lost its regional grounding and became a
means for the elaboration of a racialized taste line nationwide. This reconstruction of taste obliged southerners to resolve, at least rhetorically, their
sensory paradoxes and attune their regional way of tasting with northern,
urban sensory economies.

New Deal food writing was one of the cultural sites for the production of
a mode of sensory experience that constructed the senses as a potent way to
establish a modernized, industrialized, and urbanized color line. Southern

cuisine was at the forefront of the polarization of the U.S. racial and ethnic taxonomy in black and white, and the evolution of its taste in the interwar period is a symptom of the increasing importance of sensory methods of establishing racial difference in the first half of the twentieth century.[93] The racial taste line emerged via a creative process of interaction on the color line in different cultural, regional, and legal environments. Looking at the spatial and social circulation of southern food in the New Deal sensory economy, understood as both a set of textual representations and networks of value creation, allows documenting the role of the senses in the construction and naturalization of racial difference.

Attention to the evolving taste of southern food provides new insights on the making of black diasporic and urban identities. The interwar decades opened the path for the 1960s reconceptualization of black urban food as "soul food." As food scholar Frederick Opie points out, "it was during the civil rights and black power movements of the 1960s that the survival food of black southerners became the revolutionary high cuisine of bourgeoisie African Americans."[94] This prideful claim of a racial taste originated in the experience of the Depression and opened up a new range of debate about the relationship between taste, race, and place. At the center of this debate lies the sensitive question of determining whether people become "soulful" by eating soul food or if foods become "soulful" when eaten by "soul people." In other words, if a white person eats soul food, can this person ever taste it?[95] Interestingly, if soul food has its roots in southern cuisine, the culinary discourse around its status as race food is an often de-territorialized and somewhat atemporal one that infrequently interrogates the assumption of racially differentiated taste. Rather, this debate focuses on a discussion around "tradition," "authenticity," and "heritage making" that takes for granted food tastes that are relatively recent social constructs.[96]

Chapter 4

An American Culinary Heritage?

Mexican Food in the Southwest

In January 1942, Arthur J. Brooks advised potential tourists visiting San Antonio that they "would do well to become acquainted with the chili stands on Haymarket Plaza and the nightlife that it symbolizes." The trip from downtown to the Mexican quarter was short and with little risk of getting lost, since "one may literally follow his nose, itself beckoned by an aroma which, once sniffed, is never forgotten—the indescribable fragrance of burning mesquite, tangy as the desert air and a conjuration that evokes association with the archaic." The sensory discovery would continue as the visitor became acquainted with the "redolence" of the "pungent" foods, in this case "*chili-con-carne*." Cooked into a "mixture to assail the nostrils of the *gourmet*," the dish's unique "heat" would be "best relieved by *frijoles* and *tortillas*." While savoring the chili, the tourist could slowly and softly be "infected" by the "unhurried" atmosphere enhanced by serenade-singing "Mexican minstrels," the cooks' "rhythmic lilt," and the Spanish families' conversation, "the exquisite cadence of their voices rippl[ing] softly upon the night." "Señoritas" strolled gracefully through the scene, "all done up in the best American style except that the pretty, dark-eyed sweetheart has thrown a reboza over her head—jet black with scarlet flowers."[1]

Sensing their way through the market, tourists would be sent on a sensory, spatial, and temporal journey. In three pages, Brooks condensed a remarkable amount of clichés, sensory and otherwise, on the surviving Spanish fantasy past of the American Southwest. Eroticized descriptions of San Antonio's female chili vendors, known as "Chili Queens," were a common literary trope. Jeffrey Pilcher shows how the multisensory aura of their "dangerous yet alluring food" made palpable fears and fantasies of cross-racial sexuality.[2] (That the women's work as food vendors enabled them to assert a measure of autonomy was beyond the scope of Brooks's purportedly ethnographic essay.) Brooks conjured the evocative multisensory power of food to establish a link between performing gender and daring to partake of fiery chili. Most tourists only smelled and "look[ed] on," not daring to taste the Chili Queens' food. Only occasionally would a male tourist confidently point to the food and order "some of that . . . and that—and that" while "his womenfolk look[ed] at him with the admiration that is due the brave." By the 1940s, San Antonio's Chili Queens and their food offered a safe, if not tamed, exoticism that did not call normative gender roles into question. Years of heated municipal politics and health debates had transformed the hawker stands into a tourist attraction closer to historical pageantry than lively street market. As Brooks put it, entering the plaza was like "walking onto a Hollywood movie set" made to resemble a dreamed version of "Old Mexico."[3] Race and gender interacted in the interwar Southwest to construct the taste and smell of Mexican food as a domestic exoticism, a heritage cuisine marketable to tourists.[4]

When required to document the foods of their region, southwestern FWP workers turned to Mexican food. Indeed, such foods provided a historical, folkloric, and sensory template unique to the region, and their celebration meshed well with the anti-industrial ethos of New Deal food writing. FWP workers recognized the taste of Mexican food as the most original sensory feature of the region and highlighted it as an authentic, unspoiled taste of place. They copiously documented and enjoyed it. Only a minority of FWP workers in the region were Spanish speakers, yet most, if not all, proved their familiarity with tamales and chili. White male "Yanqui" tourists may not recognize the tasty offers of San Antonio's Chili Queens, but any FWP worker could decode that "some of that and that and that [would turn] out to be two *tacos*, two *enchiladas*, and two *tamales* on each plate, the whole buried under chopped salad greens."[5] To be efficiently promoted as an authentic sensory heritage to tourists in San Antonio, throughout the region, and on a national scale, Mexican food had to be identified, defined, and commoditized. Exploring the full scope of the FWP culinary archive, this chapter examines how New Deal food writing's effort at mapping out the history and geography of Mexican food in the United States led FWP units in the Southwest to equate the taste of race with the taste of place and the consequences of this equation on how multisensory experiences of food generated value in the region's sensory economies of tourism.

Racial categories were in flux in the 1930s Southwest, and the FWP's sensory appraisal of the region at the end of the Depression participated in making legal and vernacular categories felt realities. By the 1930s the category

"Mexican" was used rather indiscriminately to designate different groups of
Spanish speakers, from native Californios and Tejanos—families who, following the 1848 U.S. annexation of Mexico's northern territories, became,
overnight, a minority with only second-class citizenship[6]—to more recently
arrived Mexican migrants. The term was filled with semantic ambiguities
and, since the mid-nineteenth century, had oscillated between a national
and a racial category: only in the interwar period did the U.S-Mexico border
become not only an international demarcation but also a "cultural and racial
boundary."[7] Historians highlight the shifting ground on which identities
rested in the Southwest and have explored the ways in which the construction of racial categories differed in the region from the rest of the United
States. Race did not operate in terms of binary opposition between blacks and
whites in the Southwest but rather involved a series of actors: Anglo-Saxons,
European immigrants, Mexican immigrants, Spanish-speaking Americans,
Native Indians, Asian immigrants, and blacks.[8] Class formations overlapped
the plurality of race, and the interaction between structural (class) and ideological (race) factors in "historically contingent and regionally specific"
contexts assured the constant evolution of local racial hierarchies.[9] Each city,
town, and county possessed a specific racial history and terminology, leading
historian Linda Gordon to describe southwestern racial orders as "microsys-
tems."[10] In the interwar period the term "Anglo" had come to subsume ethnic
and religious affiliations under the supremacy of whiteness and tended to
include Southern and Eastern Europeans. Contributors to New Deal food
writing seldom used this category, though, preferring "American," which they
took to mean both "white" and "modern" yet left many in a grey racial area.
Whether Spanish American families—U.S. citizens since the region's mid-
nineteenth-century incorporation into the United States and often members
of the local elite—were racially white and/or American was unstable. That
the "señoritas" mixing the latest fashion with ethnic elements in San Antonio
could claim a Mexican American ethnic identity was a possibility still in
its infancy.[11] This shifting vocabulary reflects the fact that, notably different
from southern and northeastern whiteness, southwestern whiteness could,
well into the interwar period, best be defined by what it was not.[12] Defining
who was Mexican, whether legally through the introduction of such racial
category in the 1930 census or sensually in New Deal food writing, was
then of foremost importance to defining whiteness and "Americanness" in
the region. The sensory making of the Mexican racial category dialectically
participated in the making of the American identity of the region.

Not only was race neither a monolithic nor a polarized category in the
Southwest, but vastly different food cultures cohabitated in the region. Each

state had particular natural environments as well as political and demographic histories that informed local taste. FWP workers recorded—and
even insisted on—internal regional differences. Brooks, for instance, noted:
"Peculiarities . . . appear to divide the southwest itself. Tastes indigenous to
life in southern California, for example, are not readily identifiable with the
life of Texans."[13] Regional differences were intrinsic elements of a project like
America Eats since the work aimed to portray the nation as a pluralist mosaic of sensory experiences. Yet too much variety would dissolve the book's
patriotic goal and represent the country as a fragmented amalgam of eaters.
The national scope of *America Eats*, then, regulated difference and promoted
regional sensory unification by painting regions as coherent sensory units in
the New Deal sensory economy. Paradoxically, in the Southwest, this regional
sensory unification was achieved through a hyperlocalization of taste. The
regional essay, for instance, scanned the sensory span of the region on a
random pattern to offer snapshots of one particular New Mexico kitchen, a
California restaurant, or a fiesta in Arizona.[14] In this process, "Mexican food"
emerged as a central category occasionally used to refer to local creolized
sensory identities but most powerfully deployed toward the definition of
an authentic, exotic sensory other commodified for tourist consumption.
Mexican cookery evoked a strange foreignness, a familiar exoticism of tastes,
sounds, and smells apt to convince tourists to visit and come back to the
region.

New Deal food writing articulated the celebration of Mexican food as the
taste of the Southwest through a gender normative exoticism. Romanticized
Mexican women and their spicy dishes occupied a central role in the regional
culinary narrative. They were islands of sensory authenticity and embodied
racial knowledge that contrasted with the standardized produce of the food
industry. New Deal food writing's nostalgic aesthetic and the longing of a
number of FWP workers for the "real" taste of homemade food instead of the
blandness of industrial products led them to perceive the cuisine of ethnic
and racial others as purveyor of more authentic, in their words "genuine,"
culinary experiences. Anglo males, either contemporary tourists or in the
past, appeared as both protectors and conquerors of the women and their
spicy dishes; tasting their food became a crucible of white masculinity. As
Brooks put it in his description of the Chili Queens of San Antonio that opens
this chapter, "Yanqui" males would become "brave" by eating spicy Mexican
foods.

The sensory exploration and exploitation of Mexican food was not only a
way to mobilize tourist dollars but also a gendered means for the performance
of regional identity in the nation. The construction of Mexican food as the

region's racialized and gendered heritage taste provided a sensory contrast
to "American" modernity that worked to reinforce New Deal food writing's
patriotic aim. The southwestern FWP staff worked to inscribe themselves
within the U.S. national narrative of expansion and conquest by framing
enchiladas and chili as the food of a conquered people, a sensory remnant
of the past in the midst of American modernity. By the same token, the
endorsement of Mexican food as their authentic and marketable sensory
heritage allowed them to distinguish themselves from the rest of the country
and affirm regional identity. Tasting Mexican food offered the possibility to
sense the racial otherness of a conquered people while giving the region an
original and gendered sensory identity within the nation. Tasting Mexican
food was part of the American experience in the Southwest, and what was
American about the Southwest precisely was the Mexican flavor of its food.

The Taste of the Southwest

The taste of southwestern food in the 1930s was the outcome of historical
and social relations rooted in the natural environments of the borderland
region. Pre-Hispanic indigenous cultures had domesticated and mastered
the culture of corn that they turned into piki bread more often than tortillas
in what was to become northern New Spain. Native ingredients such as chile
peppers, maize, frijoles, prickly pears, pecans, and *pinones* nuts—roasted "for
eating much as Americans eat roasted peanuts"—left a long-lasting sensory
imprint on southwestern cuisines.[15] Spanish colonizers during the discovery
and conquest periods imported the culture of a host of Old World fruits,
vegetables, and cereals (grapes, olives, and wheat, to name a few) as well as
livestock, especially pork and cattle. From the sixteenth century onward,
culinary exchanges remained a decisive feature of local cuisines. The political history of the region further fostered distinct regional cultures and
foodways as the Hispanic and American frontiers "interlocked" in a North/
South dynamic.[16] Four distinct historical food cultures can be defined in
the U.S.-Mexico borderland region—Texas and northeastern Mexico, New
Mexico, Sonora, and California—and continued to influence southwestern
regional diets in the 1930s.[17] As an FWP worker remarked, diets in the region still depended "largely" upon "what [was] grown locally"; the "climate,
soil, [and] moisture" determined the taste of the food.[18] FWP workers were
aware of this geographical element of taste, even if they lacked the Tex-
Mex culinary paradigm to name it (which would not be coined before the
1960s).[19] A fieldworker named Salinas expressed a corresponding idea when
explaining that "the foods served . . . in almost any Mexican restaurant . . .

are not entirely of Mexican origin, but are rather peculiar to the Rio Grande border."[20] This everyday culinary fusion gave rise to foodways and dishes unique to the Southwest, such as wheat-flour tortillas and chili. Neither Mexican nor American per se, the foods of the Southwest were the result of human, cultural, and sensory interaction in specific natural environments.[21]

The study of Spanish American folklore, including foodways, constituted an important subfield of American folklore scholarship at the turn of the century and into the 1930s. For folklorists endeavoring to reorient their field from a search for the remnants of European folklore in the Americas to a study of the ongoing adaptation of migrants' culture in the new continent, it was an edifying case study. The FWP was at the forefront of this remaking of the field, and southwestern food traditions were a national asset that provided a vehicle for the patriotic affirmation of a liberal and pluralist civic culture. New Deal food writing often identified regional southwestern food as "Spanish American," "Spanish Mexican," or "the Mexican cookery of the United States": dishes that "ha[d] been there for centuries" and found their "source" in Spain but also "more strongly identified with materiel and ingredients easily procurable or indigenous" to the region.[22] Documenting the Spanish-speaking populations' arts, crafts, and cuisines provided the region with a local folklore—"culture, social life, foods, and dress drawing inspiration from Spain and Mexico" yet adapted to their U.S setting.[23] New Mexico's contribution to *America Eats* gave ample space to detailed essays on the culinary customs related to "Velarios (Wakes)," "La Merienda (Afternoon Lunch)," "Wedding Feast," and "Noche Buenas."[24] Antifascist politics of the 1930s encouraged this shift toward greater inclusion of groups such as Spanish Americans in the national narrative as a response to European race-based understanding of national belonging. In this context, the folkloric project potentially expressed the very modernity of the pluralist United States.

Folklore scholarship, including the FWP's own forays in the field, framed the appreciation of Spanish American culture through a broader discussion and interrogation about tradition and authenticity in the midst of modernity and progress—a modernity FWP workers often negatively perceived as "fixed upon the Concrete and the Physical" and spelling "the doom of folklore."[25] In this context, folklorists (in the FWP and beyond) and popular culture alike esteemed Spanish Americans as holders of comforting traditions and foods, a more primitive yet "soul-satisfying" society that contrasted with the exhausting American "tempo."[26] Food writing was part of a broader regional New Deal agenda to restore "almost-vanished" arts such as rug weaving or wood carving.[27] It presented Spanish American food as a reservoir of sensory experiences, a living realm of sensory memory for twentieth-century

Americans weary of the blandness of industrial life and standardized taste. FWP workers' task was one of rescue since, according to New Mexico workers, under the influence of American expansion, the "Old type Kitchen" went "missing," forcing the amateurs of "genuine native cooking and romance of its simple peasant life" to "go back into the hill towns and mountain villages" where "cooking [was] still done in pots and on flat stones in the corner mud fireplace."[28] Depression-era sensory nostalgia operated on an imperialist mode and, longing for unadulterated home cooking, seized the taste of Spanish Americans' food as an object of carnal and ideological desire.

The FWP's appraisal of Spanish American foodways was laden with ideological, sensory, and rhetorical ambiguities. Despite their acknowledgment as part of American folklore, Spanish Americans' status within the nation remained ambiguous, and, in New Mexico, the FWP celebration of "flat stones heating for the baking of tortilla" paralleled the efforts of health reformers to change local diets by eliminating the reliance on corn.[29] Similarly, in an essay on "Arizona Cuisine," fieldworkers Claire Hildman and Athlene Watson described a heritage "cookery" that possessed "centuries of tradition with a background of patient Mexican women who placed a high value on their cocinas (kitchens)" and added that "some still refuse to use commercial meal for their *tamales, tortillas,* and *enchiladas.*" Yet whether the last sentence praised the female cooks for retaining their traditional methods or belittled them for refusing to adapt to American industrial modernity is open to interpretation. The essay also operated a telling shortcut by dividing the region's food into three categories: Indian, Mexican, and modern. Hildman and Watson described Mexican food as "a blend of Spanish and Indian cultures," sometimes appreciated by "Americans too." They contrasted both Mexican and Indian foods with definitely nonfolkloric "modern" preferences enabled by the industrial production of fruits and vegetables in irrigated Arizona fields. That "modern" meant "American" was so evident for the authors that the use of both adjectives would have been redundant.[30]

Hildman and Watson's section on "Indian food" was in tune with the limited and inconsistent coverage of indigenous foodways in New Deal food writing. The focus on Mexican food took precedence over any sustained treatment of the topic. The section dealt with the game hunting, plant gathering, crop planting, and cooking techniques of "primitive Indians" before mentioning the more recent Americanization of Indian children's tastes in (often compulsory) boarding schools. They rejoiced in the fact that, though "some of the older ones cling to native habits, including their taste for raw meat," the "younger generations of Arizona Indians have acquired American eating habits" and that "government money and more accessible food give the modern Indian a chance to at least choose his diet."[31] Though such mentions were frequent, they were not the rule. The *America Eats* file for Arizona also included adequate ethnographic descriptions of the Hopi "feast of christening" and how to prepare the piki bread served for the occasion.[32] In Oklahoma, Choctaw FWP worker Peter J. Hudson contributed an essay on "Choctaw Indian Dishes." This, as well as other original Oklahoma material, news clipping, and reading notes on "Various Indian Dishes, Old and New," was integrated in the first version of the Southwest regional essay that opened with an informative, five-page historical and ethnographic report on indigenous foodways. It was edited out of the second version to make room for a Mexican motif.[33]

The FWP's sensory and cultural ambiguities toward Spanish American cuisine can be explained by the rapid demographic and culinary evolution of the Spanish-speaking population in the early twentieth century. Starting after the 1910 Mexican revolution and accelerating in the 1920s due to the need for a cheap workforce in the industrialized southwestern agricultural sector (the "modern" food identified in the aforementioned essay), a large wave of migrants moved "al norte." The interwar generation of economic migrants was a transient one, following the agricultural seasons and the labor demands. Close to 1.5 million migrants arrived in the years from 1910 to 1930, quickly outnumbering the existing Spanish-speaking population by 2 to 1.[34] Though Mexican migrants, as inhabitants of the Western hemisphere, were exempt from the mid-1920s quotas laws, they were often perceived by Anglos and, occasionally, existing Spanish-speaking populations as a threat to the region's economy and racial makeup. In New Mexico, Spanish American FWP worker Aurora Lucero White showed awareness of this sudden demographic imbalance. An early Latina intellectual of well-off Hispanic background who had been fighting for the survival of the Spanish language and local folklore in this "English only" state since the 1910s, White found her work for the FWP an efficient way to fulfill her personal goal of recording and preserving the village life of northern New Mexico.[35] She described a 1936 New Mexico "Spanish Fiesta" with alarm and pinpointed the "Mexican influence" as a definite "threat" to the "unforgettable" and "poignant" Spanish American heritage.[36] Despite being a cultural insider, White's writings for the FWP and beyond did not always avoid the hazards of cultural fetishism and xenophobia.[37] The early-twentieth-century Mexican migration to the United States heightened the debate about Mexican racial identity and classification. The anti-Mexican campaign culminated in the official "repatriation" and deportation of up to one million people by the federal and state governments after the 1929 crash and their categorization as a distinct Mexican racial group in the 1930 census.[38] The increasing size of the immigrant Mexican population had important repercussions for the region's racial taxonomy as well as its sensory economy.

When Mexican migrants cooked in the United States, they did not create a novel hyphenated cuisine but were pursuing a centuries-old culinary evolution anchored in the Southwest's natural environment and history. They did so in a constant dialogue with the home country, inventing new traditions, discarding and radically transforming older customs.[39] The interwar period was a crucial period for Mexican culinary culture and taste on both sides of the border. In Mexico itself, the period laid the foundation for the postwar turn toward a cohesive Mexican gastronomic discourse that "unif[ied] regional traditions that had formerly been divided by geography, ethnicity, and class under a national coating."[40] In the 1930s American Southwest, new tastes emerged consistent with changes south of the border, such as the "newer addition" of tacos, considered by a Texan fieldworker as "another combination of the original tortilla and meat" popular among many.[41] Mexican American ethnic foods were born out of the interaction between Mexican foodways from both sides of the border as well as with the U.S. food system in which members of the community participated as workers, entrepreneurs, and consumers. Transformed and manufactured north of the border, "tortillas, chorizos, salsas, bread, chocolate and . . . Mexican candy" took on a peculiar taste.[42] Some preferences disappeared in the adaptation to the U.S. economic and sensory conditions, such as the use of "*piloncillo*," brown cones of pressed, unrefined sugar, a sweetener deemed by a New Mexico FWP worker to be "rapidly giving way to the more easily acquired American product."[43] During the 1936 New Mexico "Spanish Fiesta" at the center of White's aforementioned fetishizing essay, "*puestos*" (booths) might have sold tacos and tamales, but a wide array of "candy, ice-cream, hamburgers, peanuts, [and] popcorns" also drew ethnic visitors.[44] The culinary and sensory interaction between Spanish American traditions, American industrial foods, and Mexican migrants' habits launched the development of new regional and ethnic cuisines.[45] But it was only incidentally that FWP workers noted the evolution of Mexican ethnic food taste or detangled its history.

The large demographic and sensory presence of Mexican migrants in the interwar Southwest destabilized the FWP documentation of regional food while enabling the glossing over of historical and sensory differences to establish a set menu of "Mexican food." No uniform terminology existed, and FWP workers used a volatile vocabulary to name and describe a consolidating ethnic cuisine. In New Mexico, for instance, Carrie Hodges switched from "Mexican-American" (an unstable, quasi-oxymoronic category in the interwar period) to "Spanish-American" in the middle of her essay when describing the foods "peculiar" to the state.[46] Others included "the recipes of our neighbor, Mexico" in the description of "Spanish food" or wrote of "Spanish-Mexican" and "Spanish-Mexican-Indian influences."[47] Overall, though, FWP workers used the Mexican racial category as an in-clusive tool to write about the evolving tastes of both Mexican migrants and Spanish American populations. Describing the fiesta held in Austin, Texas, on September 16 for the celebration of Mexican independence from Spain, an FWP worker on the Folklore Project, for instance, established a differ-ence, and related the rivalry, between the "Mexican citizens" group and the "Texas-Mexicans," but when it came to describing the foods served during the fiesta, they were simply "Mexican." We learn that, in Austin the "main Mexican foods . . . [were] tortillas, tamales, enchiladas, tacos, chili and, to a lesser degree, mole."[48] Despite their awareness of the plurality of identities, histories, and social trajectories among the Spanish-speaking population in the region, most FWP workers compounded racial and national categories in their sensory assessment of regional Mexican food. They pointed not only to the well-known *tortillas, frijoles,* and *tamales,* but also to *enchiladas, tacos, menudos, posole* ("a delicacy of Mexico"), *camotes* ("sugary sweet potatoes"), *tortillas de blanquillas* ("pancakes with fish"), *pollo con arroz* ("chicken, its golden breast flakes with rice"), *miel de tuna* ("cactus flower honey"), and a wide range of other dishes.[49] Chili was regularly evoked as well, but, as will be analyzed in the last section of this chapter, the dish's national popularity and ambiguous racial and spatial belonging complicated its classification.

One sensory characteristic united all Mexican dishes in New Deal food writing: spiciness, "the hotter the better."[50] The liberal use of chile peppers by Spanish-speaking cooks demarcated the region on multisensory grounds. FWP workers rarely failed to mention the decorative element of *ristras,* strings of chile pods hanging "like scarlet icicles" on the sides of adobe houses in their description of Mexican neighborhoods, "no matter how humble the hut." Descriptions of "typically Mexican" restaurant with "sombreros," "clusters of chile peppers," and "colorful parrots" hanging "here and there on the wall" provided a quick and efficient introductory description to many of the reports on Mexican food.[51] FWP workers considered peppers—dried, fresh, red or green—indispensable to Mexican food's "peculiar piquancy," a taste considered "as pleasing as it [is] hard to reproduce." The seasoning was considered "illusive" because the authentic flavor could not be provided by the "pulverized" chili powder marketed to Americans but required the use of home-crushed chile and access to an innate racial knowledge inherited by Mexican cooks from their ancestors in New Spain.[52] Indeed, the range of flavors distinctive to southwestern cuisines depended on a deep knowledge of chili varieties and their culinary use.

New Deal food writing linked the fiery taste of Mexican dishes not only to the use of native pepper plants but also to the work and embodied sensory knowledge of Mexican women. Aware of the inroads made by mass-produced chile flakes in American kitchens, fieldworkers used New Deal food writing as an opportunity to set the record straight. Though proud of the industrial development of the region and its capacity to export "typical" foodstuffs, southwestern FWP workers strived to highlight the traditional, authentic, and unchanging use of chili peppers by Mexican women as a unique regional feature. An anonymous FWP worker judged that "though ground and powdered chile can be bought . . . the native New Mexican would rather buy the strings of chile pods and prepare his own." Southwestern contributors to New Deal food writing established a difference between U.S. economic development and Mexican cultural retention, thus excluding the latter from the former. Only Mexican women knew how to wash and dry the pods and how to toast them on top of the stove, "turning them as they begin to blister" and until "the skin puffed way from the pulp." Once the cooking process finished, they were experts at steaming the pods between two damp cloths before pulling the skin off and removing the veins and seeds.[53] Only this labor-intensive and guarded process could produce the "stinging hotness of chili sauce."[54] This celebration of sensory authenticity and racial knowledge occasionally led FWP workers to write grossly offending pieces, such as this warning against industrial chile powder allegedly uttered by a "Mexican-American housewife": "I got no use for these kind of chile, she will say, Ees very bad for the e-stomach! Thoos pipples they grind up everytheeng those e-skeens, everytheeng they grind. Eet mack more chile to sell . . . Thoos e-skeems on the chile, they ees only gud for thoos burros [donkeys]. NO. I got no use for thet ground chile een the e-store."[55] As this diatribe makes evident, the FWP regional culinary narrative constructed Spanish speakers as sensory others on multisensory grounds and heavily recruited sound, smell, and vision as supporting elements.

Gradations of spiciness provided sensory borders to the region. The "redolent" cookery of the Southwest, "breathing Old Spain and Mexico," found its best embodiment in the myriad local barbecue-sauce recipes that, "with some omissions and remissions," usually integrated a seasoning of "salt, black pepper, dried red chili powder, garlic, *oregano*, cumin seed, [and] cayenne pepper" while "tomatoes, green chili peppers, onions and olive oil ma[de] up the sauce."[56] A Kansas FWP worker carefully copied a 1939 newspaper article by local journalist William Lindsay White that clarified the connection between current taste preferences and historical events. White explained that the spicy barbecue sauce was "as much part of the Latin heritage of the Southwest as are the crumbling Spanish missions." He pursued his sensory mapping of the Southwest by noting that, "as you come north the chili peppers weaken and finally disappear, until near the Canadian border they offer you nothing stronger than a watery scarlet store of catsup."[57] Brooks, in the Southwest regional essay, rebounded on this to note that fondness for well-seasoned barbecued meat set the region apart from "zones which serve the traveller with barbecue and hot dogs." Boosting a taste for spiciness and "virile sauces" became a way to perform a regional identity based on a mythologized territorial conquest grounded in the incorporation of an exotic, spicy other within national bounds.[58]

FWP workers identified spiciness as a signal of racial culinary authenticity and regional sensory identity, but they also linked spiciness to a specific historical narrative, namely, the American conquest of the region. Emphasizing spiciness was part of a decades-old racial discourse on the respective merits of, on the one hand, white civilization, progress, and its associated risk for degeneracy, and, on the other, savagery, racial primitivism, and its capacity to fortify degenerated, civilized men.[59] The FWP's sensory mapping of the Southwest is reminiscent of the racially inflected theory of climate developed by American scientists in their exploration of the overseas territories of the U.S. empire at the turn of the century. In *American Abyss*, Daniel Bender describes how American imperial science "defined a geography of energy and lethargy, progress and degeneration" that divided "the globe into climatic regions that corresponded with racial, not national, divisions."[60] New Deal food writing gave this climatic theory a culinary and sensory twist. FWP workers deemed the tastes of the Southwest's Spanish-speaking inhabitants responsible for their "unhurried" lifestyle, the "leisurely pace" of their trade, their "drowsy" ways, and their allegedly historically proven inefficiency at developing agriculture and industry in the region.[61] The difference in rhythm and temporality was systematically mentioned by FWP workers who insisted on comparing the agro-pastoral economy of the Spanish era with the deeds of the "last of these modern interlopers, the Yankees, who leveled the mountains for their copper, laced the face of the land with ribbons of concrete, dammed rivers to make deserts bloom, and in less than a century worked changes vaster than their predecessors had wrought in thousands of years."[62] As the *America Eats* Southwest essay explained, the American race, strengthened by centuries of adaptation to the tempered climate and pioneer frontier settlement in the New World, possessed a vigorous hunger, "welled from the lusty appetite of the hard work that settled the untameness." Though the "inhibited stomach of the Nordic[s]" might quarrel with "hot-tempered" Mexican foods, settlers conquered and incorporated these tastes with the land. American pioneers fed on the primitive tang of Mexican cookery and turned its spiciness into an asset for progress. Two races but also two stages of civilization cohabited under the same climate. According to this narrative, "Yankees" may have "assimilated many of the delights that attend the eating [habits] of the Mexican" and "acquired some of his tastes." Yet "*siesta*" still seemed "a waste of time for the energy of Americans who live on the fringe of Mexico."[63]

New Deal food writing depicted the taste of Mexican food as the codified sensory heritage of a past and romanticized way of life that now was replaced with American progress and modern food. Mexican foods and their distinctive tastes were not taboo; quite the contrary, they were omnipresent and upheld as symbols of the region. In bestowing Mexican food with easily identifiable and codified tastes, smells, and sights, New Deal food writing supervised and facilitated local Anglos and white tourists' consumption of it. Tasting Mexican food then became part of the American experience of "brave" and manly conquest in the Southwest. The male tourists eating spicy chili in San Antonio's Haymarket Plaza did not endanger their racial identity; rather, their sensory adventure reinforced and policed racial and gendered borders, demonstrating the American ability to appropriate the land and incorporate its peppery food. Like the thousands who attended an outdoor feast of "barbecued beef and Mexican beans" organized by the Sheriff's office in 1941 Los Angeles, they enjoyed the rewards of conquest and the "culinary heritage . . . from their Spanish and Mexican predecessors."[64] The codified "genuine" Mexican cuisine defined the region in the New Deal sensory economy by recounting its distinctively raced and gendered history. Spicy enchiladas were culinary and sensory landmarks that made the Southwest a unique and uniquely American region.

The "Slap, Slap Motion" of the Tortilla: Sensory Economies of Tourism

Mexican culinary traditions were part of the Southwest's sensory décor and constitutive of the sense of place sold to tourists. It provided a multisensory, romantic cultural backdrop to the FWP progressive narrative about the advent of American modernity. Modernity was palpable in the Southwest during the late 1930s and early 1940s. The period was an economic and demographic turning point as the region geared up toward a wartime economy that would eventually end the Depression.[65] The tourism sector of the economy, closely linked to the advent of the railroad in the late nineteenth century and accelerated with the birth of automobile tourism in the early twentieth century, boomed in the interwar period. As Phoebe Kropp, Marguerite Shaffer, and others have shown, the growth of tourism refashioned the region's past as "a land of enchantment" abounding with romantic, nostalgic visions of a Hispanic golden age where tourists "in search of authentic experience, therapeutic escape, and 'real' life" could travel.[66] In this context, the taste of Mexican food became a realm of sensory memory that could embody a fantasy "Spanish-Mexican" past in the present while demonstrating the American stronghold on the region. The Anglo imperialist nostalgia for all things Spanish was not a mere diversion from an anxious modernity; it was part of the regional commodity culture and corporate identity, anchoring Mexican food at the center of sensory economies of tourism.[67]

The taste of Mexican food, framed as a domestic exoticism, helped turn the Southwest from a place into a tourist destination. Culinary tourism, defined by Lucy Long as "the intentional, exploratory participation in the foodways of another," was a central tool for the region's affirmation of its sensory identity.[68] FWP workers made Mexican food safe for sensory sightseeing by establishing an unvarying menu of dishes, simplifying recipes, and providing detailed explanations on how to realize them.[69] Tortillas in particular became essential southwestern sights. Fieldworkers presented "tor-TEE-yas" as Mexican "daily bread" and "staff of life" and constantly celebrated their versatility.[70] Essays described how dexterous Mexican women soaked corn in a lime solution to produce the *nixtamal* that they then grounded into *masa* meal on their traditional stone *metate*. The dough was then flattened, "slapped from one hand to the other until it assume[d] the appearance of enormous thin pancakes," and "cooked directly on top of the stove until crisp like soda crackers." It would be served at every meal.[71] But tortillas were also easily transformed into "other delectable dishes," most notably enchiladas and tacos in the late 1930s.[72]

To make tortillas palatable to a national audience, FWP workers explained at length how to prepare and eat them. Some encouraged "housewives anywhere" to try cooking tortillas and engage in practices of culinary tourism at home. Not only the realm of the traveler to another land, culinary tourism is also an everyday domestic practice that uses food as a vehicle for traveling, experiencing otherness, and shaping one's identity.[73] A Texas contributor highlighted that tortillas "can be made about as well in Maine as in Mexico, and without the laborious grinding of grain," since one could substitute cornmeal for *masa* and even mix in a little chili powder "in true Mexican style," so that the tortilla would "resemble a thin, pink pancake."[74] We do not know whether northeastern homemakers would have followed this advice, but New Deal food writing does testify to the ways southwestern Anglo "homemakers" used "surviving influences" (in other words, Mexican food) to establish their regional legitimacy. They decorated their houses with strings of red peppers, "brightly painted gourds," and pomegranates, which could also be used as the main ingredient for "salad and ices," and served Mexican dishes as "occasional delicacies" for "luncheon."[75] Anglo housewives' temporary and playful positioning at a sensory racial threshold in the 1930s is reminiscent of the "acts of imperial buy-in" historian Kristin Hoganson analyzes in her study of the global production of American domesticity at the turn of the century. She shows how the consumption of foreign foods, fashions, and styles "[turn] the foreign into the harmless stuff of pleasure that posed no significant threat to [white middle- and upper-class women's] sense of racial, class, national, and civilizational privilege."[76] This imperialist mode of consumption and culinary exploration used a staged exoticism as a claim to regional authenticity and legitimacy.

Despite attempts to demystify their preparation, the bulk of written and visual descriptions of tortillas in New Deal food writing are multisensory depictions of Mexican women's embodied knowledge, skills, and labor. Tourists eating Mexican food in the 1930s searched for olfactory and gustatory experiences as well as auditory and kinesthetic ones. Hearing Mexican women patting tortillas into shape was the "homiest sound," a comforting marker of regional identity at the tail end of a decade of demographic and economic change and at the beginning of a new period of industrial expansion.[77] A large part of the "quite interesting" entertainment of going to the Mexican quarters resided in "watch[ing] these women in the process of making *tortillas*." Sound effects reinforced kinesthetic pleasure when the "right amount of corn meal mixture is placed in one hand, and then is transferred from one hand to the other with a slap, slap motion."[78] Most of the bakers stopped using this technique by the 1930s and thinned the dough using "dampened, cloth-covered pressing boards" but the image was still a powerful representation of Mexicanness and used as a symbol of exoticness throughout New Deal food writing.[79] Mexican women, bent over their mortars, pounding the dough with their pestles, and patting tortillas, were regional sensory symbols.

The multisensory appeal of Mexican women's cooking and baking in New Deal food writing blended desire with disgust. The 1939 California American Guide Series volume, *California: A Guide to the Golden State*, for instance, proposed an ambivalent image of a "tortilla maker" at work (figure 4.1). The image presents an orderly and idealized racial landscape, orienting our gaze toward the past and describing cooking as an immemorial gesture: the grinding of the coarse *nixtamal* dough into *masa* meal, a skill ingrained in the tortilla maker's body. Touch, texture, weight, and heat infuse the picture:

Figure 4.1. Tortilla maker, Olvera Street, Los Angeles. Federal Writers' Project of the Works Progress Administration for the State of California, *California: A Guide to the Golden State* (New York: Hastings House, 1939), courtesy of Hastings House Publishing.

the grain and vein of the wood, the heaviness of the stone pestle, the hot griddle, the fingers of the women in the background imprinting the paper-thin tortilla. The tortilla maker embodies the region's heritage; her bonnet is, for instance, more a traditional costume than protective hairnet. The woman's gaze acknowledges the presence of the photographer and seems to invite the viewer into the frame. The guidebook provides no information about who took the picture, under what circumstances, and for what purpose. It was a riff on the period's documentary aesthetic but also subverted the ethnographic codes of the genre as the woman is very obviously posing for the photographer, her frank gaze almost defiantly directed straight at the viewer.[80] The picture conveys a nostalgic sense of familiarity and comfort. Yet there is an explicit condemnation in this picture, one that relies on the senses, particularly smell. At a time when sanitary rules became the norm, we see her smoking directly over her dough; her apron is dirty, a garbage bin is under the table. The erotic potential of the phallic cigarette is latent and correlated by other FWP sources that regularly compared the expert rolling and folding of corn shucks into tamales by any "Mexican housewife" with how "she would roll a cigarette."[81] While clearly identifying her as nonwhite, the pictorial ambiguity and multisensory potency of this image leaves its meaning open: comfortable tradition or cautionary tale?

The ideological force of this photograph is both reinforced and sapped when considered in relation to the full iconographic program of the guidebook. If the region's past came alive in the image of the tortilla maker, its future was central to the upbeat, progressive, and patriotic mood that ran throughout the pages, which recorded the first effects of the increased federal investments in the defense industry. An illustration section titled "Industry, Commerce, Transportation" included pictures of a steel cargo ship, an airplane assembly line, and oil wells. Food was part of this optimistic agenda, and the section also included a photograph of a young worker in a spotless peach-canning factory (figure 4.2). The photograph, like a dozen in the guidebook, was by Horace Bristol, a young San Francisco photographer whose work with John Steinbeck was at the origin of the *Grapes of Wrath* and who would go on to be one of the first staff photographers of *LIFE* magazine.[82] The migrant workforce was key to the region's industrial and agro-industrial rise and, presenting the state as a "polyglot conglomeration," the guidebook composed a pluralist chronicle that did not shy away from exposing the labor conditions of the Mexican, Filipino, "Oriental contract labor," and migrant workers who made possible the production of "modern"

Figure 4.2. Inspecting peaches at a cannery. Federal Writers' Project of the Works Progress Administration for the State of California, *California: A Guide to the Golden State* (New York: Hastings House, 1939), courtesy of Hastings House Publishing.

and "American" agricultural commodities in the region.[83] The guidebook illustration set comprised a two-page spread that offered a stark commentary on the life of migrant agricultural workers: one of the images showed a female bean picker hanging on to her toddler (figure 4.3).[84] The links from the field to the factory and from the bodies of the migrant workers to the tortillas that might feed them were left for the reader to connect, however.

Figure 4.3. Migrant workers from many states line up on the edge of the field with their filled hampers, awaiting their turn for weighing. Near Westley, California. Photographed by Dorothea Lange. Farm Security Administration/Office of War Information Black-and-White Negatives, http://www.loc.gov/pictures/collection/fsa/item/fsa2000001828/PP (accessed September 25, 2015). Included with the caption "Migratory Workers Weighing Peas" and no attribution in Federal Writers' Project of the Works Progress Administration for the State of California, *California: A Guide to the Golden State* (New York: Hastings House, 1939).

The California American Guide Series volume's kaleidoscopic visual representation of race established the Mexican population both at the center and outside of an alleged American modernity. The photograph of the tortilla maker presents her as a sensory repository of tradition, an exotic and vanishing figure, excluded from the region's industrial development. In contrast, the guide displayed migrant workers as the essential labor force behind the states' agricultural and industrial economy. Indeed, given the racial makeup of the food-canning workforce in California, it is highly probable that the peach worker herself was of Mexican descent. But by not identifying her as such while at the same time visually highlighting the exoticism of the tortilla maker and the destitution of migrant workers, the guidebook reifies Mexicanness as an unchanging category and curtails the expression of evolving ethnic, social, cultural, and sensory identities.[85] The sensory economy of the California guidebook, the organization of the senses in text and images, remained volatile, creating tensions that ripple throughout the pages.

The guidebook did not leave industrial and sensory modernity unquestioned, however. The odd echoes between the images of the tortilla maker and the factory worker inspecting peaches falter the progressive narrative. Both illustrations represent women dealing with food, their bodies in similar position, standing up with their arms extended in front of them. Yet the two photographs are also bluntly different. Contrasting with our bodily encounter with the tortilla maker, the second image keeps the senses of smell and touch in check to promote the rationality of sight. The focus here is not on traditional cooking and daily life but instead on the modern industrial economy symbolized by the glaze of the steel and the full-bodied peaches that will feed the embattled nation proper vitamins. The caption does not mention the woman as an individual, and the presence of the photographer is not acknowledged, in effect denying her any agency in her task. She is her action. While the tortilla maker embodied a living tradition, the factory worker is using her trained eyes to inspect peaches on the conveyer belt. She is working in a sanitized, de-sensorialized environment symbolized by her rubber gloves, pristine plastic apron, and protective hat. The modernist composition of the shot—straight, almost cubist lines—can be viewed as a celebration of progress, yet it also compresses the woman. The photograph of the peach-factory worker combined the New Deal aesthetic modernist drive with the FWP's repeated insistence on the alienation induced by the modern world—a world where one eats foods denied of history and tradition. The echo between the two pictures simultaneously reinforced and undermined the modernist ethos of the guidebook. The contrast boosted the ideological charge of the industrial pictures even as it questioned the human and cultural repercussions of industrial progress. The visual similarity and the ideological discrepancy between the two pictures highlight the FWP's ambiguous attitude toward an industrial modernity achieved at the cost of substantial sensory loss. It also unveils the central role of racial and ethnic minorities in the FWP search for "real" food.

The FWP, and California boosters for that matter, were aware of the sensory deficiency of "modern food" and offered Mexican food as a remedy for locals and tourists alike. The caption locates the tortilla maker on Olvera Street, described in the Los Angeles guidebook as "a narrow, block-long alley designed to give tourists a taste of Mexico," with the "70-odd stores and booths owned and operated by Mexicans ha[ving] gay decorations and displays of Mexican foods, pottery, and trinkets." Indeed, the "alley of mud and refuse" was "reclaimed" and "restored in the manner of an old Mexican street" in 1929.[86] The ultimate instance of "theme-park-style" production of Mexican authenticity, Olvera Street served as a symbolic urban landmark, evoking the "streets of yesterday" in the midst of the "city of today." In historian Phoebe Kropp's view, the chronological disjunction at the heart of the revitalization project heightened spatial segregation, thus assuring "a sense of ethnic control" despite the contemporary image of the Mexican population as an economic and racial peril.[87] The forged Mexican market street framed the community as a "quiescent labor force that remained content in picturesque poverty, singing instead of striking," making tortillas instead of participating in regional industrial modernity and economic recovery.[88]

Despite New Deal food writing efforts to present her as a symbol of Mexican sensory and culinary authenticity, the tortilla maker was an integral part of the region's sensory modernity. As part of the Olvera Street's pageantry, she fully engaged in the contemporary regional tourist economy, as a worker and as a symbol. Moreover, she herself was working on an assembly line. An empty workstation in front of her suggests that another worker must have stepped out as the photograph was being taken (or did the photographer ask the other woman to leave?). The women in this picture were not producing tortillas for home consumption but for selling—they were running a business. Corroborating the visual elements of this picture with photographs in the Los Angeles Public Library collection helps locate this picture in the El Sol del Mayo Tortilla plant owned in the 1930s by Maria Quevedo and situated near Olvera Street.[89] Though not presented as such in the guidebook, this image was one of successful female ethnic entrepreneurship. Latent in the guidebook pictorial choices was an alternate version of sensory modernity that could potentially bypass the past/present, tradition/modernity dichotomies to establish the Spanish-speaking population at its center.

Getting a taste of the exotic within national borders became a trademark of the region. Even American Guide Series volumes that otherwise provided informative images and discussions of ethnic food businesses (the Texas guidebook, for instance) would include grossly stereotyped descriptions of Mexican quarters: "Here are odd shops, distinctive foreign odors, women wrapped in black *rebozos* huddling over baskets of freshly made *tortillas*, venders of candy, *pan dulce* (sweet bread), balloons, and brilliant paper flowers.... The somnolent atmosphere of Mexico broods over all."[90] FWP workers voiced the American identity of the Southwest through a culinary boosterism founded on the claim to exoticism. Eating Mexican food provided a medium for sensory time travel into the days of the Spanish Empire, before "Progress" and its consequences arrived. This sensory identity built on the acknowledgment of Spanish speakers as regional racial others and used their sensory difference to create a regional culinary and sensory heritage. The region was depicted as an island of sensory authenticity, a potential refuge from the alienation of modern life, and yet also a budding American region. Authentic Mexican dishes provided the region with an original sensory heritage in need of preservation amid American modernity.

Of Cowboys and "Mamacitas"

New Deal food writing coupled spicy food prepared by Mexican "mamacitas" with the sturdy food of virile cowboys, offering both for tourist consumption. If the making of the taste of Mexican food into a regional heritage resided in Spanish-speaking women's work and embodied knowledge, its valorization was often anchored in the masculine public sphere. The complex gendering of the taste of Mexican food constructed its consumption by white men as proof of manly conquest and an acknowledgment of sensory seduction. FWP workers described their region as the pinnacle of progress—the land where male pioneers absorbed Mexican women's spicy "concoction" and, re-energized by this primitive offer, conquered the land. The imagery associated with the region's conquest was laden with sexual connotation, and Chili Queen cohabitated with the no-less-mythic outdoor lifestyle of the cowboy.

FWP workers described cowboy foods as, if not a treasure of haute cuisine, indubitably American. The typical and monotonous cowboy diet was meat heavy and included forced sourdough biscuits and canned vegetables, all of it preferably "plain but well-cooked" and accompanied by gallons of coffee. Meals, prepared by the "belly-cheater" (the cook) on the "chuck wagons" that followed the men in their herding and branding journeys became part of the folklore of the "Old West."[91] Mexican dishes occasionally spiced up the dullness of cowboys' food. As an "old-timer" explained to a FWP interviewer, newly arrived Americans "didn't take [. . .] long to learn" how to "take [their] frijoles, tortillas and chili straight."[92] American interwar popular culture imagined the "West"—and here the FWP's somewhat artificial regional division between the "Southwest" and the "Far West" blurs—as a land where men living a strenuous life could acquire barbarian virtues without losing their civility.[93] In the 1930s this meant the regeneration of the "embattled masculinity" of unemployed breadwinners soon to become part of a militarizing citizenry.[94] New Deal food writing tapped into the vast pool of western imagery to write odes to the "gargantuan appetites" of the "virile, hardbitten" cowboys.[95]

Specialty dishes emerging from the cowboys' outdoor range activities had connotations of audacity, disgust, and pleasurable appropriation. "Son-of-a-gun" stew (a euphemism for its original name: "son-of-a-bitch" stew) was a favorite. No definite recipe was provided for this dish; indeed, the mystery around its exact composition was part of its sense appeal in the 1930s. The origin of the stew was a source of debate; several versions of its creation, however, involved a "ranch cook with a fearful hangover and no meat on hand." The improvident cook had noticed that, while the ranchers usually threw the "head, liver, tail and stomach or paunch . . . over the corral fence to rot away in the sun or be eaten by the coyotes at night," the "Mexican along the border utilized these parts." The cook breached the race, class, and sensory "prejudice" of the cowboys by making these taboo parts into a stew. Though at first outraged and furious at the cook—hence the stew's name—the ranch hands surrendered to its tastiness and adopted it as a beloved sensory proof of their virility.[96] Close second to son-of-a-gun stew in the pantheon of virile food were "prairie oysters" (roasted calves testicles), a delicacy appreciated by "ranch epicures" and "cooked only at branding fires or in kitchens from which women are banished either voluntarily or by diplomatic hints that what is to take place there is wholly a man's affair."[97]

The revival of Southwest fiestas and rodeos by the tourism industry in the interwar period played into the romantic and nostalgic sensory appeal of both cowboys' meat-heavy culinary specialties and Mexican dishes. Boosters in Tucson, Phoenix, or Santa Fe cast their states as "truly a land of pageantry— a land of sunsets, tradition, legendry, and romantic history." They strived to highlight local historical and sensory distinctiveness through the organization of fiestas, "combin[ing] the Spanish, Indian, and cowboy motifs" and featuring "streets fairs, parades, music, and dancing." Cities in search of a marketable past selectively highlighted "certain aspects of their frontier heritage": son-of-a-gun stew became an obligatory culinary feature of these events.[98] It even opened up the appetites of "suspicious" women who at first "thought there was something mean and ornery about it" but came back for seconds after getting "a whiff of how it smells"—"and they don't say anything about a small spoonful."[99] FWP workers were no dupes and underlined the artificiality of these events, poking fun at how the cities "[went] 'Western'" for the occasion and how "almost everyone, locals and visitors alike, don Western garb in three days of revelry."[100] Yet, fiestas and rodeos re-enacting the "flavor" of the "Sunburnt West of Yesterday" took center stage in the Depression-era Southwest's sociability and tourist sensory economies.[101] Rodeos and barbecues serving son-of-gun stew and other "frontier" dishes not only provided a distinctive cultural and sensory identity to the region but also a cathartic means to express Depression-era gender anxieties by staging overtly confident performances of masculinity.

A prime instance of the "colorful spectacle-pageant[s]" staged for "visitors" and locals alike was the yearly Los Angeles Sheriff's barbecue. Tens of thousands flocked to the event held at the Santa Anita racetracks: the 1941 edition allegedly attracted seventy thousand people. The FWP's Southern California office recorded the day in both pictures and text for the *America Eats* project (figures 2.1, 2.2, 4.4, 4.5). The food served purposely reflected the region's "Spanish-Mexican" heritage; a side dish of "Mexican beans steeped in a piquant sauce" as well as "warm, crisp rolls" and "gallons of steaming coffee" accompanied the barbecued meat. The menu used codified Mexican taste as a symbol of an idyllic and chivalric way of life, "*carne de vaca con frijoles*, their mellifluous name for beef and beans," was served "alfresco" to "*senoras* and *senoritas*, attended by mounted *caballeros*." A carefully orchestrated pageant underlined the culinary nod to Spanish California. Each sheriff entered the barbecue ground "mounted on a horse with trappings of tooled leather and silver" and wearing an "ornately Spanish costume." Their performance aimed at recapturing the "provincial" atmosphere of Spanish California, its "incomparable gaiety" and idealized "camaraderie."[102] The only trace left of the pageant aspect of the barbecue in the visual record is the oversized sombrero of the Mexican man in the background of one of the photograph (figure 4.5). The hat legitimized and authenticated the barbecue as the setting for the sensory performance of race and the invocation of a comforting mythic past; it also signaled the carnivalesque potential of the event. The satisfaction was sensorial, ideological, and financial: while the first Sheriff's barbecue held in 1924 raised $337.60, the 1941 edition grossed $45,000. The value of Mexican tastes appreciated fast in the Southern California sensory economy.

The set of pictures that accompanied the written description of the Sheriff's Barbecue provides a complementary record to the written sources. The

Figure 4.4. Removing the barbecued beef from the pits, Los Angeles Sheriff's Barbecue, 1941. Federal Writers' Project photographs for the *America Eats* project, Library of Congress Prints and Photographs Division Washington, D.C., LOT 13328 (F).

Figure 4.5. Prepared beef, ready for the barbecue pits, Los Angeles Sheriff's Barbecue, 1941. Federal Writers' Project photographs for the *America Eats* project, Library of Congress Prints and Photographs Division Washington, D.C., LOT 13328 (F).

photographic reportage captured the exclusively male cooking staff but also offered a more complex view of race relations at the event. The anonymous photographer concentrated on taking snapshots of the impressive amount of meat and the men proudly preparing and providing it to the hungry crowd. This iconographic program corroborates the strong triangular relationship between barbecued meat and embattled masculinity explored in chapter 2.[103] Moreover, the pictures unveil a visible generational difference, suggesting the initiation of younger males into the local gendered sensory economy through their participation in the barbecue preparation (figure 2.2). This process simultaneously made them the symbolical culinary heirs of the "Spanish-Mexican" and of the later American conquerors. The 1941 edition of the Sheriff's Barbecue also added patriotic mobilization to the cathartic function of eating "*carne de vaca con frijoles.*" In the regional pageant of the mobilizing nation, California contributed defense plants and a romantic gendered past of conquest. Yet here again the photograph rebels against the written word and the description of the orderly pageant, providing us with a glimpse of California's multiethnic population. Behind the Mexican cook an Asian American man takes his place in the homosocial U.S. barbecue culture, posing, cigarette in his mouth, in the background of the group photograph (figure 4.5). What this photograph also starts to unveil, then, is the extent to which food in the Southwest was part of an ongoing multiethnic sensory exchange.

"Fiery Texan-Mexican Border" Dishes: Defending Southwestern Regional Authenticity

The portrayal of Mexican food as the region's sensory heritage in New Deal food writing regularly masked the fact that southwestern food was the result of a long-lasting, ubiquitous, and ongoing regional culinary exchange. Newly arrived Mexican migrants added to the local cuisine, while regional dishes had a decidedly distinctive taste, "a suggestion of dried mint leaves, a sprinkling of celery salt, a spring of greens, perhaps parsley from the backyard patch, the stain of tomato, a nuance of oregano, a reminder of onion or the more recollective garlic, a twist of chile, a bit of sherry, the garnishment of ripe or stuffed olives."[104] New Deal food writing documented the existence of a regional cuisine with both past and present incarnations. FWP workers themselves occasionally wrote about their own taste. Lorin Brown, a worker in the Santa Fe office, son of an Anglo father and a Latina mother, for instance, reported his enjoyment of "*chicharonnes* . . . sizzling hot, wrapped in a hot tortillas, sandwich fashion, plentiful salted with a good glass of wine to wash them down."[105] A dynamic web of sensory interactions and commodification, culinary borrowings, and cultural relationships animated southwestern sensory economies. Although still adopting a temporal metaphor, Brooks, the author of the Southwest regional essay wondered: "Where does the Spanish influence end and the American begin?"[106]

Mexican food had been popular across the region and beyond before the interwar period. In Arizona as in Texas, "most restaurants . . . serve[d] one or more Mexican dishes." Most popular of these were tamales and chili con carne, two "delicacies" for which Anglo Americans had "gone strong."[107] The former were described as "steaming edibles" and a staple of street pushcarts throughout the West, and, in local versions, the Midwest and the South already in the late nineteenth century.[108] The popularity of tamales, as well as the dexterity required to prepare them, explain why the stuffed cornhusks were one of the earliest ethnic foods to be canned and mass-produced in the United States. As one FWP worker advised readers, "strangers to the art of making tamales are advised to buy them in cans or take some time to practice."[109] According to several fieldworkers, within the span of a few years, tamales became "popular dishes in the homes of many . . . not of Spanish or Mexican descent." Another "favorite" among Arizona's "American" population was tamale pie, consisting of *masa* combined with "cut-up chicken or beef, onions, tomatoes, fat, chili and olives . . . cooked in a baking dish." But for those desiring to avoid the trip to the Mexican store, hominy grits could be substituted in the making of the "mixture."[110]

Food entrepreneurs, restaurant owners, and industrialists seized some of the Mexican tastes most enjoyed by local "Americans," tamed them down, and branded them successfully. Sensory sightseeing did not require an actual visit to the region. FWP workers were aware of this commodification of Mexican taste and sheepishly participated in it. A Texas FWP worker on the *America Eats* project, for instance preceded a report on Mexican recipes in the state by stipulating that "these recipes, not being credited to any particular host, cook, or authority (but in fact based upon the use of chili *powder*, which is a commercial product) are not in accord with editorial suggestions as to the handling of such material."[111] The most successful brand in the interwar period was Gerbhardt, whose slogan, "That Real Mexican Tang," was known nationwide. Fieldworker Carrie Hodges used (and plagiarized) their 1908 advertisement cookbook in her essay on New Mexico cuisine, although she cut out direct mention of the brand to write an ode to Mexican women's embodied knowledge. The resulting essay was a palimpsest circling from advertisement copy to ethnographic notation with ease. She concluded her essay with recipes calling for chili powder and "drops of Tabasco sauce" such as "Scrambled Eggs Con Chile," "Chile Meat Loaf" and "Meatballs—Mexican style," all of which she declared having "collected" and "personally tested."[112] Readily available cornmeal and chili powder would provide a sensory template for the nation to taste "genuine" Mexican food.[113]

The national success of southwestern food, especially chili con carne, spurred local concerns about the dilution of regional culinary and sensory identity in the standardized American diet. Chili was the only dish clearly identified in the FWP archive as not only Mexican but above all regional and southwestern, and FWP workers took it upon themselves to protect the "fiery Texas-Mexican border [dish]."[114] By the late 1930s chili was falling victim to its own sensory success and becoming a contested sensory icon. Put simply, the problem was that "most cheap restaurants throughout the country [now served chili con carne], which consist[ed] of a mixture of cheap ground beef and beans, seasoned with chile powder and cooked into a thick soup."[115] This "poor imitation" of the authentic recipe became a staple in the interwar Midwest. There, "chili joints" attracted eaters because of the low price of their food; wholesomeness rather than exoticism was the main sensory appeal. A lengthy description of chili in Kansas noted that despite its Spanish name, "it [was] difficult to state with authority that its popularity is due entirely to the influence of Mexicans residents" and went on the mention that the "few" Mexican restaurants who put the dish on their menu used "much more pepper than the American cooks." The latter could be sophisticated amateurs who "pride[d] themselves on their skills in preparing a steaming kettle of *chili con carne* with *frijoles*" and proved their cosmopolitanism by serving it "with dill pickles on the side or perhaps a lettuce and tomato salad with French dressing, coffee, and no dessert." But chili cooks were more often operating at "chili parlors" where they offered a watered-down version of the dish accompanied by vinegar ("to cut the grease"), soda crackers, and tomato ketchup for a five-cent supplement. And then, the "chili devotee" in Kansas also had the possibility of ordering the "mongrel dish" of chili and spaghetti, known as "spaghetti red." If some prepared chili for its exotic entertainment value, most cooked and ate the dish "because it [was] cheap" and warming during the winter months. The Kansas FWP worker therefore did not fail to mention the popularity of the dish among "Negroes" in Topeka, who allegedly even had a song about chili, the chorus of which went: "If yo' can't git po'k chops, chili will do." The Americanized chili was a comfort food of the Depression across race, class, and geographical lines.[116]

The dish offered in chili parlors across the nation stirred up the scorn of southwestern FWP workers, who made clear that "real chili-con-carne should not be confused with the food now served as such" across the country.[117] If well known by name to most Americans, they ignored its genuine taste. Chili recipes considered acceptable by young New Mexican fieldworker Reyes Martinez, for instance, did not usually include beans nor tomatoes and required experience and skill.[118] We can speculate on the reasons FWP workers safeguarded the authenticity of southwestern Mexican foods. A fair number of the workers, such as Lorin Brown, Reyes Martinez, or Aurora Lucero White, were Spanish speakers themselves, their families having lived in the region for decades, if not longer. Although they often penned romanticized narratives of the Spanish past themselves, they also aimed at truthfully describing the taste of their food in the midst of its industrialization and commodification. Defending regional sensory authenticity in the face of sensory standardization also guaranteed that the integration of chili into national food preferences would not deprive the region of a sensory attraction monetized through tourism. "Real" chili could still only be found in the Southwest. The creation of the "Tex-Mex" culinary category in the postwar period would eventually reduce the threat of sensory dilution while simultaneously allowing the national and international growth of Mexican-inspired fast food and frozen dinners as well as inscribing Mexican taste within an American regional culinary narrative. This latter development shows how taste can be delocalized while still infused with exotic sensory significance and informed by practices of culinary tourism originating from a specific historical and geographical place. This handy tag, however, was not available to FWP workers.[119]

*   *   *

Further interpretation of the essay that opened this chapter is needed in light of our exploration of the taste of Mexican food in the southwestern and New Deal sensory economies. In his description of a group of white tourists' visit to San Antonio's Chili Queens, Brooks blatantly stereotyped the Mexican community as a peaceful and backward American sensory exotic. He also placed himself as a regional insider by providing a recipe that, though more flexible in its list of ingredients, agreed with the general regional understanding of what "genuine" chili should look and taste like (although contemporary foodies might wonder at his equation of chili and mole poblano). The recipe read: "Properly made chili-con-carne is a delectable combination of ox-tongue or tender beef. This is boiled. Thus, the liquor and the meat stock, with onions and chili sauce identifies [the] dish. . . . Variants may be prepared with chicken, called *mole poblano*, or with mutton, beef or pork, with ripe tomatoes and various condiments." He took great care to differentiate this "soul-warming dish" from the "soupy gravy, wholly without any convictions of its own" that one might be served in "New York, New Haven or Hartford."[120] As narrator

of the story, he removed himself from the staged encounter between the female Mexican cook and the male "Yanqui" tourist. He poked fun at the latter
and highlighted the snobbishness of most tourists, who, thinking they knew
everything about chili could be heard saying to the vendors: "Anything but
chili-con-carne, please. I tasted that in Kansas City." This remark was followed
by a typical complaint about the "counterfeit" and "spurious" dish that passed
for chili outside of the region.[121] Brooks managed in this excerpt to simultaneously romanticize the sensory (and sensual) appeal of the Chili Queens as
part of a gendered and racialized tourism sensory economy *and* to side with
the Mexican women by implicitly inscribing himself in a shared regional food
culture. His defense of chili was a reaffirmation of regional sensory expertise
that worked to reclaim its taste and to demonstrate American control over the
region. Mexican food constituted the heritage taste of the Southwest, a taste that
was economically and culturally exploited by the tourism industry but whose
authentic character also needed protection against overt commodification and
delocalization. The debate over chili con carne, then, also contributed to change
the region's sensory perception of itself from a land of racially differentiated
taste to an intermingled regional food culture.

The sensory, culinary, and cultural meanings woven around Mexican food
in the Southwest made the taste of tamales, tortillas, and chili con carne valuable currency in 1930s sensory economies. The codification of Mexican dishes
provided the region with an original sensory heritage in need of preservation
in the midst of American modernity. This directly played into the FWP's
sensory nostalgia for real and authentic food and celebrated Mexican food
as local traditions while concealing the ongoing regional sensory hybrid-
ization. The protective tone of some FWP workers, as well as their defense
of the genuine taste of Mexican food in the face of its commodification by
the food processing industry, was also heavily gender coded and put female
Mexican cooks under the guardianship of white males. New Deal food writing
paradoxically articulated the American identity of the Southwest through a
culinary boosterism founded on the claim to sensory exoticism. Recognizing Mexican food as the taste of the Southwest did not mean opening up the
fold of cultural citizenship to Spanish speakers; rather, eating Mexican food
became a means to feel, and really embody, the region's history of conquest.
This set of sensory and historical entanglements explains how, in the Southwest, the taste of race became the taste of place.

Chapter 5

A "Well-Filled Melting Pot"

In June 1938, Robert Gaurino of the Connecticut FWP interviewed Charles Fusco, a forty-one-year-old Italian American worker whose family emigrated to the United States when he was three months old. Fusco recalled his employment in munitions plants during World War I and his time as a Works Progress Administration (WPA) worker in the mid-1930s. Answering Gaurino's questions, Fusco mentioned his views on U.S. politics and the New Deal, European fascisms, the evolution of gender roles, the Catholic Church and, more broadly, the changes brought by "new inventions like the radio and a lot of other things" to various aspects of his life, including diet and taste. Fusco had internalized a difference between so-called "American" and "Italian" food but reported partaking in both, signaling the incorporation of the latter into the former. He did not elaborate on what exactly was "American" food and left its meaning unstated—he probably had in mind classic dishes such as apple pie, roast, and mashed potatoes, as well as more recently introduced food and drinks such as Jell-O, hot dogs, and soft drinks. He explained to Gaurino: "Well, the kind of food I like is plain enough although some of our dishes are very rich. I like American food but not to eat everyday." Fusco reported enjoying spaghetti "now and then," though he noticed that some families had it up to four times a week, a frequency he judged excessive and potentially unhealthy. The dish had been a luxury food of the Italian elite in the old country, rarely eaten by the masses of southern Italian peasants who left for North America. By contrast, its affordability in their new home quickly made it a favorite dish of Italian Americans and an object of sensory conspicuous consumption.[1]

Fusco's interview illustrates the process through which ethnic taste, rooted in histories of migration and immigrant ghettos, evolved in sensory interaction with U.S. food culture. Fusco and the millions of ethnic Americans the FWP's taxonomy labeled "foreign white stock" arrived at America's gates between the late 1880s and the mid-1920s. Most important among these new populations were Southern and Eastern Europeans, known as "new immigrants." Only through the Great Depression did these populations secure the category "white" and the new terminology of "ethnic" for themselves, however. The whitening and "ethnicization" processes intensified for Southern and Eastern Europeans in the period after the 1921 and 1924 quota laws that drastically restricted immigration from Europe. Paradoxically, the halt to new entries, a result of xenophobic impulses, facilitated the acceptance of the new immigrants within American society. The coming of age of second- and third-generation ethnics, their participation to the New Deal era labor struggles, and interwar consumer culture, as well as their inclusion in the liberal welfare state and its safety net, accelerated the whitening of Southern and Eastern Europeans. The dearth of new arrivals encouraged sensory syncretism and the emergence of ethnic cultures invented in interaction with U.S. political culture, social life, and cultural evolutions, such as the growth of mass culture and the industrialization of the food system.[2] Immigrants did not Americanize and let go of their food and culture, but rather they ethnicized and created new syncretic sensory identities that used specific food as symbol of ethnic identity while acquiring more specifically American tastes—for instance, a penchant for sweets and rich desserts.[3] This process of sensory syncretization was also a generational shift. Fusco was concerned that the trend would endanger the physical strength of the U.S.–born generation. He blamed what he viewed as the bodily weakness of the Italian American youth on new eating habits such as the substitution of "soft sweet desert and coffee" in place of "good old wine."[4]

Fusco's culinary observations provide insights into the role of ethnic food in the circuits of economic and cultural exchanges that shaped interwar sensory economies. While immigrants and their offspring adopted novel ingredients to prepare foods reminiscent of their homeland for bodily and psychological comfort, the taste of their syncretic dishes became mainstream. Fusco spoke of the influence of ethnic food on "American" taste and noted that "more American people [were] eating Italian food" than anybody else was by 1938. A fact that astonished him: "Everybody used to make fun of our food . . . today these same people invite themselves in—especially when it comes to spaghetti."[5] The taste of immigrants' food proved a potent currency during the Great Depression, prompting the syncretization of not only immigrants' taste but American food culture in general. This moment of heightened sensory circulation caused, according to Donna Gabaccia in her expansive exploration of the place of ethnic food in American culture, "cultural confusion."[6] New Deal food writing fell into some of the pitfalls of this moment of sensory and ideological turmoil while preparing the way for the anchoring of ethnic taste at the center of American sensory economies.

Throughout the 1930s, the notion of ethnicity progressively dissociated from that of race, reflecting the growing black and white dualism of American race relations and leaving groups like Asians, Mexicans, and Filipinos in a gray zone as members of "foreign races." The FWP's consideration of these communities is a case in point. Asian Americans were documented as part of the Social-Ethnic Studies Project that also covered Southern and Eastern Europeans. The FWP bureaucratic classification used the term ethnic to designate any group apart from African Americans; however, the treatment of "foreign-born whites" and Asians regularly diverged. New immigrants were increasingly considered as whites and therefore Americans, while Asians remained "impossible subjects."[7] A 1941 letter from an Idaho FWP worker discussed Chinese food as part of the state's "ethnic elements" but quickly added, in brackets, "non-American."[8] The strong chauvinistic sentiments that had led to the Chinese exclusion act of 1882 and the restriction put on Japanese immigration in 1907 extended well into the 1930s, despite the continued growth of these communities in the early twentieth century. By the 1930s the dish of chop suey, created by Chinese cooks in the United States, was a customary city taste. Sukiyaki had lost some of its foreign edge, though the fact that it would be unfailingly prepared at the table was still enjoyable. It could be had in Chicago, New York, and California, where "those already initiated who crave variety and something out of the ordinary" could instead order "tastily prepared dishes . . . such as raw fish—usually sliced bass, tuna, rock-cod, devil-fish, squid."[9] This chapter follows the FWP filing system and integrates Asian Americans in its discussion of ethnic taste, if only as not to underestimate the black and white divide reflected throughout New Deal food writing. Doing so allows developing a comparative analysis of European groups and Asian communities that illuminates how the senses shaped notions of identity and difference in the New Deal era.

This chapter combines two types of analyses to explore how syncretic ethnic tastes came to occupy a central place in 1930s sensory economies, and, despite the reticence of some, in New Deal food writing. Continuing the work of previous chapters, I open with an analysis of the evolving place of ethnic taste in the New Deal's search for American food and look at how the motley crew of FWP workers across the country conceived of ethnic

Americans' taste as well as the tropes they used to document it. Although, as explored in chapter 1, the federal editors of the *America Eats* project had in theory excluded nineteenth- and early-twentieth-century immigrants' food from their study of regional food "of the nostalgic variety," documentation on ethnic food in *America Eats* and the FWP material in general is abundant. Many FWP workers described ethnic food using well-known keywords such as "the melting pot" or "cosmopolitanism," keywords that had acquired various, and often contradictory, meanings by the mid-1930s. While admonition to Americanize at times surfaced, FWP workers collectively provided a cultural pluralist version of the melting pot that recognized the role of sensory exchange in shaping U.S. food cultures. New Deal food writing updated the paradigmatic metaphors by portraying a sensory cosmopolitanism grounded in culinary encounters and working-class solidarities. Throughout the country, they reported on local, multiethnic sensory economies that pioneered the everyday diversity that characterizes American eating today.

Beyond the FWP's sensory and cultural politics, New Deal food writing provides key elements toward a social history of ethnic taste in the 1930s. To produce a textured account of ethnic taste in the New Deal era, I develop, especially in the second half of the chapter, an ethnographic reading of the FWP culinary essays. These sources allow investigating the significance of the senses, especially the sense of taste, in the making of ethnic identities in the 1930s. Ethnic sensory economies were syncretic, the result of intergenerational compromise and intra-ethnic sensory unification, and heavily influenced by the industrial food system. This was not a unilateral process, and the ripple effects of the evolution of ethnic taste were felt throughout American food culture. The narrative then focuses on sites of culinary and economic exchange, such as restaurants, supermarkets, and workplaces, that emerged as catalysis for the sensory syncretization of American taste.

Documenting Ethnic Taste, Reconfiguring the Melting Pot

FWP staff, both federal editors and local workers, used several intellectual frameworks to describe ethnic life in the 1930s but never settled on which one was the most appropriate. Early projects like "Pockets in America," which sought to present "samples of odd, strange, or unusual national groups, religious sects, festivals and fiestas, fisherfolk and hillbillies, idealistic communities, and survivals of early cultures," presented racial, ethnic, and cultural groups as unchanging and insular communities contributing selected "gifts," such as handicraft and food, as tribute to their new nation.[10] This rhetoric led FWP workers at times to describe urban ethnic neighborhoods and rural settlements as foreign gustatory and sensory "colonies."[11] By 1938, however, the FWP was promoting a more participatory narrative in projects such as "Cosmopolite America" and "Hands that Built America." The editor of a Social-Ethnic Studies project on Greeks in America, for instance, warned state offices not to "overstress the separateness and peculiarities of the group." Rather, local workers were encouraged to consider the "community as . . . a living entity in which all elements, including immigrant elements, are in a state of flux and fusion" and to understand that "even in semi-segregated colonies of the large cities it is not true that immigrants have little contact with the larger community life—such immigrants are really in constant contact at work, on the streets, in shops, movies, etc. They are inevitably being molded by the community, while, at the same time, producing cultural changes in the community itself."[12] This pluralist, inclusive, and dynamic viewpoint reverberated on the culinary work of the FWP, which took off in the final years of the program. Projects like America Eats would be inclined to consider sensory perceptions, such as taste, as categories evolving through exchange and interaction rather than contribution and appropriation.[13]

Detangling the diverse tropes used by FWP workers and mapping out the varying intellectual frameworks from which they borrowed, sometimes in the same essay, is a complex yet necessary task toward understanding New Deal food writing to its full potential. The constrictive temporal and demographic guidelines of the America Eats project fostered ideological and sensory discordances. As earlier chapters detail, America Eats did not attempt to be a comprehensive survey of the food cooked and eaten in the United States in the late 1930s but rather a celebration of "traditional cookery [kept] alive" and of indisputably "American" food, such as clambakes, baked-bean suppers, apple pies, and a large variety of flapjacks and other griddle cakes.[14] This nostalgic overtone disqualified "National Group Eating" (what we would today describe as ethnic) from being part of the FWP culinary project. The chronological and spatial framing of America Eats created sensory exclusions that left many ethnic foods on the threshold of American regional traditions and skewed the FWP's culinary search. For instance, a fieldworker in charge of assessing the influence of "nationality groups" on Indiana's food specified that "where Italians have settled in the mining district of the southwest . . . excellent Italian spaghetti and red wine are to be found," and that "in the industrial Calumet area centering in Gary, with its vast population of foreign born from every part of the world, are an abundance of foreign dishes, of course." Yet the paragraph concludes with a rather arbitrary judgment, possibly aimed at reassuring the reader as well as at demonstrating compliance with the federal editors' guidelines: "But these have exerted little influence on the balance of the State, and almost none at all upon its eating habits."[15] The anonymous FWP worker who crafted this description simultaneously included immigrants' cuisine in his enumeration of Indiana's food while considering them as foreign to the state's food culture. The acknowledgment of ethnic taste neared its sensory confinement.

To avoid in-depth discussions of the place of immigrants in U.S. regional food cultures, FWP workers often resorted to using the metaphor of the melting pot. This metaphor was extremely seductive, given the topic that FWP workers had to research—food—combined with the need for quick turnaround of essays and the lack of literary experience of most writers. Yet FWP workers inherited an unstable concept, explaining why their recurrent use of it lacked consistency. Playwright Israel Zangwill originally coined the term melting pot in 1908 in order to describe what he identified as "an all around give and take" between American and immigrant cultures.[16] Progressive Era thinkers further shaped the melting-pot ideal in the wake of the massive arrival of Southern and Eastern European migrants at the turn of the century. The term became an important means for thinking about the effects of mass migration on American society while shunning the two extremes of xenophobia and cultural pluralism. Literary scholar Sarah Wilson describes how, contrary to the latter concept, which considered the nation as a "collection of culturally different communities united by political bonds," the melting-pot trope offered a "version of assimilation imagined as cultural fusion."[17] However, two versions of the melting-pot concept evolved from this original meaning. The "repressive" melting pot, admonishing immigrants to assimilate and Americanize, had general prevalence in the 1920s public and political understanding of the trope.[18] However, a more "flexible" version, defining the melting pot as "a process through whose action both individuals and cultures would be made flexible, multiple, and continually changing," survived decades of ubiquitous nativism. The melting-pot metaphor arose in a time of "cacophony" about the consequence of immigration on American cultural, social, and political life, and never lost its ambiguity.[19] Both the repressive and the flexible melting-pot metaphors appeared in New Deal food writing. Frequently switching from one intellectual framework to the other, FWP workers fostered sensory confusion.

Under the influence of the rhetoric developed by the repressive melting pot, FWP workers often recounted the progressive culinary Americanization of immigrant communities, though not without a tinge of nostalgia for lost sensory experiences. While they situated the "pronounced" and "odd" tastes of immigrants' cuisines at the margins of American food culture, the fact that "some races continue[d] to cook in foreign style" was not as strong a blame or threatening a danger as it had been during the nativist decades of the 1910s and 1920s.[20] Rather, fieldworkers considered ethnic foodways as quaint habits ultimately doomed to disappear as communities slowly Americanized. Serbian picnics in the Midwest might still feature Balkan-style barbecued lamb, but the roasted meat was "waging a losing fight" with the "American hot dog." The Darwinian "fight for survival" was "not over" in the interwar period, but taste evolution dictated the increased "attachment to cold sodas and hot dogs eaten together" of the American-born generation.[21] Despite the attachment to traditional holiday dishes, European ethnic communities were, as a general rule and to the nostalgic dismay of some, on the way to complete culinary and sensory Americanization. Though "romanticists" may be tempted still to see, smell, hear, and taste foreign enclaves, the modern American tourist could now travel across the country and "pass through [places that were once colonies of foreign-born whites] without seeing any distinguishing marks to set it apart from any hundred villages similar in size and location."[22] FWP workers nostalgically deplored the perceived abrasion of ethnic enclaves' sensory difference yet also held it as a sign of modernity and as an attestation of the country's ability to assimilate immigrants.

The paradoxical coupling of nostalgia for a lost exoticism with the celebration of immigrants' Americanization was less present in essays about Asian Americans since, to most FWP workers, the exotic character of America's Chinatowns and Little Osakas was never lost. In San Francisco, home to the largest Asian population during the Depression, the American Guide Series volume explained that Chinatown, despite being "Americanized to a degree," still embodies the color, the romance, the fascination of the Orient," meaning that "distinctive sounds and odors give Chinatown its atmosphere of the unchanging East."[23] Sensory arguments were primordial in this depiction of Asian Americans as denizens of immutable enclaves. But while only a decade earlier Chinese food would have been commonly considered as filthy or dangerous, FWP workers often compared it to artistic creations.[24] A Chicago FWP worker, for instance, provided a full sensory account of Chinese cuisine, detailing how the food felt on the tongue and how it crackled to the ear. The author explained that "the Chinese eat food for its texture, the elastic or crisp effect it has on the teeth is very important, as well as the fragrance, flavor and color. The idea of texture may be hard to understand, but to the Chinese the great popularity of Bamboo shots is due to the fine resistance that bamboo shoots give to their teeth."[25] Descriptions and photographs of mysterious Chinese ingredients and picturesque vegetable stands included, for instance, in the American Guide Series guidebooks on California cities, reinforced the culinary and sensory otherness of Asian Americans. Despite regularly praising the art of Chinese cooking, FWP workers effectively excluded this cuisine from American food culture.

The casting of Chinese, and Asian Americans in general, as sensory others interchangeably conjured the repressive and the flexible melting-pot ideal. An anonymous New York FWP worker used the repressive paradigm to authoritatively state the impossibility of Asian integration within the American population: "The Chinese in New York City, as in every other metropolis of the Western hemisphere, constitute an indestructible and distinct colony, one which is impervious to melting pot ideas."[26] His colleague, Strong, adopted a more affirmative version of the melting pot in which the Chinese contributed to the city's sensory mosaic, providing a "picture of a colorful and different bit of New York which has more than done its part in contributing to the city's well-filled 'melting pot.'"[27] But even in this more pluralistic appreciation, Chinese cuisine remained apart and "different" despite its avowed centrality in the city's sensory economy.

Not surprisingly, New Deal food writing more frequently and unambiguously recovered the original, flexible meaning of the melting-pot trope when focusing on European immigrants instead of Asian Americans. More innovative and unexpected was their geographic focus. Descriptions of 1930s food culture as the result of a blending of tastes rather than a melting into an American mold came often, as would be expected, from the Eastern Seaboard and large immigrant-receiving cities. A New York State worker, for instance, deemed that, by the 1930s, "the pot pourri of peoples" had a "chance to simmer down to an even consistency."[28] However, reports of sensory and culinary fusion were most salient and eloquent in essays covering the rural Midwest and Far West. The *America Eats* Midwest essay opened on an evocation of the melting-pot metaphor without concluding on the tastiness of the results: "If each, of all the races of men which have subsisted in the vast Middlewest, could contribute one dish to one great Middlewestern cauldron, it is certain that we'd have therein a most foreign, and most gigantic, stew."[29] A left-wing "radical regionalism" flourished in the western states during the Depression, encouraging descriptions of local syncretic food cultures determined by multiethnic sensory crossovers.[30] One such example was a recipe for barbecue sauce prepared by "Whithey," a second-generation Yugoslavian immigrant from Wallace, Idaho, described by FWP worker Edward B. Reynolds in the Far West regional essay. The young man's will to conform to a loosely defined American ideal and his eagerness "to prove that he belongs" went hand in hand with his syncretic taste. His secret barbecue seasoning exemplified this sensory "mixture." His garlicky sauce was "definitely Old country," but his methods were "Western," meaning "picked up from Western story magazines, books and conversations with cowboys." In this version of the nation's culinary history, American food was the result of a series of sensory interactions adopting unforeseen shapes; it was born during a multiethnic "hilarious party . . . drinking and wisecracking in the American summer," that took on "segments of this culture, portions of that, all put together in a new and original way."[31] In depicting this local syncretic taste, Reynolds recovered the original purpose of the melting pot as an ideal of cultural fusion, albeit one that here unconventionally equated ethnic influences, mass culture, and local traditions.

FWP workers' description of syncretic and multiethnic sensory economies participated in what Michael Denning considers the period's working-class "pan-ethnic Americanism," a "paradoxical synthesis of competing nationalisms . . .—pride in ethnic heritage and identity combined with an assertive Americanism."[32] To describe the foods of the American industrial democracy inhabited by the masses of new immigrants, New Deal food writing accordingly drifted away from the ambiguous melting-pot trope as well as the notion of culinary cosmopolitanism typically used to describe the middle-class and elite urban restaurant scene. Instead, some FWP workers proceeded to describe American food as the result of widespread working-class, localized cosmopolitanisms. From Butte, Montana, Reynolds described miners' lunch buckets, from the "conventional sandwich and coffee" faced by "native" Americans, to Cornish miners' pasties and "yellow saffroned bread," Italians' and Austrians' "homemade, red and white mottled salami sandwiches with their throat-burning seasonings," and Mexicans' "hot-tempered frijoles and tortillas." He highlighted cross-ethnic eating at several points in the piece, which culminated in the judgment: "It is undoubtedly through these lunch hours, and the interchange of food articles among the workers, that has made larger mining camps some of the most cosmopolitan of cities in their food tastes." Not only a masculine sensory exchange, multiethnic tastes followed the miners home, since the "average housewife" regularly "include[d] any of a dozen foreign foods in her weekly menu."[33] This assessment of women's place still relegated them mainly to a domestic role, yet it also shows the impact of the Great Depression years on the conceptualization of crossover tastes as a central element in a united working-class culture.[34] If New Deal food writing upheld the conservative partition of the feminine private sphere and male public life, it also portrayed workers and their families as part of interactive, cosmopolitan sensory economies.

Working-class sensory cosmopolitanism, like pan-ethnic Americanism, was unstable. Documenting the sensory exchanges that triggered the making of local multiethnic sensory economies presented FWP workers with challenges often left unresolved. A comparative reading of two draft versions of the "Cuisine" section of the Minnesota American Guide Series volume by St. Paul worker Marjorie Ottaway unveils the roadblocks she encountered in the field and the volatility of her appraisal of the role of ethnic taste in shaping local preferences. The first version of Ottaway's essay powerfully depicted how local interethnic sensory exchange functioned. She asserted that "inhabitants of St. Paul and vicinity comprise a great many nationalities, hence a conglomeration of foreign dishes, cosmopolitan taste in food prevails for the most part." An important part of Minnesota's ethnic foods were those of Scandinavian origins: "smoked dried fish, lutefisk, canned fish balls and fish puddings, goose liver, gaffelbitar, Swedish blood puddings, lingon berries." These items were so popular that they could "be purchased as ordinary commodities of the everyday day menu." She also referred to French, Russian, Italian, Greek, Syrian, and Jewish cooking, as well as the "delicious dish" of gumbo prepared by "colored people from Louisiana." Overall, she estimated that "Minnesota women not only excel in preparing dishes of their ancestors, but because they have adopted many food customs of other nationalities who have settled in the same district, they have attained a cuisine which is unique and most palatable." Sensory circulation thus drove the creation of a local syncretic sensory economy. Restaurants directly catered to local tastes. Although most eating places "usually have a standardized café menu," the "wise ones" had started to understand the value of ethnic foods and occasionally served them. These were not advertised, though, and Ottaway's culinary search proved strenuous, since "to find the expert cooks and the rare local dishes served up by them, one must have patience and a dash of effrontery, and in interviews, one must ask questions interminably."[35] The legacy of the Americanization paradigm can be felt in this last remark, as cooks and consumers tended to hide their syncretic food tastes. Yet the use of the word "local" instead of "ethnic" also created a strong connection between taste and place, elevating ethnic dishes as regional sensory cushions against the standardization and industrialization of American food.[36] This also highlights that one of the most efficient ways immigrants could become American and claim the privileges of citizenship in the New Deal era was by acquiring local identities.

Ottaway maintained many of her astute remarks on cosmopolitan taste in the second version of her essay but framed it somewhat differently. She opened with the remark, "St. Paul and Minnesota contains many races of the old world, each with their favorite food dishes from the homeland, American food prevails, however."³⁷ Two key changes occurred in the rewriting of the piece. "Nationality" became "race," a symptom of the evolution of the taxonomy of difference in interwar America. Second, the non-described category of "American food" superseded mentions of both "cosmopolitan" tastes and "foreign" dishes, crushing the possibility of sensory exchange and downplaying the endurance of ethnic preferences. One can only speculate about why Ottaway edited her essay to conform to the Americanizing injunction developed in the repressive melting-pot rhetoric. But her revisions enjoin us to remain cautious about the numerous FWP materials that portrayed a cohesive food culture united along "American" standards. Sensory habits and clichés framed FWP workers' engagement with local foodways, and idiomatic phrasing surfaced in most essays, rendering the combined analysis of New Deal food writing as a source *and* an object of inquiry key to unlocking its potential.

Taking stock of the inconsistencies and contradictions of New Deal food writing is necessary to appreciate the role of ethnic food in late 1930s sensory economies. The repressive melting-pot rhetoric was an easy fallback for most FWP workers pressed to produce their copy for the various FWP projects. In the case of *America Eats*, constraining editorial guidelines tended to foster clichés. Yet FWP workers also modified the formula, and their essays highlighted the inadequacy of the old culinary paradigms to the evolving shape of 1930s sensory economies. They slanted the conventional Americanizing, repressive version of the melting pot by describing it not as a homogenizing device but as a collaborative process. Doing so, they recuperated an earlier trend that had conceived the melting pot as a blending of cultures. Especially in the trans-Appalachian region, fieldworkers proudly displayed the numerous influences that shaped local foods and described "vigorous" eating habits "based in the tradition of a recent frontier past, softened by eastern U.S. and Old World refinements, tempered by modern dietetics, and blended by the many cosmopolitan influences of the immigrants."³⁸ Followed zealously, the editorial demand to "not give much attention to Nationality Group Eating" in the largest of the FWP culinary effort, *America Eats*, would have significantly reduced, if not annihilated, the relevance of the final book to contemporary American food culture. Thankfully, the content of the archive significantly exceeds these constrained goals and documents ethnic foods as central currencies of the New Deal sensory economy. If the records of New Deal food writing are at times puzzling, or even contradictory, key features of the evolution of ethnic taste can be fleshed out of the culinary and ideological confusion of the fieldworkers and editors.

"Drinking Soda Pop the American Way": 1930s Ethnic Sensory Economies

Despite the ideological hesitancies of New Deal food writing, the FWP culinary archive can be successfully used to look at the evolving tastes of ethnic communities during the Great Depression, as migrants and their children underwent the hand-in-hand process of Americanization and ethnicization. First-, second-, and third-generation migrants forged syncretic diets and tastes that reflected the cuisines of their homelands as well as American ingredients (often industrially produced), habits, and preferences. "Drinking soda pop the American way" became central to ethnic Americans' newly forged identities. The Life Histories interviews conducted by the FWP's Social-Ethnic Studies Project among Italian American families in New England provide a macro-level view of the making of ethnic tastes in the 1930s. These interviews document the generational sensory shift witnessed by most ethnic communities and some of the anxieties spurred by the dual processes of culinary ethnicization and Americanization over several generations. A New Jersey Italian mother explained to FWP worker Mari Tomasi in November 1938 that, though her late husband would "laugh at pie an' cakes an' sof' sweet food" and preferred "meat an' potato, an' rice, an' the spaghetti—everything to make him strong an' make him muscle," satisfying her son Johnnie was a different task. "He like the strong food an' he like he sof, an' everyday he want both." The two poles of "strong" and "soft" were two recurrent qualifiers in migrant interviews for, respectively, Italian and American food, translating in gendered terms the malaise immigrant parents sometimes encountered when facing their children's taste for "fancy food." The European-born parents' unease was centered on the potentially harmful and feminizing consequences of sodas and confectionaries on their children. They predicted that "the sweets would soften their bodies."[39]

Ethnic cuisines often resulted from intergenerational sensory compromise within the community. The American-born generation coming of age in the 1930s acquired a sweet tooth that amazed and disconcerted their immigrant parents. These tastes were, however, central to new ethnic identities. For instance, young Italian Americans adopted a nutritional and sensory strategy of integration and established a powerful connection between American foods, American identities, and American bodies.[40] While working-class fathers valued their wives' cooking because it "makes the muscle for these hours of hard-work," their sons defied their parents' prediction and geared their bodies toward playing American sports by enjoying "pudding, cake and pie." In his interview, one father, Giacomo Coletti, expressed his "amazement" at his sons' vitality but "continue[d] to nurse a silent suspicion that if he lives to see grandchildren—or better still great-grandchildren, their bodies will prove this theory of his." Mothers, on the other hand, attempted to satisfy everyone, baking dessert following "the lessons from [their] American neighbors."[41] Indeed, in New England in particular, social workers and reformers targeted housewives as the main agents of dietary change in migrant households since the late nineteenth century. Through these reform attempts, migrant women became self-conscious of their sensory difference but also acquired knowledge of American cooking and ingredients that pleased their children's tastes.[42]

Asian Americans went through a similar process of generational change that located identity in sensing bodies. In the 1920s and 1930s, Chinese American youth strove to promote a renewed vision of their community based, in the words of historian Nayan Shah, on "the management of space and the care of the body [as] an index of American cultural citizenship and civic belonging."[43] FWP sources describing life in San Francisco's, New York's, and Chicago's Chinatowns insisted on the generational gap within the Chinese community, describing the "younger generation" as "carefully neat in their appearance, so invariably well-groomed, so anxious, apparently, not to be mistaken for anything less than Chinese-Americans, with the accent on 'American.'"[44] According to the San Francisco guidebook, this careful differentiation from their parents was cultural and sensory; it led American-born Chinese to adopt "the dress, the slang, and the commercial methods of [their] American compatriots." They created a new Chinatown along Grant Avenue, where educated ethnic youth of "both sexes" met at Fong-Fong's, a "widely patronized 'Joe-College' hangout" that offered "a soda fountain, lunchroom, and bakery."[45] Chinese American youth still partook of and enjoyed Chinese food, but they understood sensory conformity to mainstream American standards in speech, appearance, and taste as an important cultural tool for their political and cultural claims to American belonging.

The rise of Italian American cuisine provides a paradigmatic example of how taste was recruited to support the "invention of ethnicity."[46] In the case of Italian Americans, the process of sensory ethnicization required not only forging a new cultural identity and food culture but also inventing the geographic and national notions of "Italy" and "Italianness."[47] If FWP workers considered New York's little Italy the "hottest melting pot" in the country, it was not because migrants were learning American ways but because Italy itself had been a "melting pot for 3,000 years."[48] As the New York

City unit explained, once in the United States, the difference between the northern "artist, adventurer and exile type of immigrant" and the "swarthy," "picturesquely dressed peasant from the warm Italian southland" receded, especially given the demographic preponderance of the latter on the former in the early-twentieth-century migration wave.[49] FWP workers still occasionally highlighted the allegedly "insurmountable gastronomic prejudice" between Northern and Southern Italians, describing the then-novel dish of "pizzaiola" as "one of the pet aversions of the Northern Italians." Only in the postwar period did pizza emerge as a shared culinary symbol.[50] Overall, Italian American foodways in the 1930s were, in the words of food historian Hasia Diner, "a fusion of some southern Italian staples with a hodgepodge of foodstuffs and dishes from other regions, mixed with American styles of consumption, particularly of eating meat, creat[ing] a cuisine that combined new and old."[51]

The spaghetti supper held annually by the Italian community in Tontitown, Arkansas, is an example of the syncretic character of ethnic sensory economies in the 1930s: it featured fried chicken, industrial bread, and spaghetti (figures 1.1 and 1.2). As detailed in chapter 1, the federal guidelines of the *America Eats* project contributed to bar this annual festival from publication on the grounds that this event was not "traditional" and "regional" enough, despite its forty-year history. This community was not exceptional. Writing about Italians in the Ozark Mountain in 1937, fieldworker Laura Earley remarked that "[Italians] are Americans and proud of it," although "when it c[ame] to their feast days, they revert[ed] to the customs of the motherland." This was only partially true. On holidays, members of the "old families" met at the schoolhouse after Mass; they filled the school basement with "laughter and babel" and enjoyed sodas "while their children consume[d] ice-cream cones." Then, at mid-day, the hall became engulfed with the "enticing odor" of the plates "piled high with steaming Italian spaghetti," participating in the sensory buttressing of ethnic identity.[52] Indeed, spaghetti dishes had become the main taste markers of "Italianness" in the United States but cohabited in the community's sensory economy with industrial foods, drinks, and regional specialties.

Evolving taste but also economic concerns drove ethnic Americans food choices during the Depression. This period played an evident role in the sensory resistance and spread of ethnic cuisines as they offered tasty yet cheap meals. Yet for the vast majority, the economic downturn also accelerated sensory evolution as working-class ethnics learned how to use the discounted products of the food industry. By the end of the 1930s, ethnic grocers in ghettoized neighborhoods could not compete with the new food retail model implemented by supermarket and chain stores. Ethnic shoppers stayed somewhat faithful to local ethnic grocers through the 1920s despite the advent of the chain stores, in part because ethnic entrepreneurs started carrying brand-name products but also because grocery shops served as community gathering centers throughout the period of mass migration and, through credit, became an important financial buffer during hard times. Yet ethnic grocers did not fare well during the Depression, as self-serve supermarkets, launched for the first time during the 1930s and offering discounted products and steady quality, started to attract ethnic consumers. Canned and standardized products remained at a consistently low price throughout the Depression, benefiting from the development of new retail techniques based on bulk purchasing and self-service. Throughout the decade, the food industry gradually integrated ethnic Americans into its consumer base, thanks to evolving taste but also to changes in food retailing.[53]

To weather changes in the industry, ethnic grocers adopted the chain-store and supermarket models and their products. Elita Lenz in New York explained in an article counter-intuitively titled "cosmopolitan markets" that "more and more chain-stores, with their made-in-America stocks, are appearing in the once foreign neighborhood, to satisfy the newly acquired taste for things American."[54] Her colleague in Chicago, Marie Fisher, noted after a visit to a "Russian store" that, "while the proprietor and clerks were evidently of that nationality, [she] saw little to distinguish this from the average corner grocery and meat market." Fisher concluded her essay on the "interesting communities [of] little Europe" by noting that stores' "stock of merchandise must appeal to people of all classes," and that ethnic items were offered only as an add-on, "as in the case of the chain store at Walton and Western, managed by Sam Giglio, where *spumoni* and Italian sausages and other delicacies dear to the hearts of Italians" were available amid the regular offerings of breakfast cereals and canned pineapple.[55] The Depression increased ethnic consumers' consumption of mass-produced industrial foods, and ethnic products progressively became an adornment rather than a central sensory feature in grocery stores and supermarkets. But industrialized versions of ethnic foods also found their way onto the supermarket shelves, where, "near the cans of Boston baked beans and codfish cakes . . . [stood] cans of spaghetti and chop suey." Ethnic entrepreneurs played an important role in the industrialization of the U.S. food culture, sometimes marketing foods of widely different origins than their own. Chicago FWP worker Elizabeth Drury, for instance, disparagingly advised visitors to Chinese restaurants to ask the waiter for "Italian chop suey or whatever brand he has for the day."[56] Her remarks were part of the Chicago unit's extensive coverage of the city's restaurants, ranging from the "Jerusalem Oriental Café" (1907 South Wabash Avenue) that served "only veal with an Arabian Argeelah pipe" to a "Jewish-American style restaurant" (78 West Randolph Street) where "no emphasis [was] placed on kosher meat at all," to "Shalimar Tea Garden" (64 East Walton Place), a "cozy, homelike restaurant specializing in the dishes of India."[57]

Beyond Cosmopolitanism?
Ethnic Restaurants in the 1930s

Restaurants are choice sites to close our exploration of the workings and evolution of 1930s sensory economies. Restaurants are sites of economic flow and sensory circulation. A successful dining experience results from a transactional process anchored in the sensorium as restaurateurs and clients yoke their senses, both culinary and aesthetic (decoration, presentation, service).[58] They are places of encounters, cross-cultural exchange, and satisfaction of the senses; yet restaurants are also sites for the expression of authority through claimed connoisseurship and straightforward economic power so that the aesthetic and sensory demands of patrons can dictate, or at least influence, what is on the menu.[59] Throughout New Deal food writing, restaurants emerged as key sites in the shaping of American food culture out of the sensory and economic circulation of food and taste between ethnic restaurateurs and their patrons of various classes and ethnicity.[60]

New Deal food writing offers a rich corpus for an ethnography of ethnic restaurants in a period when eating out had become for many, especially in urban environments, a solidly anchored habit rather than an occasional luxury. FWP workers documented a wide range of restaurants: modern lunchrooms, cafeterias, automats, tea rooms, hotel dining rooms, haute cuisine establishments in New York, San Francisco, or New Orleans, street stands, early drive-in and fast-food chains, southern (and increasingly northern) barbecue joints. Finally, one could visit "foreign restaurants," which, especially numerous in cities, proposed French haute cuisine but most often immigrants' food, what we would call ethnic cuisine. The shifting use of the term "foreign" to qualify these establishments testifies to the fast evolution of their role in American life and the blurring of categories in the period. The 1939 New York City guide used the qualifier "foreign" to characterize places ranging from *Bengal Tiger* to *Janet of France*, *Zucca's*, famed Chinatown *Port Arthur*, and *Keen's English Chop House*, while places offering the likes of "Italian-French-American" food, such as a restaurant named *Firenze*, were listed under the "American" category.[61] Such unstable categorization captures the diversification of U.S. urban dining scenes in the interwar period and the ascent of cosmopolitan fare *as* American cuisine.[62]

Ethnic restaurants were heavily diversified and defied generalizations. The FWP documented different types, corresponding to different price ranges and audiences. Foreign-themed nightclubs capitalized on the continued yet somewhat tamed exotic appeal of Italian, Russian, or Chinese food and culture, and they offered dinner and floorshows in colorful décors to middle- to upper-class urban dwellers.[63] In Chicago, "Oriental Gardens" offered "Chinese and American food. Dance orchestra with floor show."[64] Ethnic restaurants of more modest ambition attracted middle-class eaters in search of convenient and economical alternatives to increasingly standardized American food and conceited French restaurants.[65] For ethnic working-class patrons, unassuming neighborhood restaurants provided sensory familiarity and comfort in the midst of the economic depression. An increasing numbers of these establishments served "standard" American fare—"soups, roasts, vegetables"—alongside ethnic food at various price points.[66] The FWP documented the evolution of ethnic restaurants through various projects, most notably American Guide Series volumes focusing on specific cities, which often included restaurant lists, and the New York–based unfinished *Feeding the City* project. A study of "all phases of production, transportation, and marketing of all food commodities forming the yearly supply for the Metropolitan area of New York," *Feeding the City* aimed at painting a comprehensive view of the city's foodways. The author of the volume's draft, Fredrick Clayton, director of the New York City unit, showed an awareness of the daunting character of the task and remarked that "the food tastes and needs of these twelve million people cannot be standardized" before somewhat regretfully noting that "racial and religious influence complicate the supply problem."[67]

Most of the documentation on ethnic restaurants came from the urban areas, where even the *America Eats* editors had to admit that the "influences spreading form the larger immigrant groups" could not be "overlooked."[68] In cities, FWP workers often moved away from the melting-pot metaphor to favor instead the cosmopolitan paradigm, which was not without its own ambiguity. By the 1930s cosmopolitanism was infused with a range of meanings. A popular alternative to the Americanizing (or repressive) melting pot, cosmopolitanism emerged at the turn of the century as a model for the articulation of "an ideal of American national identity capable of balancing the principles of individuality and cultural inclusiveness with a sense of civic

solidarity." Forged by Progressive Era thinkers, it evolved along, and sometimes rejoined, ideals of cultural pluralism and the flexible version of the
melting pot, as in the case of the working-class cosmopolitanism abounding
in western New Deal food writing.[69] Yet, cosmopolitanism in its vernacular
usage also came to characterize a middle-class, "appropriative," often elitist
and urban standpoint. Historian Kristin Hoganson explored how the "ad-
vanced pluralistic conceptions of citizenship" that animated the cosmopolitan ideal also participated in the reification of ethnic life "by appealing to
consumerist valuation of novelty and difference." Enjoying a cosmopolitan
lifestyle, or, rather, being part of an imagined community of cosmopolitan
consumers, constituted a powerful tool for class distinction and the affirmation of national superiority.[70]

Cosmopolitanism in its early-twentieth-century vernacular usage reflected
an appropriative mentality that, far from a multiethnic ideal, presupposed
racial, ethnic, class, and taste distinctions. The practice of slumming in urban
ethnic neighborhoods established in the last decade of the nineteenth century
was a central feature of the cosmopolitan worldview as it offered commodified
multisensory experiences of racial others. Foreign languages, exotic food, traditional garments, and supposedly licentious sexual practices attracted white
middle-class men and women who slummed around the Bowery in New
York and the historic red-light Levee district in Chicago, later in Greenwich
Village and Towertown, nowadays Chicago's Near North Side. Negotiating
and crossing spatial and sensory borders was a potent way for middle-class
cosmopolitan slummers to perform race and exercise their economic power
by requiring authentic—in the lingo of the time, "real"—ethnic food.[71] FWP
worker Fitzgerald was part of this trend when he described the "Spanish"
restaurant El Chorrito, located at the end of the Brooklyn Bridge, as a "ren-
dez-vous of picturesque peasant type, frequently patronized by Americans
who would see a bit of Spain in the rough and enjoy genuine Spanish fare at
modest prices."[72] The world was at hand for the white middle-class visitor to
consume and the culinary aesthete to taste.

Notions and practices of cosmopolitanism forged at the turn of the century
stretched into the interwar period and prompted the metaphoric depiction
of urban dining scenes as offering "the world on a plate," each exotic bite
providing a taste of cosmopolitan pleasure. Metropolises such as New York,
San Francisco, and Chicago promoted cosmopolitanism as their main tourist
attraction. Ethnic and racial differences were central to urban tourist sensory
economies as potential purveyor of sensory thrill and objects of consumption. In the case of the Southwest explored in chapter 4, the consumption of
tacos and chili in Mexican quarters was a way for visitors to feel and sense

the domestic exoticism of American cities. In New York, ethnic enclaves became one of the many urban sights of the commodified city, and well into the 1930s FWP workers invited visitors to enjoy "the Gotham phantasmagoria of exotic food."[73] Mary H. Weik, from the New York City unit, exemplified this stance when she claimed that the "gourmet of genuinely cosmopolitan tastes" would not be disappointed by a visit to New York. She encouraged potential visitors to "slum a bit" and aroused their appetite with an exhaustive list of the city's offerings. Every fancy could be satisfied; one could sample, among other repasts, "shrimp-and-pineapple in a tiny Chinese restaurant . . . melting *apfel strudle* or spicy *brauernwursten* in a real German brauhaus . . . chicken paprika in a gay Czechoslovak café; tiny dried herring with a Scandinavian meal; . . . scallopine marsala, huge bowls of minestrone and frosty *zabaglione* in a friendly Italian restaurant, with an accordion and a guitar wagging a spirited battle somewhere in the rear." The "horizon ha[d] no limit" for the would-be cosmopolitan urbanite searching for an evening of titillating entertainment.[74]

New Deal food writing on Chinese American restaurants and the dish of chop suey tested the limits of the "world on a plate" cosmopolitan paradigm. Chinese entrepreneurs had historically been staging performances of sensory exoticism to attract tourists to their establishments.[75] But as chop suey, chow mein, and egg foo yong became ubiquitous, this marketing strategy deflated. Weik's and Fitzgerald's colleague in the New York FWP, Harry Zahn, made of point of debunking the Chinese origins of the dish and wrote about the alleged "trick" perpetrated by Chinese restaurant owners "upon gullible Americans in the matter of chop suey" and instead highlighted its American roots, highlighting that it "originated in San Francisco."[76] Indeed, historians Samantha Barbas and Andrew Coe provide an account of the birth of chop suey as a pragmatic sensory adaptation and culinary invention of single Chinese male migrants' to the West Coast in the nineteenth century, later widely spread by Chinese restaurateurs catering to the tastes of white slummers.[77] From New York to San Francisco, home to the largest Chinese communities in the 1930s, FWP workers described chop suey as the symbol of the commercialization of Chinatowns at the expense of white Americans. Adopting a didactic stance, the San Francisco guidebook sharply explained that "beneath the pagoda-like cornices, electric chop suey signs perpetuate the popular notion that this dish . . . is more exotic than its name—the Chinese word for hash—indicates." They harshly depicted the Chinese neighborhoods as "palpable fake[s]" perpetuated by "sight-seeing companies" and "Chinese business men."[78]

The cosmopolitan argument could also take an unexpected twist when the same FWP workers who debunked the Chinese origins of chop suey attempted to convince readers that the dish was still authentically Chinese. Zahn reassured his readers by noting that "the truth of the matter is that the name, chop suey, is unknown in China, but the substance, which is meat with mixed vegetable, is prepared everyday in millions of Chinese homes."[79] Worldliness would replace the thrill of mystery in triggering New Yorkers' sensory appreciation of the dish. His co-worker, Nathan Ausubel, opted for a less-edifying route when he "melancholic[ally]" regretted the lack of information on the origin of the dish before affirming that "one thing is certain: the dish is a great favorite with New Yorkers and generally with the American people; it has helped made gourmets of those accustomed to unexciting home cooking only." For this Jewish FWP worker, chop suey's sensory attraction did not reside in its exoticism anymore but rather in its tamed difference and recognizable taste.[80]

The trajectory of chop suey is representative of the evolution of interwar urban sensory economies in which the taste of ethnic food was no longer valued for its exoticism but instead for its familiarity, making the experience of sensory difference less an adventure and more overtly an everyday act of consumption. In the first two decades of the twentieth century, working-class ethnic neighborhoods had been the destination of choice for restaurant goers in search of cosmopolitan dining, bohemian entertainment, and ethnic sensory exoticism. The slumming vogue receded by the late 1920s as the end of mass migration and the increased presence of American-born ethnics made working-class immigrant neighborhoods more reassuring but also less foreign and thrilling to white middle-class tourists.[81] By the late 1930s, it was only awkwardly that FWP workers could cling to sensory difference. In an essay titled "Eating in New York among Foreign Background," Maryse Rutledge noted that "in dress, speech, and thought, foreigners become American but each transplanted nation clings to habits of cooking with combinations of meat and vegetables, and seasonings."[82] The exotic sensorium had been reduced to "seasonings." The Depression, in fact, accelerated what historian Chad Heap has identified as "the general progression of slumming from a place-oriented activity to an amusement that determined the character of the spaces upon which it converged."[83] FWP workers explicitly made the connection between the "lean years" of the Depression and the active courting of a new clientele outside of ethnic neighborhoods, explaining how some "foreign restaurants" choose to leave their original locations and reopen in midtowns as full-fledged nightclubs, offering dance shows, music, and food, "with a little racial flavor thrown in."[84] Successful black-and-tan cabarets joined them, providing white audiences with "a glimpse of Harlem sans inconvenience" and further reifying racial difference.[85]

Descriptions of foreign-themed restaurants in New Deal food writing participated in the development of a version of middle-class cosmopolitanism that incorporated, rather than appropriated, ethnic food into American food. The displacement of the "gyp'" restaurants of the Prohibition-era by nightclubs with "foreign mise-en-scène" institutionalized ethnicity within American entertainment and tamed ethnic cuisines as part of a "night out."[86] Ethnic entrepreneurs adopted different sensory niches: some offered reassuring American alternatives to the ethnic menu while others located themselves within the cosmopolitan world of international cuisine. In particular, the "smartly appointed establishments" in midtowns across the country simultaneously capitalized on and regulated their own sensory difference by choosing to offer entertaining floor shows and ethnic dishes "seasoned and served to American taste."[87] This was done in interaction with the clientele but also through guessing as the dishes were "doctored to accord with what is thought to be the American taste."[88]

Restaurant owners' strategies to satisfy the taste of their clients ran the gamut from purposely staged ethnicity to the creation of international menus. Patrons yielded an important sensory and economic power and looked for entertainment and taste satisfaction, in part through the consumption of what they perceived as sensory authenticity and, occasionally, the enforcement of exoticism. Leonard E. Strong, for instance, noted in his review of the "Syrian" restaurants *Mocca* and *Haddad* that he was "slightly hurt" when offered an English menu, thought to be more suited to his taste by the "Arabian waiter." This did not deter him from enjoying the thrill of the moment as he "easily pictured [him]self being wined and dined by an Arabian sheik of the desert" while in the middle of Brooklyn.[89] Meeting customers' sensory expectations sometimes meant inventing brand new pan-ethnic cuisines and performances. At New York's Dubonnet, a "French Hungarian" restaurant that opened in 1933, one could "order Hungarian food prepared by a chef from Budapest, French food prepared by a chef from Naples, and last but not least southern food prepared by a real southern chef." The entertainment accompanying such a syncretic dinner would consist of a shrewdly marketed mix of racial authenticity and entertaining internationalism. Zimmerman's, a popular Times Square restaurant, for instance, proposed "real Hungarian entertainment" in the form of a "six-piece gypsy band," a prima donna singing "native Hungarian songs," and a soprano who "ke[pt] up the cosmopolitan spirit with her German and Italian songs."[90] New Deal food writing substantiates historians' suggestion that foreign-themed restaurants reframed the consumption of cosmopolitan food as a sign of the rising consumer power of the middle class while enabling immigrants to claim American cultural citizenship because of their sensory contribution.[91] All were not happy with this evolution. Adopting a posture close to the contemporary foodie in search of authentic food, New York fieldworker Harry Zahn warned his reader: "When you order *spaghetti alla milanese* your hopes that this is the real thing are doomed to be shattered. Ask an Italian from Milan if the sauce you get ever tasted like that in his hometown. His reply will consist of an expletive denotative and emotional, No."[92]

The move to midtown of some ethnic restaurants and their transformation into lavish, foreign-themed nightclubs did not eliminate the implantation of ethnic restaurants in working-class neighborhood and their role in their communities. FWP workers established a clear distinction between the two types of ethnic restaurants—downtown ethnic nightclubs, often owned by members of ethnic groups but not necessarily, and working-class establishments. They reported on both.[93] Patronized by migrant families, ethnic restaurants often got their start as boarding houses catering to male migrants in the late nineteenth century and were agents of cultural preservation and transmission throughout the interwar period.[94] Reporting on Romanian restaurants, a FWP worker noted that some "[went] for . . . good food and cabaret," but that the majority still "[went] in for just good, simple food."[95] Harder for the visitor and tourist to locate, "obscure eating places" catering to specific "national groups" occupied a central place in ethnic life as meeting places where one could enjoy comforting foods at a modest price. Humble spots with their "sawdust floor, unwashed windows and crude decoration," they provided favorite homeland dishes and in a number of cases regional cooking; southern Italians could, for instance, enjoy genuine pizzaiola, a "dish resembling pie-crust decorated with cheese and tomatoes."[96] Rarely accessible from the street, these restaurants were a "secluded retreat" for "serious-minded Russian workers gather[ed] to discuss union affairs fraternal problems, political questions and other matters of interest," and for Greek men "to sit long over cups of black coffee and discuss with acquaintances political affairs of their homeland as well as of their adopted country."[97] Lack of sources makes the estimation of the gender distribution of the clientele problematic; yet a couple of essays hint at the preponderance of men in these eating places. In New York, "if women [were] seen in . . . [Greek] restaurants, [they were] usually American-born."[98] More than simply eating places, ethnic restaurants were sites of community gathering that seem to have upheld conservative social values, serving as either male working-class clubs or family-based institutions.

New Deal food writing occasionally hints at the difficulties encountered by owners of working-class ethnic establishments during the Depression.

Although they provided affordable sensory and psychological comfort, some had difficulties surviving the economic downturn, as "people found it economically expedient to eat at home," and the taste of the American-born generation evolved.[99] A FWP worker in New York further remarked that "poverty allow[ed] no color line" and that the economic downturn had encouraged sensory mingling as well as "friendliness between the races, of which they are many."[100] In New York, the Bowery was the hub of these "minimum-priced restaurants" where "the commonest order [was] doughnuts and a bowl of coffee for 5 cents, next [was] the hamburger 'steak,' not too full of flour, with roll, coffee or tea, for a dime."[101] Poverty shrank taste differences and regulated working-class senses to fit a standard and cheap urban diet with only a hint of ethnicity, here in the form of "goulash." Moreover, working-class ethnic restaurants lost some of their clientele as second- and third-generation urban ethnics divided their loyalties between ethnic establishments and "modern" restaurants. They patronized luncheonettes, automats, and diners serving classic American fare such as hamburgers but also crossover inventions such as "spaghetti red," a mixture of chili and spaghetti.

The Depression also created new sites of sensory trade. Not all culinary and economic transactions around ethnic food described in New Deal food writing happened in urban environments or in established restaurants. Several Life Histories interviews transcribed by the Vermont Social-Ethnic Studies Project, and a subsequent *America Eats* essay, focused on the widespread practice among Italian stone carvers' widows of hosting "Italian feeds" in their homes. Reporting on these feeds was Mari Tomasi, a second-generation immigrant employed by the FWP in Vermont, where she notably contributed to a project on the Italian stoneworkers of Barre, titled "Men against Granite." Building on this research, she later published two novels on Italian American working life in the state. The FWP's unprecedented mandate to document U.S. cultural, social, and artistic lives inclusively was for Tomasi a unique opportunity to find support in a lifelong project and produce groundbreaking ethnographic work that considered foodways as integral to ethnic American life. Food was central to her sustained interest in immigrant lives and her interviews with stoneworkers' widows, and descriptions of the Italian feeds they organized give us a glimpse of the status of Italian food in the 1930s. Tomasi took care to mention that "contrary to common belief, the cook who prepares an Italian feed uses that pungent bulb, garlic, with no lavish hand, but with a light epicurean artistry": for most, Italian American cuisine was known and occasionally sought after, though it was still a somewhat sensorially suspicious novelty.[102]

The widows of Barre, Vermont, used their cooking skills as a means of survival during the Depression and opened up their kitchens and homes to private dinners, much like their African American counterparts throwing "chittlin' dinner" and "rent parties." They "had to do it" to take care of elderly parents and send children to school. Each private party consisted of an average of a dozen "Americans": "government official, professional, clerk, or truck driver." The dinners could also be a more diverse set; "Italians, Swedes, Yankees, Scotsmen" were eating and drinking "elbow to elbow" when FWP worker Roaldus Richmond visited Mrs. Gerbati, a widow and second-generation migrant. These dinners were more frequent (up to twice a week) in winter than in the summer months, when customers would rather enjoy modern drive-ins. As one cook explained: "They like to get out . . . in their cars and stop at different places to eat." Once the reservation was made, the menu was set in accordance to the customers' desire. A fixture of the meals was a "mountain of white spaghetti, quivering under a dusky tomato sauce, and capped with grated Parmesan cheese" as well as "*ravioli*"; the "diminutive derbies of pastries, the crowns stuffed with a well-seasoned paste" were the "most popular of Italian dishes." Italian cooks might have judged it "foolish to have both at the same dinner," but they complied with their customers' tastes and demands. The cooks would even use "packaged cheese already grated," even though they "scoff[ed]" at the dryness of the American parmesan whose "spirit" was, as one of them put it, "gone." Tomasi informed her reader that the cooks might "justifiably frown at dessert, but, if you wish . . . will serve you *spumoni*, an Italian ice cream." These small-scale, Depression-era entrepreneurs plainly laid out their reason for sensory compromise: "If that's what they want—me, I don't care. It means more money for me." In this case, economic exchange was straightforwardly driving sensory trade.[103]

*   *   *

FWP workers, pressed for time and pages, used well-known and somewhat ill-fitted models to describe the evolution of taste in the United States in the second half of the 1930s. Yet if their use of keywords such as "the melting pot" or "cosmopolitanism" was rhetorically conservative, it could also be ideologically innovative. When FWP workers dotted their essays with references to the melting pot, they contributed to reviving an ideal based on cultural fusion rather than coercive Americanization. Similarly, reduced to seasoning, sensory exoticism and difference could hardly be considered the core element of cosmopolitanism anymore; rather, a refurbished definition of cosmopolitanism grounded in sensory circulation and working-class identity emerged in New Deal food writing. This renewed appraisal of how taste was made in the United States had racial limits. A three-way distinction between blacks, white ethnics—in the FWP's words, "foreign white stock"—and racialized groups such as Asian Americans, Mexican Americans, or Arab Americans animated New Deal food writing. The case of Chinese food illustrates how FWP workers kept a cuisine popular with American consumers outside their narrative on American food while Chinese entrepreneurs capitalized on the exotic attraction of their cuisine. The taste of Chinese food was an integral part of 1930s sensory economies but not recognized as American per se and left at the margin of the FWP's culinary archive. In contrast, and despite the editorial line of a project like *America Eats*, the syncretic tastes of white ethnic groups found increasing legitimacy within the realm of American food. An ethnographic appraisal of New Deal food writing reveals how such tastes developed through the passing of generations and in interaction with developments in food processing and the industrialization and standardization of the U.S. food system so that, in effect, taste ethnicization *was* sensory Americanization, bringing to a close debates about the meaning of the melting pot.

Iconic ethnic dishes—spaghetti, chili, chop suey—once regarded as foreign and exotic became familiar and comforting staples of the Depression era. New Deal food writing on metropolitan restaurants documents how ethnic cuisines were "invented" in a dynamic process of sensory interaction between different players representing specific social aspirations. Foreign-themed nightclubs replaced slumming trips as signs of middle-class cultural capital and cosmopolitan good taste. Pragmatic sensory and business adaptation to the conditions of the Depression launched a sensory exchange that anchored ethnic food within the realm of American food. This sensory interaction defused the classic urban cosmopolitan paradigm. By the late 1930s, it was not so much the thrilling promise of sensory slumming among authentic members of the Italian "race" that attracted customers to Italian American restaurants but the anticipation of the comfort taste of "spaghetti and meatballs," "macaroni," and "salami sandwiches." A French-Irish waitress working in an Italian-owned restaurant in Maine explained in August 1940 that, though the migrant generation usually would "stick to Italian food," ethnic youths went "about fifty-fifty for Italian and American cooking." She added, "Lots of people who come here like Italian food, even if they're not Italian themselves. Funny, isn't it? I go for spaghetti and meatballs, and macaroni, myself."[104] Searching for America's food, the FWP encountered and documented the legions of cross-ethnic eaters whose daily choices and interactions in local sensory economies made ethnic food a stalwart symbol of American identity.

Conclusion

How Taste Is Made

Taste of the Nation concerns a period of American history often remembered in popular culture through iconic and haunting images of starvation and soup kitchen lines, but the book deals instead with the reassuring images of community gathering and public eating produced by the New Deal state. It delves into the rich food archives of one New Deal agency, the Federal Writers' Project, home of the ambitious *America Eats* project, in order to explore how the state envisioned the nation's collective sensory identity in the midst of the Great Depression and as the country geared up for war. New Deal food writing's program of anchoring national identity in the senses and in regional cuisines was only partially successful as local sensory constructions of race and ethnicity challenged some of the project's core assumptions. The narrative then tracks how the senses functioned as agents in the making of the modern U.S. racial taxonomy and highlights how eating and tasting the food of racial or ethnic others could be a way to create, reinforce, resist, blur, negotiate, and ultimately undermine difference. In doing so, the book proposes a new vocabulary for the study of the senses, centered on the notion of sensory economies, which enables exploring the web of sensory, cultural, social, textual, affective, and economic networks generated by food.

Our exploration of New Deal food writing combined analysis of taste, race, and place. The FWP set out to document the nation's regional cuisines, aiming at no less than overturning the blandness of a national standardization of taste, the product of more than fifty years of the industrialization of the U.S. food system. This search was regularly defeated, however, and the analysis reveals how nostalgia, prescriptive gender ideals, and racial stereotypes informed the FWP's culinary narrative and circumscribed how it was able to reframe regional foods as national symbols. A project such as *America Eats* reified and commodified regional "tastes of race," anchored in the sensing bodies of racial others, as sensory islands of unchanging local authenticity. For instance, sensory sightseeing as it operated in the Southwest, and to a lesser extent in the South and in northern ethnic neighborhoods, depended on fixed, often staged sensory authenticities that simultaneously reinforced and silenced contemporary racial politics. Tasting spicy Mexican food in the American Southwest then became a means for the performance of masculine whiteness and for the redefinition of the category Mexican away from a national category and toward a naturalized racial identity. Only occasionally would the reader get a glimpse, or taste, of the fast-evolving Mexican American ethnic cuisine. Similarly, eating southern food in New York's Harlem or Chicago's South Side, and imbuing its taste with blackness, could be a way for northern whites, of ethnic origins or not, to consolidate whiteness. The work of black FWP workers provides a needed alternative to the majority of New Deal food writing, giving us a sense of how southern food was also fast becoming an object of sensory pride in interwar northern black metropolises. New Deal sensory economies rested on the dynamic, intimate link between tasting place and sensing race.

New Deal food writing not only recorded the evolution of vernacular and legal notions of race and ethnicity, but it also had a formative role in shaping the sensory politics of race. *Taste of the Nation* captures the federal editors' and local workers' deliberations over which and whose regional foods would be worthy of integration into the American culinary narrative, and why. Analyzing the making of the FWP sensory and culinary archive provides a novel look into the New Deal cultural apparatus and unveils some of the incoherence of the liberal views on race, ethnicity, and national identity. The federal editors envisioned the book as the patriotic recording of regional, pre-industrial, and pre-mass-migration foodways. In *America Eats* the theoretical exclusion of communities central to New Deal sensory economies, such as Chinese Americans but also occasionally Southern and Eastern Europeans, was a limit inherent to the project's guidelines, with important ideological consequences. These guidelines left a large part of the population on the threshold of American traditions and in the archive's limbo. This was all too easy to do, as the archival mode of sensory memorialization tended to reify racial and ethnic identities by defining their supposedly authentic taste and to downplay the role of multiethnic, syncretic tastes in shaping New Deal sensory economies.

Yet, the implementation of the New Deal's search for American food also signaled a change in the national culinary paradigm and the progressive acceptance of ethnic food as well as industrial products *as* American. Donna Gabaccia casts the interwar period as one of "food fights" resolved at the brink of World War II by an ideological ceasefire between food experts in search of American culinary values and ethnic foods.[1] New Deal food writing was not so much a battlefield in this struggle as a remarkable stalemate. Attuned to paradox, the book explores how racial and ethnic categories shaped local sensory economies and charts the role of the senses in policing racial lines, all the while sensing between the lines of the archive to track the rise of multiethnic tastes. New Deal food writing recorded the rise of multiethnic eating habits in which Italian food can be had for lunch, a taco as a snack, and sushi as dinner. Local FWP workers described, and sometimes praised, a pluralist and cosmopolitan food culture to which all contributed. They depicted Americans' taste as the result of a dense sensory syncretization that combined ethnic foods with the standardized products of the food industry. The commodification of food has most often been talked about in relation to the food-processing industry and the development of a national marketplace of standardized foodstuffs.[2] The FWP's search for traditional regional cuisines was also part of this process as workers and editors looked for emblematic regional tastes to be sold on the national marketplace of food, taste, and ideas. New Deal food writing participated in the birth of a commodified culinary diversity. Analyzing the role of the senses in 1930s nation-building efforts, then, deepens the current narrative of Americanism as consumerism.[3] With New Deal food writing, the state attempted to present the nation as a consumable object, sensorially, symbolically, and materially. Taste, rather than food, became a commodity in the economic, affective, and symbolic networks of New Deal sensory economies, networks of value creation and social relations.

Taste of the Nation is a reflection on the making of a sensory archive and explores how societies remember and record taste. It is an invitation to sense between the line, to attune our senses to the archive and what it might reveal about past ways of sensing the world. I offer a methodological reflection on the status of the archive as a repertoire of sensory experiences and examine how the interaction between federal editors and local workers produced sensory and culinary knowledge about the nation's regions and peoples. Racialized and imagined regional sensory pasts became ideological and sensory commodities actively shaping New Deal sensory economies, on the ground and in the archive. The notion of sensory economies is an analytical tool to explore how FWP workers sensed the food they wrote about *and* to conduct archival sensory analysis. The narrative explores the textual representations of the senses to chart the economy of the senses in New Deal food writing (the interaction and hierarchy of smell, sound, vision, touch, and kinesthesia in the appreciation of food) and directs attention to the processes of production and organization of sensory knowledge inherent in the creation of a sensory archive like the FWP's. Doing so allows a combined analysis of the value of the senses and how the senses create value.

A sensory analysis of New Deal food writing highlights the last years of the Depression as a cornerstone period in the making of modern American taste. The celebration of gendered, and often staged, racial and ethnic sensory authenticity present throughout New Deal food writing was, in part, the expression of interwar anxieties over both the potential lack of food and the encroachment of industrial foods on American taste. *America Eats*, in particular, can be considered as a cathartic site for the acceptation of the standardized products of the food industries as American food. Histories of food often link major transformations in American food culture and taste either to the late-nineteenth-century rise of giant food companies or to post-1945 technological advances in food processing.[4] Situated at the hinge of these two major changes and straddling decades of hunger and restrictions (real or imagined, in economic depression and war) and heavy usage of food symbolism, New Deal food writing culturally and sensorially paved the way for the postwar food and eating culture. This moment of acclimation to the changes brought by the development of the food industries at the turn of the century was the condition of its success in the postwar era. As a food historian recently put it, FWP workers were part of the generation of Americans that slowly, hesitantly "attuned to industrial flavors and textures" and participated in the emergence of a new "collective national palate."[5] The chronological focus on the late 1930s and early 1940s emphasizes the role of race and ethnicity in the making of U.S. taste but also underlines the origins of the war and postwar gendered domestic ideology. This book participates in a broader scholarly literature that seeks to unveil the ideological continuity between the interwar debate about women and their ability to provide proper nutrition to their families and the contemporary blaming of women for succumbing to the food industry's advertising campaigns.[6] New Deal food writing provides us with a framework to understand how the nostalgic longing for the foods of an imagined past work to inscribe racism and domesticity at the core of our contemporary sensory economies.

Selected passages of the *America Eats* archive recently made it into print under the eloquent title *The Food of a Younger Land: A Portrait of American Food before the National Highway System, before Chain Restaurants, and before Frozen Food, When the Nation's Food was Seasonal, Regional, and Traditional, from the Lost WPA Files.*[7] The *America Eats* editors might have agreed with this title; indeed, they did search for "traditional" and "regional" dishes, promoting a sensory nostalgia for the food of a utopian past. But they did not find "the foods of a younger land" (if these had ever existed), and a close reading of the not-so-lost archive underlines the national marketplace of foodstuffs, ideas, and sensory perceptions as a main determinant of American taste in the 1930s. A critical appraisal of the words and goals of New Deal food writing highlights that it was the very encroachment of mass-produced industrial food that triggered a project like *America Eats* and its nostalgic search for regional culinary traditions. Yet this mislabeling of the archive is also informative, as it layers the 1930s sensory and ideological craving for "real" foods with an early-twenty-first-century sensory nostalgia, and moral judgment, about the contemporary food system. The 1930s here becomes the Golden Age of untainted American eating that the FWP editors situated in the early to mid-nineteenth century. New Deal food writing pioneered anthropological research on foodways but also contemporary searches for "the time before the fall, before greed, gluttony, and sloth." A time of pure, clean food and eating without feeling of guilt or shame. In reaction to the hold-up of scientific nutrition on American understandings of food in the first decades of the twentieth century, federal editors aimed to *not* tell their readers what they "ought to" eat while admonishing them to *not* care about calories or vitamins. Instead, they choose to celebrate tradition and taste, pointing to the sensory past as a solution for the future. But despite this original stance, they became enmeshed in the moral discourses woven around food, the dichotomy between real and fake, good and bad food—however defined—that continues to animate American food culture.[8]

The pages of New Deal food writing are often surprisingly reminiscent of contemporary celebration of local, homemade food. Queue this description of a Delaware church dinner at which "only vegetables raised in the neighborhood, and meats dressed by local butchers, and poultry raised and dressed by local people are used."[9] New Deal food writing echoes contemporary exhortations to forgo the processed products of the global food industry for local food that, to paraphrase food writer Michael Pollan's now classic adage, our great-grandmothers would recognize as food.[10] It also falls into some of the same trappings by setting "good" food as both a goal and an object of sensory nostalgia in which women's and nonwhites' labor and bodies occupy an ambiguous place. What if, as editors and fieldworkers repeatedly complained, our great-grandmothers fed their families not with homemade stews and apple pies but with "canned foods and factory bread"? How should we consider the triumphant remark, emanating from the South regional essay that, on Sundays, "the ghost of a confederate soldier's grandmother could walk into the dining room of some New Orleans or Mobile residences and feel perfectly at home at the sight of the food awaiting the worshippers upon their return from church"? The work and knowledge of the absentee mammy who cooked while her "white folks" prayed loomed large on the sensory economy of the southern dining room heralded to the nation. As Amy Trubek reminds us: "Plantation slavery, patriarchy, and malnourishment are also part of our shared food past," despite our dreams of wholesome repasts.[11] Curiosity for the taste of race can lurk behind hankerings for a taste of place.

The FWP's drive to record, protect, and publicize regional food resonates with twenty-first-century enthusiasm for local food, including in its gendered and raced limits. Developments in food activism and food politics over the past twenty years have often been "hungering for authenticity" and steeped in nostalgia for a "romantic pastoralism," heightening the symbolic virtue of women's nurturing role while sidelining the labor of people of color in the daily workings of the American food system and sensory economies.[12] New Deal food writing, like some contemporary food writing, depicted women as simultaneously responsible for the deterioration of food quality as they yield to the food industry when entering the workforce *and* the last buffer against its economic and sensory supremacy.[13] The work of nonwhites, and in particular women of color, was essential to this argument, as they became symbols of local sensory authenticity, superior cooks due to their very closeness to the lower senses of taste, smell, and touch. New Deal food writing, despite its groundbreaking focus on taste and foodways, did not often question racial hierarchies established through the senses. But this sensory superiority put nonwhite cooks, somewhat unexpectedly to FWP editors and workers, at the center of New Deal sensory economies, their present food work hidden in plain view as a historical foil.

What are we to make of these parallels? New Deal food writing provides us neither with lessons in how to eat better nor with cause to dismiss it as a misplaced, bigoted, or even failed nation-building attempt. Rather, it offers a reminder that contemporary anxieties about the sensory, political, environmental, social, and moral consequences of the global industrial food system as well as the drive toward the celebration of local traditions and knowledge are not a late-twentieth and early-twenty-first-century affair but part of a longer, in fact largely repeating, historical trend. (After all, the introduction of wood and then gas stoves in the nineteenth century triggered a wave of nostalgia for the good old days of the pre-industrial hearth, glossing over the bending, lifting, and the potential for catching on fire that accompanied this method of cooking.[14]) New Deal food writing provides us with a tool to better understand, at a distance, the challenges of establishing sustainable, pleasurable, and equitable food systems. This is not to disparage efforts at changing industrial foodways in the twenty-first century but to highlight how social and sensory histories of food can create spaces for debates about the social, cultural, and environmental equity challenges posed by the industrial food system and its critics.[15]

Notes

Introduction

1. Bessie A. Carlock, "Camp Chuck," January 16, 1942, Arizona: Notes, Essays, Reports, LOC-AE, A830. Donna Gabaccia's work (*We Are What We Eat: Ethnic Food and the Making of Americans*) on the *America Eats* archive was the inspiration for this book; see also Levenstein, *Paradox of Plenty*, 40–45.

2. Carlock, "Camp Chuck," emphasis in original; Gladys Gregg, "Colorado Eats," 24, Colorado: Notes, Essays, Reports, LOC-AE, A830.

3. My use of the expression "New Deal" here and throughout mirrors cultural critic and historian Michael Denning's remark that the expression "New Deal" is "at once" the name of "[Franklin D.] Roosevelt's successful political alliance and the common term for the United States in the 1930s and 1940s." Denning, *Culture*, 159.

4. Hirsch, *Portrait of America*, 212. On cultural nation building and the FWP, see also Schindler-Carter, *Vintage Snapshots*. On the social, political, and economic features of the New Deal order, see Gerstle and Fraser, *Rise and Fall*. On the American Guide Series, see Bold, *WPA Guides*; Shaffer, *See America First*, 170–220.

5. "Brief Description of Proposed Book,"1, Administrative Material, LOC-AE, A829.

6. *Gourmet* started publication in 1941; on the magazine's early history, see Neuhaus, *Manly Meals*, 104–5.

7. Women writers in particular used food as a central practical and metaphorical issue in Depression-era fiction. Paula Rabinowitz's study of women's revolutionary literature in the decade has shown how these writers, taking their cue from Meribel Le Sueur, situated "the differentials between male and female bodies [. . .] in the belly." While the male body (along with the masculine text) was "hungry, an empty space once filled by its labor," the female body was "pregnant with desire for 'children,' for 'butterfat' to feed them, and most significantly, for 'history' to change the world for them." Rabinowitz, *Labor and Desire*, 3 and 36.

8. For recent appraisals of Lange's iconic *Migrant Mother* photograph, see Gordon, *Dorothea Lange*, 235–43; DePastino, *Citizen Hobo*, 215–17. Lange was working for the

State-sponsored Farm Security Administration (FSA) when she took this photograph. The FSA employed dozens of photographers who produced an extensive pictorial record of American life in the period, including foodways. These photographs can be consulted online at http://www.loc.gov/pictures/collection/fsa (accessed August 15, 2014). For more perspective on the FSA photographs, see Daniel et al., *Official Images*.

9. Levenstein, *Paradox of Plenty*, 60–62. On black and white southern sharecroppers' foodways, see Ferris, *Edible South*, 166–87.

10. Le Sueur, "Women on the Breadlines," 166–71.

11. On the "paradox of want amid plenty" and political and social reactions to the Agricultural Adjustment Act (AAA), see Poppendieck, *Breadlines*, especially 109–21; on cultural responses to the AAA, see White, *Plowed Under*.

12. For a broader view of the 1930s documentary aesthetic and the central role of the New Deal art programs in its development, see Stott, *Documentary Expression*; Fleischhauer et al., *Documenting America*; Daniel, *Official Images*.

13. White, *Plowed Under*, 205.

14. Marling, *Wall-to-Wall America*, 21; see also Melosh, *Engendering Culture*, 33–81.

15. Melosh, *Engendering Culture*, 67–76. On race, see also Williams-Forson, *Building Houses*, 71–79.

16. Denning, *Cultural Front*, 133–34. See also Dorman, "Revolt of the Provinces," 8; and, generally, Dorman, *Revolt of the Provinces*.

17. Scholars have highlighted examples of the dialectic relationships between regional and national cuisines, tradition and modernity in varied geographical settings. On India, see Appadurai, "National Cuisine"; on France, see Julia Csergo, "Emergence of Regional Cuisines"; on Italy, see Montanari, "Regional versus National Cuisine in Italy"; on Mexico, see Pilcher, *Que Vivan Los Tamales!* and Pilcher, "Tasting the Patria"; on China, see Swislocki, *Culinary Nostalgia*.

18. McWilliams *Revolution in Eating*; Gabaccia, *We Are What We Eat*, 10–35.

19. "Brief Description of Proposed Book," 1–2. On the industrialization of the U.S. food system, see Horowitz, *Putting Meat on the American Table*; Gabriella M. Petrick, "Arbiters of Taste"; Levenstein, *Revolution at the Table*; Freidberg, *Fresh*; Cronon, *Nature's Metropolis*, 97–147 and 207–59.

20. FWP, *U.S. One: Maine to Florida*, xvii–xviii; Abrahamsen, "Culinary Goodies, Cape Cod Style," 1–2, Massachusetts: Notes, Essays, Reports, LOC-AE, A831.

21. Studying the visual arts and theater programs of the Works Progress Administration (WPA), cultural historian Barbara Melosh explains the "containment of feminism" over the decade as a reaction to a "sense of manhood in crisis" caused by widespread unemployment and the masculine incapacity to fulfill the role of exclusive family providers. The Depression increased women's presence on the job market to the extent that "female independence threatened an embattled masculinity." Alice Kessler-Harris, in her analysis of the legal and social "gendered limits" of the period, further highlights that New Dealers "reconstructed and perpetuated notions of individualism by protecting male independence and autonomy in the labor market, reinforcing traditional notions that rights are defined by position in the family, and affirming women's status as dependent." She demonstrates how New Deal reforms such as Social Security "drew on a deeply gendered, racialized, and sometimes nostalgic vision of the past that was ultimately rooted

in Lockean perceptions of individual freedom and economic opportunity, untrammeled by government intervention." Defining independence as the primary condition for full citizenship, New Deal reforms had widespread gendered and racial consequences since they established "a concept of dignity and of rights in which most women (black or white) and many African American males were expected to have no part." Melosh, *Engendering Culture*, 1 and 30. Kessler-Harris, "In the Nation's Image," 1253, 1256, and 1264. For further perspective on women during the Great Depression and the New Deal, see also Faue, *Community of Suffering and Struggle*; Ware, *Holding their Own*.

I am paraphrasing contemporary food writer Michael Pollan's food rule, "Don't eat anything your great-grandmother wouldn't recognize as food." Pollan, *Food Rules*, 7–8. For a more thorough discussion of the links between New Deal food writing and the contemporary food movement, see the conclusion to this book.

22. On the evolution of definitions of whiteness, ethnicity, and race, see Jacobson, *Whiteness*; Barrett and Roediger, "Inbetween Peoples." Studies of how Italian Americans became whites are especially numerous; see, for instance, Guglielmo, *White on Arrival*; Guglielmo and Salerno, *Are Italians White?*; Guterl, *Color of Race*. On the reconstruction of race in immigration law in the twentieth century, see Ngai, *Impossible Subjects*. For an example of a group changing cultural and political strategies in the twentieth century, see Sanchez, *Becoming Mexican American*.

23. Roediger, *Working toward Whiteness*; Cohen, *Making a New Deal*.

24. Jacobson, *Whiteness*, 110; Sugrue, *Origins*, 15–87.

25. Roediger and Barrett, "Inbetween Peoples," 12.

26. Mangione, *Dream and the Deal*, 331–33.

27. Bold, *WPA Guides*, 91.

28. Michael Denning estimates that approximately 10 percent of the FWP employees were "non-relief." He identifies the WPA art programs, such as the FWP, as a key organ of the state cultural apparatus and an important creative source for the Cultural Front. According to Denning, it represented a crucial hope for the advent of a "cultural democracy" in the United States, that is, "a bureaucracy that would provide 'culture' for the people." Though this hope faltered in the face of the capitalist power of the "Advertisement Front" and the "American Century," it left an "indelible imprint on the modern cultural apparatus." Denning, *Cultural Front*, 77–83. On the federal editors, see also Bold, *WPA Guides*, 22–29; Hirsch, "Cultural Pluralism," 50.

29. Kellock, cited in Mangione, *Dream and the Deal*, 73.

30. State directors, fourteen of whom were women, were physicians (Mabel Ulrich, Minnesota), editors (W. T. Couch, North Carolina), local writers (Lyle Saxon, Louisiana), sports and pulp fiction writers (James W. Egan, Washington), local reporters (Dorris May Westall, Maine), or held English doctorates (John J. Lyons, Wisconsin; John T. Frederick, Illinois). The process by which federal staff and state directors were selected and appointed as well as detailed background information on their professional and social lives is described by former FWP worker Jerry Mangione in his memoir of the period, *The Dream and the Deal* (see esp. 53–93). On John J. Lyons, see Edmonds, "Federal Writers' Project in Wisconsin."

31. Bold, *Writers, Plumbers, and Anarchists*, 25.

32. On the "heterogeneity of employee profiles" and their few "shared characteristics," see Bold, *WPA Guides*, 20–22. Bold highlights that the inclusive definition of "writers"

adopted by the FWP breached traditional class and cultural lines by including literature in the world of labor. I follow her lead in referring to them as "FWP workers" rather than "writers." This wide recruitment policy posed repeated problems concerning the literary quality of the FWP copies, much to the chagrin of the federal office. *Writers, Plumbers, and Anarchists*, 11–30 and 99–126. See also Szalay, *New Deal Modernism*, 28.

33. Women occupied important positions in the FWP as federal editors and state directors; they were also well represented among fieldworkers. Most FWP's branches were inclusive and employed second-generation immigrants and African Americans. But if work with the FWP proved empowering for many black intellectuals, Southern branches were segregated, and when African Americans were on the payroll, they wrote in segregated offices or from home. On African Americans in the FWP, see Sklaroff, *Black Culture*, 83–122, as well as chapter 3 of this book.

34. Bold, in her detailed study of the making of the American Guide Series, explains how such things as "the tensions between federal bureaucracy and regional difference; the competing claims of 'specialized' versus 'local' knowledge; the effects of 'official' sponsorship on the setting of cultural norms and the jostling of local groups and narratives for recognition within the national framework" regularly sapped the FWP's goals. Bold, *WPA Guides*, xiv–xv. On the tensions between civic and racial citizenship in the New Deal period, see Gerstle, *American Crucible*, 128–86.

35. John D. Newsom to Robert W. Allan, September 29, 1941, Correspondence, August–October, 1941, LOC-AE, A829.

36. On archives being simultaneously sources and subjects, see Stoler, *Along the Archival Grain*, 44–49. On the necessity of analyzing New Deal archives in particular as both sources and subjects, see Fleischhauer et al., *Documenting America*, 43–74.

37. For a multidisciplinary account of the "sensory turn" since the late 1980s, see Howes, "Expanding Field." The work of historians Alain Corbin, Constance Classen, and Mark Smith and of anthropologist David Howes in particular influence the practice of sensory history developed in this book. See, among their many works, Corbin *The Foul and the Fragrant*, *Villages Bells*, and *Time, Desire, and Horror*; Classen, *Worlds of Sense* and *The Deepest Sense*; Howes, *Sensual Relations* and *Varieties of Sensory Experience*; Howes and Classen, *Ways of Sensing*; Smith, *How Race Is Made* and *Sensing the Past*.

38. On the "economy of the senses," see Ong, *Interfaces of the Word*, 135–36; Jütte, *History of the Senses*, 14–16.

39. Howes, "Expanding Field."

40. On the method of sensory history, see Smith, "Producing Sense"; Corbin, *Time, Desire, and Horror*, 189–90; Howes, "Can These Dry Bones Live?" 442–45.

41. Mitchell, "Rethinking Economy," 1117. The notion of sensory economies builds on and expands Nils Lindahl Elliot's exploration of economies of multisensuality. He writes:

Here I refer not so much to the modern notion of "economy"—though certainly many zoos attempt to commodify their most explicit multisensualities—but to two older meanings of the word: economy as a certain arrangement of something, and, in the archaic sense of the word, as the management of household affairs. Derived from *ménage*, meaning "household" in the original French, and also household management in English, the older name for zoos is, of course, "menagerie." The notion of an economy of multisensuality might thereby be described as the sensual equivalent of a collection of animals: the different senses themselves appear to be "collected" and "managed," if not "domesticated." (Elliot, "See It, Sense It, Save It," 205)

On the evolution of "economy" from the private affairs of the household to the modern meaning of economics and "the economy," see also Williams, *Keywords*, 110.

42. Mitchell, "Fixing the Economy," 91. On New Deal programs, see Mitchell, "Economy," 94.

43. Probyn, "In the Interests of Taste and Place," 70. On economies as "sets of entanglements," see also Ahmed, "Affective Economies"; and Highmore, "Bitter After Taste."

44. Howes develops "a full-bodied, multisensory theory of the commodity and consumption" in his chapter titled "Material Body of the Commodity," in *Sensual Relations*, 204–34; quote is on p. 227.

45. Howes, *Sensual Relations*, 228. On the need to analyze "the conditions under which economic objects circulate in different regimes of value in space and time" and how commodities, including food commodities, are embedded in specific historical, cultural, and, I would add, sensory milieus, see also Appadurai, "Introduction," 3.

46. Wright, *Native Son*, 69, emphasis in original. Wright was employed successively by the Chicago and New York FWP units; see Mangione, *Dream and the Deal*, 124.

47. On the role of bodily performances in the commodification of blackness, see hooks, "Eating the Other"; Lott, *Love and Theft*; and more recently, Brown, *Babylon Girls*; Heap, *Slumming*; Tompkins, *Racial Indigestion*.

48. On African Americans as "sonic beings" and the role of sound in the making of the black modern public sphere, see Corbould, "Streets, Sounds and Identity." On the racial politics of listening, see Miller, *Segregating Sound*.

49. Williams-Forson, *Building Houses*.

50. Smith, *How Race Is Made*, 6. Scholarship on imperialism and domesticity in the United States and beyond has shown the critical role of domestic spaces and intimate contact in establishing racial lines; see, for instance, Hoganson, *Consumers' Imperium*; Stoler, *Haunted by Empire*; Stoler, *Carnal Knowledge and Imperial Power*; McClintock, *Imperial Leather*.

51. For varied perspective on the evolution of the meaning of taste in the modern period, see Ferguson, "Senses of Taste"; Fitzgerald and Petrick, "In Good Taste," 80–83.

52. Bourdieu, *Distinction*, 190.

53. Ibid, 177–200.

54. For more perspective on the "Negro Vogue" among white urbanites in the interwar United States, see Heap, *Slumming*, 189–230.

55. For a critique of Bourdieu's "static" and "passive sociology of taste," see Probyn, *Carnal Appetites*, 27–30, and Hennion, "Pragmatics of Taste."

56. Highmore, "Bitter After Taste," 120.

57. In her analysis of the cultural politics of emotion, Sara Ahmed writes:

[W]hile emotions do not positively reside in a subject or figure, they still work to bind subjects together. Indeed, to put it more strongly, the non-residence of emotions is what makes them "binding." . . . Rather than seeing emotions as psychological dispositions, we need to consider how they work, in concrete and particular ways, to mediate the relationship between the psychic and the social, and between the individual and the collective. (Ahmed, "Affective Economies," 119)

58. Tompkins, *Racial Indigestion*, 6.

Chapter 1. America Eats

1. "Brief Description of Proposed Book," 1, Administrative Material, LOC-AE, A829.

2. "Editorial Report to Regional Editors of America Eats," 2, Administrative Material, LOC-AE, A829, emphasis in original.

3. "Memorandum," 3, Administrative Material, LOC-AE, A829.

4. "Editorial Procedure for America Eats," 2, Administrative Material, LOC-AE, A829.

5. "General Notes to Regional Editors of *America Eats*," 1, Administrative Material, LOC-AE, A829.

6. "Virginiaham Is One Word," in "The South," 5, Section Essay, LOC-AE, A833.

7. Boym, *Future of Nostalgia*, 15.

8. On the renewed attack on the New Deal State in the mid- and late 1930s, see Brinkley, *Voices of Protest*; on the contested nature of the New Deal food and agriculture policy, especially the Agricultural Adjustment Act, see White, *Plowed Under*.

9. Trachtenberg, *Reading American Photographs*, 247.

10. Katherine Kellock, "Editorial Report: Illinois," November 24, 1941, Correspondence, November–December, 1941, LOC-AE, A830. On the relationship between the FWP federal staff and the field of anthropology, especially through many of the editors' Harvard and Columbia University educations, see Hirsch, *Portrait of America*, 23–24. The use of the expression "eating pattern" is preponderant in "Editorial Report on State Copy," January 30, 1942, 3, Correspondence, 1942, LOC-AE, A830; John D. Newsom to James H. Crutcher, September, 4, 1941, Correspondence, August–October, 1941, LOC-AE, A829.

11. "General Notes to Regional Editors of *America Eats*," 1.

12. "Editorial Report: Illinois."

13. John D. Newsom to Robert W. Allan, September 29, 1941, Correspondence, September–October, 1941, LOC-AE, A829.

14. "The Northeast," unpaginated, Section Essay, AE-LOC, A829.

15. I thank Franca Iacovetta for alerting me to the multiplicity of these possibilities and for pushing me to refine my argument on this point. The quote is in Iacovetta, "Immigrant Gifts," 60, emphasis added.

16. "Editorial Procedure for America Eats," 1.

17. Stoler, *Along the Archival Grain*, 49.

18. Chas J. Finger to Henry G. Alsberg, October 28, 1937; Eudora Ramsay Richardson to Henry G. Alsberg, November 12, 1937; Correspondence, 1937–1938, LOC-AE, A829.

19. John D. Newsom to Robert W. Allan, January 2, 1942, Correspondence, 1942, LOC-AE, A830; letter sent to several states that had not sent in essays to Washington yet on November 29, 1941, Correspondence, November–December, 1941, LOC-AE, A830.

20. John D. Newsom, to Floyd Sharp, September 25, 1941, Correspondence, September–October, 1941, LOC-AE, A829. On the revamping of the Federal Writers' Project into the Writers' Project and then the Office of War Information, see Hirsch, *Portrait of America*, 197–228 (quote is on p. 212), and Mangione, *Dream and the Deal*, 289–348.

21. The Library of Congress received the vast majority of the *America Eats* material at the end of the project. Some regional archive centers also hold *America Eats* material in their collections; Montana State University Library, for instance, holds two boxes of *America Eats* material as part of its WPA collection; see http://www.lib.montana.edu/collect/spcoll/findaid/2336.html (accessed September 16, 2014). It is worth noting that these collections often contain carbon copies of essays already sent to Washington.

22. John D. Newsom to Lyle Saxon, August 26, 1941, Correspondence, August–October, 1941, LOC-AE, A829

23. Mangione, *Dream and the Deal*, 66.

24. On Kellock's intellectual education and her work with the FWP, see Bold, *WPA Guides*, 25 and 64–91 (quote is on p. 89); Hirsch, *Portrait of America*, 52–56.

25. Bold, *WPA Guides*, 76

26. Succinct notes accompanied some of the empty files, such as: "Nothing from West Virginia except what the Louisiana Writers' project has been able to dig up." West Virginia: Notes, Essays, Reports, LOC-AE, A832. Charles Camp notes that in the case of Illinois and Louisiana, the units were in charge of collecting material from other states before sending a blended regional essay to Washington. They probably did not bother sending their own contributions and reworked them directly into the regional essays. See Camp, "*America Eats*," 124; on *America Eats*, 93–250; checklist of *America Eats* manuscripts, 127–60. The *America Eats* material from New York City was never sent to Washington but is included in the archive of the *Feeding the City* project in the New York City Department of Records, Municipal Archive's Collection.

27. A large selection of photographs taken for the *America Eats* project is available online: http://www.loc.gov/pictures/item/00649983 (accessed May 29, 2015).

28. The five *America Eats* regions were as follows ("key states" would be in charge of the final regional essays): Northeast: New Jersey (key state), Maine, New Hampshire, Vermont, Massachusetts, Rhode island, Connecticut, New York City, New York State, Pennsylvania; Middle West: Illinois (key state), Indiana, Ohio, Michigan, Wisconsin, Minnesota, Iowa, Missouri, North Dakota, South Dakota, Nebraska, Kansas; South: Louisiana (key state), Delaware, Maryland, Virginia, West Virginia, Kentucky, Tennessee, North Carolina, South Carolina, Georgia, Florida, Alabama, Mississippi, Arkansas; Southwest: Arizona (key state), Southern California, New Mexico, Oklahoma, Texas; Far West: Montana (key state), Wyoming, Colorado, Utah, Idaho, Nevada, Washington, Oregon, Northern California.

29. Lyle Saxon to John D. Newsom, August 20, 1941; John D. Newsom to Lyle Saxon, August 26, 1941, Correspondence, August–October, 1941, LOC-AE, A829; "Editorial Procedure for America Eats," LOC-AE, Administrative Material, A829. On Lyle Saxon's work for the FWP, see Lawrence N. Powell, "Lyle Saxon and the WPA Guide to New Orleans"; Ferris, *Edible South*, 180–82.

30. "Editorial Report on State Copy," 3.

31. "The South," 3, Section Essay, LOC-AE, A833.

32. "The Northeast," unpaginated, Section Essay, LOC-AE, A833.

33. Edward B. Reynolds, "Far West," Section Essay, 1; 56; Arthur J. Brooks, "America Eats (Southwest Section)," version 1, 9, Section Essay, LOC-AE, A833. Two versions of the Southwest section essay are conserved in the Library of Congress files. The earlier, unedited version will be cited as, "America Eats (Southwest Section)," version 1.

34. Nelson Algren (?), "America Eats, a Short History of American Diet," 80, Middle West Section Essay, LOC-AE, A832. Although the manuscript conserved at the Library of Congress is unsigned, it has been attributed to and published under Nelson Algren's name. Algren and Schoonover, *America Eats*.

35. For a discussion of the difficult task of estimating how many writers were involved with the FWP on a short- or long-term basis, see Gross, "American Guide Series," 85 and 104–5. Bold states a high estimate of ten thousand during the course of the project, the size of which was considerably reduce after 1939 (*Writers, Plumbers, and Anarchists*, 13).

36. Samuel Y. Tupper Jr. to John D. Newsom, October 8, 1941, Correspondence, August–October, 1941, LOC-AE, A829. The complex bureaucratic organization of the FWP led to occasional cacophony, as can be inferred from John D. Newsom reassuring 1941 letter to Lyle Saxon: "You will be glad to learn that the National staff is so organized now that such calamities [misunderstandings] need not be anticipated . . . and the delightful possibility that half a dozen persons will issue conflicting instructions no longer exists." John D. Newsom to Lyle Saxon, August 28, 1941, Correspondence, August–October, 1941, LOC-AE, A829. See also, Hirsch, *Portrait of America*, 111.

37. William R. McDaniel to John D. Newsom, October 3, 1941, Correspondence, August–October, 1941, LOC-AE, A829.

38. Eudora Ramsay Richardson to Henry G. Alsberg, November, 12, 1937, Correspondence, 1937–1938, LOC-AE, A829.

39. Eudora Ramsay Richardson, "Family Reunion," 4, LOC-AE, Virginia: Notes, Essays, Reports, A832. On Eudora Ramsay Richardson, see Perdue, Barden, and Phillips, *Weevils in the Wheat*, xxi–xxiii; Kurlansky, *Food of a Younger Land*, 133–34.

40. "Colorado Contribution to America Eats," 1, December 2, 1941, Correspondence, November–December 1941, LOC-AE, A830.

41. John D. Newsom to James H. Crutcher, December 6, 1941, Correspondence, November–December, 1941, LOC-AE, A830. New Deal food writing was a precursor to the study of foodways and the multidisciplinary field of food studies. Food became part of the field of folklore in the 1970s, in part through the scholarship of folklorists Don Yoder, and has grown into a subject of academic inquiry since the early 1980s. See Yoder, "Folk Cookery."

42. FWP, *Missouri*, 133.

43. On travel literature and tourist guidebooks, see Shaffer, *See America First*, especially 169–220, on the FWP American Guide Series. For additional perspective on armchair tourism at the turn of the century, see Hoganson, *Consumers' Imperium*, 153–208.

44. Though most folklorists ignored the FWP's Folklore Project in the following decades, the shift from the study of folklore in America to American folklore it operated was instrumental in the transformation of folklore into a professional and academic field in the postwar period. For an introduction to the history of folklore in the United States, see Bronner, "In Search of American Tradition." On the FWP Folklore Project and B. A. Botkin's leading role in particular, see Hirsch, "Folklore in the Making"; Hirsch, "Cultural Pluralism."

45. "Outline Indicating Approach to Subject"; "Brief Description of Proposed Book," 2, Administrative Material, LOC-AE, A829.

46. Kammen, *Mystic Chords of Memory*, 303.

47. Becker, *Selling Tradition*, 222.

48. Denning, *Cultural Front*, 78, 134–35, and 227. For additional perspective on the making of folklore in the period, see Whisnant, *All That Is Native*.

49. Henry Alsberg to Vardis Fisher, March 21, 1938, Correspondence relating to Folklore Studies, 1936–1940, RG 69, P157 22, box 1.

50. Becker, "Revealing Traditions," 19–22.

51. Gladys Gregg, "Colorado Eats," 23, Colorado: Notes, Essays, Reports, LOC-AE, A831; "Colorado Contribution to *America Eats*," 1.

52. On the evolution of the field of anthropology and the concept of culture, see Williams, *Keywords*, 87–93 (quotes are on pp. 90 and 92).

53. Susman, *Culture as History*, 150–83; Williams, *Keywords*: on civilization, see 58–59; on progress, see 244–45.

54. "Editorial Report on State Copy," January 30, 1942, Correspondence, 1942, LOC-AE, A830; "Editorial Report: Illinois," November 24, 1941; John D. Newsom to Charles P. Casey, November 5, 1941, Correspondence, November–December 1941, LOC-AE, A830. For additional perspective on the FWP federal editors' and directors' adoption of the anthropological concept of culture, see Hirsch, *Portrait of America*, 109. On the rise of the anthropology of food in the 1930s and the role of Margaret Mead in this trend, see Macbeth and MacClancy, *Researching Food Habits*, 2. On Mead's sensory scholarship, see Howes, *Sensual Relations*, 10–14.

55. John D. Newsom to Edward Gatlin, November 21, 1941, November–December 1941, LOC-AE, A 830.

56. Pilcher, *Que Vivan Los Tamales!*, 156.

57. Mintz, "Eating Communities," 26, emphasis in original.

58. Jessie L. Duhig, "Camp Cookery of Southern Big Horn Basin, Wyoming," 1936, 30–31, LOC-AE, Wyoming: Notes, Essays, Reports, A832.

59. On nations as imagined communities and the role of invented traditions in cementing them, see the seminal works of Benedict Anderson, *Imagined Communities*; Pierre Nora and Lawrence D. Kritzman, *Realms of Memory*; and Eric J. Hobsbawm and T.O. Ranger, *The Invention of Tradition*. On food and nation building, see among others, Pilcher, *Que Vivan Los Tamales!*; Appadurai, "How to Make a National Cuisine."

60. Fischer, *Albion's Seed*, 792. Lucy Long proposes a similar definition of regions as "cultural landscapes shaped by and resulting from specific natural environments and the particular cultures using them," in Long, "Culinary Tourism," 24.

61. On the history of regional cuisines in the British colonies and early United States, see McWilliams, *Revolution in Eating*; Gabaccia, *We Are What We Eat*, 10–34.

62. Levenstein, *Revolution at the Table*.

63. On the late-nineteenth-century changes to the American food system, see Levenstein, *Revolution at the Table*, 30–43; Freidberg, *Fresh*; Cronon, *Nature's Metropolis*, 97–147, 207–59; Petrick, "Arbiters of Taste." On meat, see Horowitz, *Putting Meat on the American Table*. On baby food, see Bentley, *Inventing Baby Food*. For a taste-centered analysis of food industrialization, see the case of the iceberg lettuce in Fitzgerald and Petrick, "In Good Taste."

64. See Levenstein, *Revolution at the Table*, 30–43; Shapiro, *Perfection Salad*, 192–216; Strasser, *Satisfaction Guaranteed*, 252–85. The history of white bread is particularly representative of how the food industry played on consumers' fears of adulteration to sell highly processed, and indeed adulterated, products; see Bobrow-Strain, *White Bread*.

65. "Processed Meats, the Sausage," Various Commodities and Products, Feeding the City, FWP-NYC, roll 137.

66. Claire Warner Churchill, "Please Pass the Potatoes," Oregon: Notes, Essays, Reports, LOC-AE, A832.

67. Ayers et al., *All Over the Map*, vii. For more perspective on the ideological diversity of regionalisms in the 1930s, see Denning, *Cultural Front*, 133.

68. Dorman, "Revolt of the Provinces," 2, emphasis in original.

69. Swislocki, *Culinary Nostalgia*, 26. Swislocki tracks the role of regional cuisines and nostalgia in the process of place making in Shangai, China.

70. William Lindsay White, "Beef Tour," 5, Kansas: Notes, Essays, Reports, LOC-AE, A831, clipping from newspaper article originally published in the *Emporia Gazette* on August 15–16, 1939.

71. Bold, *WPA Guides*, 10–11.

72. *U.S. One: Maine to Florida*, xvii–xxvii.

73. Florence Kerr, letter sent to seven states, July 18, 1941, Correspondence, August–October, 1941, LOC-AE, A829

74. John D. Newsom to James H. Crutcher, September 4, 1941. This remark was a perspicacious one; on the tripartite Texan racial organization see the work of historian Neil Foley (*White Scourge*, 1–2).

75. Eudora Ramsay Richardson to Henry G. Alsberg, November 12, 1937, Correspondence, 1937–1938, LOC-AE, A829.

76. John D. Newsom to James H. Crutcher, September 4, 1941; "Editorial Report on State Copy, Montana: The Herder," November 26, 1941, Correspondence, November–December 1941, LOC-AE, A830.

77. Rudolph Umland to John D. Newsom, December 1, 1941; Pearl Gimple to Florence Kerr, December 10, 1941, Correspondence, November–December 1941, LOC-AE, A830. On this "buckwheat controversy," see also Gabaccia, *We Are What We Eat*, 140

78. "New Hampshire," 2, New Hampshire: Notes, Essays, Reports, LOC-AE, A831; "The Northeast," unpaginated, Section Essay, LOC-AE, A832.

79. The motto first appeared on the state's license plates in 1940. Mark Mutt to Florence Kerr, redirected to Kellock, December 1941, Correspondence, November–December 1941, LOC-AE, A830.

80. Cohen, *Consumer's Republic*; McGovern, *Sold American*.

81. Gross, "American Guide Series."

82. "Editorial Report to Regional Editors of America Eats," 2; John D. Newsom to A. E. Michel, November 3, 1941, Correspondence, November–December 1941, LOC-AE, A830; John D. Newsom to Henry Armory, September 4, 1941, Correspondence, August–October 1941, LOC-AE, A829.

83. John D. Newsom to James H. Crutcher, September 11, 1941, Correspondence, August–October, 1941, LOC-AE, A829.

84. "Editorial Report to Regional Editors of America Eats," 2.

85. "Coca-Cola Parties," Georgia: Notes, Essays, Reports, LOC-AE, A831; Lyle Saxon to John D. Newsom, October 8, 1941, Correspondence, August–October, 1941, LOC-AE, A829.

86. "General Notes to Regional Editors of *America Eats*," 4.

87. Katherine Kellock, "Editorial Report," October 16, 1941, correction made on October 18, Correspondence, August–October, 1941, LOC-AE, A829.

88. Jacobson, *Whiteness*; Barrett and Roediger, "Inbetween Peoples"; Jacobson picks up the narrative in the early 1960s in his book *Roots Too*.

89. See Roediger, *Working toward Whiteness*, as well as his earlier *The Wages of Whiteness*; Cohen, *Making a New Deal*; Sugrue, *Origins of the Urban Crisis*, 10.

90. Gerstle, *American Crucible*, 128–86.

91. Lipsitz, *Rainbow at Midnight*, 339. For more insight on the racialized effects of New Deal policies on African Americans, see Ferguson, *Black Politics*.

92. The goals, staff, work, and archival material of the Negro Studies units is further analyzed in chapter 3 of this book. See also Sklaroff, *Black Culture and the New Deal*, 83–122.

93. Roi Ottley, "Cooking," November 5, 1938, New York, LOC-NSP, A885. During his time with the FWP, Ottley conducted research for two books that he later published, *New World A-Coming* (with W. J. Weatherby) and *The Negro in New York*. On Ottley's time with the FWP, see, Mangione, *Dream and the Deal*, 261–63; on his role in the intellectual life of the black metropolis, see also Gregory, *Southern Diaspora*, 115–16.

94. The Social-Ethnic Studies Project, for instance, documented Italian stone carvers and Portuguese fishermen in New England, as well as Southern Greek restaurateurs. The main outcome of this research was the anticipated but never-achieved publication of a series of books whose eloquent titles, such as "Hands that Built America," transmitted the pluralistic ideal of the New Deal era and the "laboring" of American culture over the course of the decade, identified by Michael Denning in *The Cultural Front*. The work of the Social-Ethnic Studies Project is archived in the Federal Writer's Project collection at the Library of Congress.

95. "Memorandum on the Albanians of Massachusetts," May 2, 1938, Massachusetts: Albanians, LOC-SES, A747.

96. Kellock, "Editorial Report," October 16, 1941.

97. "Outline Indicating Approach to the Subject," 8; "Memorandum," 2.

98. "General Notes to Regional Editors of *America Eats*," 4.

99. Edward B. Moulton to John D. Newsom, October 20, 1941, Correspondence, August–October, 1941, LOC-AE, A829.

100. John D. Newsom to Robert W. Allan, September 29, 1941, Correspondence, August–October, 1941, LOC-AE, A829.

101. "General Notes to Regional Editors of *America Eats*," 4.

102. Nora, *Realms of Memory*, 7–8.

103. Fitzgerald and Petrick, "In Good Taste," 393. For more insight into the elusiveness of taste, see Ferguson, "Senses of Taste," 383; Hoganson, *Consumers' Imperium*, 136. On the method of sensory history, see Smith, "Producing Sense," 849; Howes, "Expanding Field"; Howes, "Can These Dry Bones Live?"

104. Stoler, *Along the Archival Grain*, 38.

105. "Brief Description of Proposed Book," 4.

Chapter 2. Romance of the Homemade

1. "Big Thursday," 1–2, Delaware: Notes, Essays, Reports, LOC-AE, A830. The *America Eats* essay built on the description included in the 1938 American Guide Series' *Delaware: A Guide to the First State*, 402.

2. "Outline Indicating Approach to Subject"; Don Dolan, "Food a la Concentrate," California: Notes, Essays, Reports, LOC-AE, A830.

3. Levenstein, *Revolution at the Table*, 30–43. See also chapter 1 of this book.

4. FWP, *Delaware*, 403. In her discussion of the "racial contradictions" of southern consumption (*Making Whiteness*, 168–97), Grace Hale has powerfully demonstrated that although "whiteness became the homogenizing ground of the American mass market," both whites and blacks were coveted consumers of mass-produced consumer goods, including food.

5. Bentley, *Eating for Victory*. For a comparative perspective, see Mosby, *Food Will Win the War*.

6. Gabaccia, *We Are What We Eat*, 144.

7. On the construction of the black sensory apparatus as coarse and primitive and the role of this stereotype in the making of race in U.S. history, see Smith, *How Race Is Made*; Bederman, *Manliness and Civilization*, 170–215.

8. "Editorial Report: Illinois," November 24, 1941. Michael Denning, in his landmark study of 1930s culture, insists on the discrepancy between populist politics and populist rhetoric and considers the "people" as a "rhetorical stake in ideological battle" between the diverse brands of 1930s populism, namely, the social movements of the Right (such as those of Huey Long and Father Coughlin), the Popular Front and the CIO proletarian version of "the people," as well as, finally, the official "cultural populism" of the New Deal State, incarnated here by New Deal food writing. The FWP vision of the American people at the table can also be understood in light of historian Michael Kazin's bare-bones definition of U.S. populism as the conception of the citizenry as a "noble assemblage not bounded narrowly by class" but by its reverence to a mythic, national founding creed. Though the content of this creed was an object of political contention between the Right and Left of the political spectrum, it provided a stylistic framework to 1930s writers. As Kazin argues, the populist mode was "a grand form of rhetorical optimism" and "impulse" rather than an "ideology" that posed that, "once mobilized, there is nothing ordinary Americans cannot accomplish." The founding creed of sensory populism in New Deal food writing would be the belief in the moral superiority of so-called traditional foods compared to industrial foodstuffs. Kazin, *Populist Persuasion*, 1–3, and, on the 1930s in particular, 109–64; Denning, *Cultural Front*, 124. On reactionary populism during the Depression decade, see also Brinkley, *Voices of Protest*. For a Gramscian interpretation of the "cultural populism" of the New Deal Art Project, see Harris, *Federal Art and National Culture*, esp. 28–43.

9. "General Notes to Regional Editors of *America Eats*," 3.

10. On interwar food writing, see, Levenstein, *Paradoxes Of Plenty*, 9–38; Neuhaus, *Manly Meals*, 57–97; Helen Zoe Veit, *Modern Food, Moral Food*, 157–80.

11. On the figure of the hobo in 1930s America, see DePastino, *Citizen Hobo*, 200–220.

12. The term "Progressive Era" is used to describe the period from the 1890s to the 1920s in U.S. cultural, social, and political life. The period was a time of social activ-

ism and political reforms aimed at curtailing the excesses of capitalism. The movement cut across political lines and was marked by a rise of what historian Daniel Rogers has dubbed the "interventionist state" and of the role of professional experts in American life. Home economists and nutritionists are examples of such experts. Rogers stretches the chronological limits of the Progressive Era from the 1870s to the New Deal. See Rodgers, *Atlantic Crossings*, 1–6.

13. Veit, *Modern Food, Moral Food*, quotes are on p. 5; see also her discussion of vitamins and calories on pp. 45–49. For more insights on the Progressive Era nutritional order and the rise of scientific nutrition, see also Biltekoff, *Eating Right in America*, 12–50; Levenstein, *Paradox of Plenty*, 9–24.

14. Shapiro, *Perfection Salad*, 73, and see also 91–95.

15. Levenstein, *Revolution at the Table*, 147–60; Levenstein, *Paradox of Plenty*, 9–23.

16. Levenstein, *Paradox of Plenty*, 60–62; Veit, *Modern Food, Moral Food*, 25; Biltekoff, *Eating Right*, 48–50.

17. "Brief Description of Proposed Book," 2.

18. "Delaware Eats," October 1941, Delaware: Notes, Essays, Reports, LOC-AE, A830. Dolan, "Food a la Concentrate."

19. Levenstein, *Paradox of Plenty*, 25.

20. Longstreth, *Drive-In* (quote is on p. 112). On the changes in food retailing during the Depression, see also Deutsch, *Building a Housewife's Paradise*, 73–154; 144–49.

21. Donald McCormick, "Personal Information on Maine Food," 1, December 1, 1941, Maine: Notes, Essays, Reports, LOC-AE, A831.

22. Deutsch, *Building a Housewife's Paradise*, 52; Cohen, *Making a New Deal*, 235–38.

23. Biltekoff, *Eating Right in America*, 23–24; for more insights on sensory hierarchies and modernity, see Smith, *Sensing the Past*, 1–18.

24. "Editorial Report: Illinois," November 24, 1941; Katherine Kellock, "Editorial Report: South Dakota," November 22, 1941, Correspondence, November–December, 1941, LOC-AE, A830.

25. The FWP editors explicitly referred to the "light" tone of the book in three documents: "Brief Description of the Proposed Book;" "General Notes to Regional Editors of *America Eats*," 3; John D. Newsom to Henry Armory, September 4, 1941.

26. "Church Supper," 2, Delaware: Notes, Essays, Reports, LOC-AE, A830.

27. A box dinner was a popular social event in the early 1900s and into the 1930s. Each participating girl brought a boxed meal for one or two; the boxes were auctioned off to the participating men, who would then eat their meal in the company of the girl who had prepared it. See, "Box-supper," Georgia: Notes, Essay, Reports, LOC-AE, A831; "Box Social," "School Box Supper," Nebraska: Notes, Essays, Reports, LOC-AE, A831; "Box and Pie Dinner," Texas: Food, Celebrations, LOC-FP, A681.

28. "Fish Fry," Nebraska: Notes, Essays, Reports, LOC-AE, A831; Luther Clark, "Rodeo with Barbecue," 2, Alabama: Notes, Essays, Reports, LOC-AE, A830.

29. "All Day Preaching and Dinner on the Ground," Alabama: Notes, Essays, Reports, LOC-AE, A830.

30. E. J. Moss, "School Picnic," Nebraska: Notes, Essays, Reports, LOC-AE, A831.

31. T. S. Ferree, "North Carolina Camp Meeting Dinner," North Carolina: Notes, Essays, Reports, LOC-AE, A831.

32. Jean Winkler, "Cypress Ridge Singing Convention," Arkansas: Notes, Essays, Reports, LOC-AE, A830.

33. See for instance, George Round, "Fun Feeds," *Lincoln Sunday Journal and Star*, April, 15, 1934, Nebraska: Notes, Essays, Reports, A LOC-AE, A831

34. As James Gregory explains, "World War II, still a distant nightmare for most Americans in 1941, was nevertheless beginning to rearrange the economy and political priorities, especially on the strategically important West Coast." Gregory, *American Exodus*, 99.

35. Reynolds, "Far West," 57–59.

36. The essay on Yankee "penny-pinchers" explains that "to be thrifty is to avoid unnecessary waste, and in cooking to be ingenious is to devise ways and means of being thrifty with wholesome and tasty results. Thrift, born of necessity, has become a Yankee tradition which, unfortunately, has given rise to the idea among the uninitiated that the Yankees are penny-pinchers." Untitled essay, New Hampshire: Notes, Essays, Reports, LOC-AE, A831.

37. On community meals and church dinners in particular, see "Chicken Pie Supper," Vermont: Notes, Essays, Reports, LOC-AE, A832; Donald McCormick, "The Maine Church Supper," November 29, 1941, Maine: Notes, Essays, Reports, A831; "Church Fellowship Dinner," Kansas: Notes, Essays, Reports, A831; "The Church Dinner or Supper," Indiana: Notes, Essays, Reports, LOC-AE, A831.

38. "Church Fellowship Supper," 2.

39. "Wyoming Eats," 7, Wyoming: Notes, Essays, Reports, LOC-AE, A832.

40. "Brief Description of Proposed Book," 2 and 8.

41. Boym, *Future of Nostalgia*, 12, 42.

42. I am borrowing here Mark Swislocki's frame of analysis in his study of the culinary nostalgia for Chinese regional food in Shanghai from the fifteenth century onward. Swislocki, *Culinary Nostalgia*, 1–11.

43. Rosaldo, "Imperialist Nostalgia," 108.

44. "Brief Description of Proposed Book," 2.

45. Untitled, 4–5, New Hampshire: Notes, Essays, Reports, LOC-AE, A831; Brooks, "America Eats (Southwest Section)," version 1, 35, Section Essay, LOC-AE, A833; "All Day Preaching and Dinner on the Ground," 3.

46. Sutton, *Remembrance of Repasts*, 125–56.

47. On heritage cookbooks in the 1930s, see Mendelson, "Cookbooks and Manuscripts."

48. J. Willis Kratzer, "The School Picnic," Nebraska: Notes, Essays, Reports, LOC-AE, A831. For more insight into the tension between authenticity and imitation in interwar American cultural life, see Orvell, *Real Thing*.

49. The comments on ham are, respectively, from "Cypress Ridge Singing Convention," and Eudora Ramsay Richardson, "Virginia (Food along U.S. 1)," 2, Virginia: Notes, Essays, Reports, LOC-AE, A832.

50. Reynolds, "Far West," 94; Gladys Gregg, "Colorado Eats," 7, Colorado: Notes, Essays, Reports, LOC-AE, A830.

51. Reynolds, "Far West," 73.

52. "Chicken Pie Supper," Vermont: Notes, Essays, Reports, LOC-AE, A832.

53. "Rhode Island Johnny Cakes," Rhodes Island: Notes, Essays, Reports, LOC-AE, A832; "American: National Dish," 2, Wisconsin: Food, LOC-FP, A694; "Paul Bunyan Dines," Washington State: Notes Essays, Reports, LOC-AE, A832.

54. Thige, untitled, December 3, 1941, 3, Pennsylvania: Notes, Essays, Reports, LOC-AE, A832, capitalization in the original.

55. Abrahamsen, "Culinary Goodies," 2.

56. The description is from Donna Gabaccia, who discusses lutefisk in the *America Eats* archive in *We Are What We Eat*, 142–43.

57. "The Lutefisk Dinner," Wisconsin: Notes, Essays, Reports, LOC-AE, A832. Lutefisk and smorgasbord dinners are documented in a series of essay in the *America Eats* archive; see "America Eats: A contribution written by members of the North Dakota Writers' Project for the publication of the WPA Writers' program entitled America Eats," 5–9, North Dakota, Notes, Essays, Reports, AE-LOC, A830; Ethel Bristol, "Church Smorgasbord," 2, Nebraska: Notes, Essays, Reports, LOC-AE, A830; "Racial Traditions and Customs," 17, Idaho: Notes, Essays, Reports, AE-LOC, A831; Reynolds, "Far West."

58. For more insight on ethnic food, the senses, and authenticity, see also Hoganson, *Consumers' Imperium*, 10 and 121; such construction of ethnic sensory authenticity omitted the fact that, by the 1930s, canned and ready-to-eat versions of preferred ethnic dishes were already available for U.S. consumers to purchase (Gabaccia, *We Are What We Eat*, 64–121).

59. "America Eats: A contribution written by members of the North Dakota Writers' Project," 10.

60. "Barbecue, Fourth of July," 1, Indiana: Notes, Essays, Reports, LOC-AE, A831.

61. Abrahamsen, "Culinary Goodies, Cape Cod Style," 2. A similar argument appears in FWP, *U.S. One*, xvii–xviii.

62. Melosh, *Engendering Culture*; Kessler-Harris, "In the Nation's Image."

63. "Footwashing at Lonely Dale," Alabama: Notes, Essays, Reports, LOC-AE, A830; "Family Reunion and Sunday Dinner," Mississippi: Notes, Essays, Reports, LOC-AE, A831.

64. Thige, untitled, 3. This same description of an egg salad can be found in the cookbook *Pennsylvania Dutch Cook Book: Fine Old Recipes Made Famous by the Early Dutch Settlers in Pennsylvania*, published in 1936, suggesting that Thige, the author of this FWP essay, plagiarized his source.

65. White, "Beef Tour," 5. The newspaper article was originally published in the *Emporia Gazette* on August 15–16, 1939.

66. "Editorial Report: Illinois," November 24, 1941.

67. White, "Beef Tour," 5.

68. Bentley, *Eating for Victory*, 5. On the continuity between the 1930s and the postwar period, see also May, "Cold War–Warm Hearth," and Neuhaus, *Manly Meals*, 137.

69. Deutsch, "Memories," 170; see also Deutsch, *Building a Housewife's Paradise*.

70. Elaine Tyler May coined the notion of "domestic containment" in reference to the 1950s Cold War tactic of "containment" that aimed at curtailing the spread of communism: see May, *Homeward Bound*. On cookbooks and gender in the postwar era, see Neuhaus, *Manly Meals*, 161–259.

71. Reynolds, "Far West."

72. Gregg, "Colorado Eats," 7.

73. Amy Bentley notes that, "despite the overwhelming emphasis on private war aims, it was important to offer glimpses of a more communally oriented vision of America . . . to ensure that the country would maintain enough unified sense of itself to win the war. While wartime rhetoric in the United States focused on private material and

familial interests, the lens somewhat broadens when it comes to wartime food rationing and women's role as family food manager." Overall, if the food rationing propaganda emphasized the common good, women would foster it not by cooking together but by making patriotic choices when shopping and cooking for their families. Bentley, *Eating for Victory*, 3–6 and 59–84 (quote on p. 3).

74. "Brief Description of Proposed Book," 8.

75. "General Notes to Regional Editors of *America Eats*," 1.

76. Franck Bardon, "Barbecue," November 16, 1937, Texas: Folklore, LOC-AGF, A443.

77. Ibid.; Clark, "Rodeo with Barbecue," 2.

78. Reynolds, "Far West," 86–87.

79. The "gusto" leitmotif is especially perceptible in Brooks, "America Eats (Southwest Section)," version 2.

80. Reynolds, "Far West," 1–2 and 86–87.

81. White, "Beef Tour," 5.

82. On manliness in the New Deal era, see Melosh, *Engendering Culture*; Kimmel, *Manhood in America*, 127–46.

83. John D. Newsom to State Directors, December 12, 1941, Correspondence, November–December 1941, LOC-AE, A830.

84. On wartime food rationing and food propaganda, see Bentley, *Eating for Victory*; Biltekoff, *Eating Right*, 50–79.

85. On the FWP "Negro Units," the FWP Negro Studies Project as well as African American foodways in New Deal food writing, see chapter 3.

86. Jennifer Stoever-Ackerman theorizes the "sonic color-line" in her article "Splicing the Sonic Color-Line," 65–67.

87. John W. Thomas, "Chicken," 1, Virginia: Notes, Essays, Reports, AE-LOC, A832. On stereotypes associating blacks and chicken, see, Williams-Forson, *Building Houses*.

88. "William Wheeler Talk," Mississippi: Notes, Essays, Reports, AE-LOC, A831.

89. Katherine Palmer, "Chittlin Strut," North Carolina: Notes, Essays, Reports, LOC-AE, A832;

90. Ibid.; "Fish Fry On the Levee," Mississippi: Notes, Essays, Reports, LOC-AE, A831.

91. "The South," 53 Section Essay, LOC-AE, A833. See also "Big Quarterly," Delaware: Notes, Essays, Reports, LOC-AE, A830.

92. FWP, *Delaware*, 263–64. This was already a tamed version since, to his credit, federal director Henry Alsberg had dismissed a 1936 draft by noting that "'mob' is hardly a word to describe an orderly crowd, or even a noisy crowd of religious folk, and there is no more reason to use this group as a laboratory than there would be to use a gathering of Nordic Rollers or Episcopalians. The Negro is no longer considered a pathological specimen except among the prejudiced." Henry Alsberg to Jeanette Eckman, November 6, 1936, Correspondence relating to Folklore Studies, 1936–1940, Alabama to Mississippi, RG 69.

93. Katherine Palmer, "Tobacco Barn Brunswick Stew," 4, North Carolina: Notes, Essays, Reports, LOC-AE, A831.

94. J. B. Cook, "Richmond, Virginia, 1919–1941, Sergeant Saunder's Brunswick Stew," Virginia: Notes, Essays, Reports, LOC-AE, A832.

95. Louise Jones Dubose, "Chicken Bog," October 10, 1941, South Carolina: Notes, Essays, Reports, LOC-AE, A832.

96. Williams-Forson, *Building Houses*, 45; Palmer, "Tobacco Barn Brunswick Stew," 24.

97. Stetson Kennedy, "A Ton of Rice and Three Red Roosters," 1, Florida: Notes, Essays, Reports, LOC-AE, A830.

98. Stetson Kennedy's biography is detailed at http://www.stetsonkennedy.com (accessed November 19, 2014). His books include *Southern Exposure* and *The Klan Unmasked*, first published as *I Rode with the Ku Klux Klan* in 1954. Kennedy wrote an informative introduction to the Florida Folklore material collection in the Florida Folklife Archive in which he details his and others' work, including Zora Neale Hurston's, see Kennedy, "Florida Folklife and the WPA."

99. Kennedy, "Ton of Rice," 4.

100. Williams-Forson posits how the cliché of the harmless and obedient ex-slave existed in conjunction with an "over-sexualized image of black men whose presence was a threat to white womanhood." The figure of the threatening black man was at the root of the southern argument for the need of legal racial segregation and triggered violent lynchings in the region. See Williams-Forson, *Building Houses*, 45–48 and 50. For further perspective on gender and lynching in the New South, see Gilmore, *Gender and Jim Crow*, 82–89. For further insight into sensory stereotypes, see Smith, *How Race Is Made*, especially pp. 88–89 on taste.

101. Warnes, *Savage Barbecue*, 6 and 103.

102. Clark, "Rodeo with Barbecue," 1.

103. "The South: Women Stop the Meat From Breathing," 1–2, Section Essay, LOC-AE, A833. The regional southern essay builds on a Mississippi essay titled "Political Barbecue," prepared by Frances Watkins Bruguiere and Harrison Saunders, Mississippi: Notes, Essays, Reports, LOC-AE A831. The FWP worker, in all probability Lyle Saxon, who composed the regional essay was enrapt enough with the gendered detail of the piece to change the title from the descriptive "Political Barbecue" to the sensationalist "Women Stop the Meat from Breathing."

104. Bruguiere and Saunders, "Political Barbecue," 2.

105. "Harlem Negro," Feeding the City: Eating Out, draft, roll 144, FWP-NYC. "Suggestion for Characteristic Meals," 2, Kentucky: Notes, Essays, Reports, LOC-AE, A831. On chitterlings in the *America Eats* archive, see also, Gabaccia, *We Are What We Eat*, 141.

106. "Chitlin' Supper," Indiana: Notes, Essays, Reports, LOC-AE, A831; "Menu for Chitterling Strut (A North Carolina Negro Celebration)," North Carolina: Notes, Essays, Reports, LOC-AE, A832.

107. For more perspective on the history of chitterlings, see McDearma and Abbott, "Chitterlings," 143–45; quote is on p. 145.

108. "Mississippi Chitlins," Mississippi: Notes, Essays, Reports, A831.

109. "Suggestion for Characteristic Meals," 2, Kentucky: Notes, Essays, Reports, LOC-AE, A831, emphasis in original.

110. Dixon, "A Picnic Dinner in Fairfax County," 2, North Carolina: Notes, Essays, Reports, LOC-AE, A832.

111. Probyn, *Carnal Appetites*, 127–46, quotes are on pp. 140 and 141; Korsmeyer, *Savoring Disgust*, 61–86. Wazana Tompkins, *Racial Indigestion*.

112. FWP, *Louisiana*, 230. On Madame C. J. Walker, see Peiss, *Hope in a Jar*; Baldwin, *Chicago's New Negroes*, 53–90.

113. Sharpless, *Cooking*, 177–176.

114. Bentley highlights the role of black cooks in assuring the "psychic security" of white households in wartime; see Bentley, *Eating for Victory*, 63 and 78–80. On the "mammy" stereotype, see Manring, *Slave in a Box*; McElya, *Clinging to Mammy*; Witt, *Black Hunger*, 21–53; Hale, *Making Whiteness*, 98–115 and 155–60. See also chapter 3 for more insight on the place of black cooks in New Deal food writing.

115. "The South: We Refreshes Our Hog Meat with Corn Pone," 2, Section Essay, LOC-AE, A833; "Menu for Chitterling Strut"; "Chitlin' Supper."

116. "Fish Fry on the Levee," 1.

117. In *Building Houses out of Chicken Legs*, Psyche Williams-Forson explores the role of black women's small-scale food businesses in sustaining African American communities. She presents black women as community entrepreneurs who, "while [their] lives were being caricatured using food . . . were learning valuable skills in cooking and catering" and highlights how "the trading and selling of theses foods for commerce also provided relative autonomy, social power, and economic freedom" (*Building Houses*, 65 and 35, see especially chapter 1, "We Called Ourselves Waiter Carriers," 2–37).

118. This is the broad narrative adopted in Harvey Levenstein, *Paradox of Plenty*, 101–30; Bentley, *Eating for Victory*, 171–79; Gabaccia, *We Are What We Eat*, 149–74; and more recently in Biltekoff, *Eating Right in America*, 45–79.

Chapter 3. Tasting Place, Sensing Race

1. Chalmers S. Murray, "WPA Road," Edisto Island, South Carolina, January 1939, ALH online, http://www.loc.gov/item/wpalh002105 (accessed November 17, 2014).

2. On Chalmers S. Murray, see Spencer, *Edisto Island*, 165–66. Seven of his essays are available on the Web site for the Library of Congress's American Life Histories.

3. Smith, *How Race Is Made*, 88.

4. "Miscellaneous Notes for Mr. Saxon," Administrative Material, LOC-AE, A829.

5. Ferguson, "The Senses of Taste," 371.

6. Smith, *How Race Is Made*, 4,

7. Gerstle, *American Crucible*, 162–86.

8. Classic texts on the Great Migration are James R. Grossman's *Land of Hope* and James N. Gregory's *The Southern Diaspora*. See also Baldwin, *Chicago's New Negroes*.

9. On soul food, see Opie, *Hog and Hominy*; Witt, *Black Hunger*; Poe, "Origins of Soul Food"; Mosley, "Cooking Up Heritage in Harlem."

10. Smith, *How Race Is Made*.

11. Jack Kytle, "Alabama Eggnog," Alabama: Notes, Essays, Reports, LOC-AE, A830.

12. Sharpless, *Cooking*, 141–45; Smith, *How Race Is Made*, 88.

13. Smith, *How Race Is Made*, 6.

14. Kytle, "Alabama Eggnog;" FWP, *New Orleans City Guide*, xvi.

15. On the "branding" of the "edible Old South" for tourist consumption, see Ferris, *Edible South*, 188–242, and on New Orleans in particular, 218–27. For examples of the treatment of food in the American Guide Series, see "Eating and Drinking," FWP, *North Carolina*, 101–6; "Cuisine," FWP, *Louisiana*, 225–31; "Cookery," FWP, *South Carolina*, 152–56.

16. FWP, *New Orleans City Guide*, liii. Southern cuisine was the result of local relationships between cultural, social, and racial groups—from enslaved Africans and Indigenous

people to Spanish, French, and British explorers and planters—living and working in ecosystems shaped by the "Columbian Exchange," which designates the exchange in foodstuffs, animals, disease, and people after the arrival of Christopher Columbus in the Caribbean. See Crosby, *Columbian Exchange*. On the Creole history of southern food, see Gabaccia, *We Are What We Eat*, 10–35; McWilliams, *Revolution in Eating*, 89–166.

17. Kennedy, "Florida Folklife and the WPA, an Introduction."

18. Sklaroff, *Black Culture and the New Deal*, 2; on African American writers in the FWP and Sterling Brown's work in particular, see pages 83–122.

19. The archives of the Negro Studies Project are part of the Federal Writers' Project collection at the Library of Congress, the bulk of which can be found in boxes A649 through A890. The papers of the Harlem Negro Unit are part of the New York Public Library collection at the Schomburg Center for Research in Black Culture as well as the New York City municipal archives. The bulk of the correspondence for the project is part of the National Archives and Records Administration Record Group 69.

20. "The Household of Ruth Annual Meeting and Dinner," 2, Alabama: Notes, Essays, Reports, LOC-AE, A830. An earlier version of the essay, titled "Annual Household of Ruth," dated from June 21, 1938, and signed by Ila B. Prine concludes on the racist note: "One has never heard the old time darkies sing in their own church has missed a stirring occasion." Prine was a white FWP worker who worked on a series of the FWP's project in the state, notably conducting interviews with ex-slaves; digital copies can be found on the Library of Congress's website, http://memory.loc.gov/cgi-bin/query/S?ammem/ mesnbib:@field(OTHER+@od1(ila+b+prine))::heading=Interviewer--Ila+B.+Prine (accessed October 2, 2014).

21. Sharpless, *Cooking*, 144; Smith, *How Race Is Made*, 88.

22. "Alabama Barbecue," 3, Alabama: Notes, Essays, Reports, LOC-AE, A830; "The South: Family Reunion in Lay-by Time," Section Essay, LOC-AE, A833.

23. "Alabama Barbecue," 3.

24. On the cultural and racial politics of wheat bread and cornbread in the region, see Engelhardt, *Mess of Greens*, 51–82.

25. Smith, *How Race Is Made*, 6.

26. *Ibid.*, 50. On the "separation or ritual 'break' between black food preparation and white food consumption," see also Mary Titus, "'Groaning Tables,'" 16. Grace Hale describes the southern white home as an "island of racial mixing in a sea of separation" and explores its role in the enforcement of racial segregation in *Making Whiteness*, 85–119 (quote is on page 87). See also, Sharpless, *Cooking*, 135 and 143. For a similar argument about black men cooking in the army in the 1940s, see Williams-Forson, *Building Houses*, 71–79.

27. "Virginiaham Is One Word," 5.

28. "A mimeographed pamphlet prepared by Eudora Welty for the Mississippi Advertising Commission and distributed by them," Mississippi: Notes, Essays, Reports, LOC-AE, A831. Mrs. T. C. Billup from Columbus, Mississippi, shared this recollection with African American FWP worker Eudora Welty, who included it in her pamphlet, making its interpretation tricky. Was Welty's goal to expose the myth of the benevolent, peaceful "Old South" constructed by the white South? Was she catering to a white audience? She probably did both at once with her remark about the culinary glory and "charm of the Old South." It is also worth noting that Welty's pamphlet was not written for *America Eats*

but rather added as documentation to the project's file. She participated in other FWP projects: see Kurlansky, *Food of a Younger Land*, 115.

29. Richardson, "Virginia (Food along U.S. 1)," 4.

30. John E. Doar, "King Oyster," Norfolk, Virginia: Notes, Essays, Reports, LOC-AE, A832.

31. Blight, *Race and Reunion*; Silber, *Romance of Reunion*; Hale, *Making Whiteness*, 43–84. The "New South" refers here to a place, a time, and an ideology. The "New South" emerged gradually from the ashes of the Reconstruction period; it was, at its origin, a blueprint for the region's economic development after slavery, a blueprint designed by a renewed industrialist white elite. It became synonymous with racial segregation and the white supremacist ideology. See Woodward, *Origins of the New South* and *The Strange Career of Jim Crow*.

32. "Kentucky's Table," 5, Kentucky: Notes, Essays, Reports, AE-LOC, A831; Kytle, "Alabama Eggnog."

33. Manring, *Slave in a Box*, 140–41; McElya, *Clinging to Mammy*, 72; Grace Hale notes that the popularity of Aunt Jemima ragdolls assured that "not every child could have a servant but all but the poorest could have her very own pancake mammy." Hale, *Making Whiteness*, 98–115 and 155–64; quote is on p. 161. On the mythic figure of the mammy, see also Manring, *Slave in a Box*; Witt, *Black Hunger*, 21–53.

34. McElya, *Clinging to Mammy*, 16.

35. Swilling, "North Georgia Cookery," September 1937, Georgia: Cuisine, LOC-AGF, A70.

36. Smith, *Sensing the Past*, 8–11; Ferguson, "Senses of Taste," 376–81.

37. Bower, *Recipes for Reading*; Avakian and Haber, *From Betty Crocker*; Theophano, *Eat My Words*.

38. "Kentucky's Table," 1.

39. Tompkins, *Racial Indigestion*, 43–52; Kaplan, "Manifest Domesticity."

40. McElya, *Clinging to Mammy*, 144.

41. FWP, *North Carolina*, 103.

42. "A mimeographed pamphlet"; Southern historian Anthony Stanonis, among others, explains that "blacks' reluctance to write down recipes suggested that they understood the power of their cooking skills under Jim Crow" (*Dixie Emporium*, 212); See also Sharpless, *Cooking*, xxi; Witt, *Black Hunger*, 13.

43. Kytle, "Alabama Eggnog"; "Wilmore Camp Meeting," Kentucky: Notes, Essays, Reports, LOC-AE, A831.

44. Smith, *How Race Is Made*.

45. "Cuisine Peculiar to the State, Southeast Missouri, Sikeston District," February 17, 1936, Missouri: Foods, LOC-FP, A628.

46. Smith, *How Race Is Made*, 6.

47. "Mullet Salad," Mississippi: Notes, Essays, Reports, LOC-AE, A831; Demmon, "Eating Prejudices," May 1, 1938, "Foods, Celebration," Indiana, LOC-FP, A600.

48. Mary H. Weik, "Introduction to Restaurant in New York," FWP-NYC, roll 19.

49. Wayne, "Migrant Women's Modernity."

50. "Feeding the City: Draft," "Eating Out: Inexpensively," FWP-NYC, roll 153.

51. Sarah Chavez, "Feeding the City: Eating Out," "Harlem Restaurants," October 1, 1940, FWP-NYC, roll 144.

52. I am inspired here by Eric Lott's classic study (*Love and Theft*) of the role of black-face performance in the construction of white identity in the United States. On blackface performances of the mammy character, see McElya, *Clinging to Mammy*, 63–66.

53. Franck Byrd, "The Ofay Problem in Harlem," 3, New York, LOC-NSP, A885; Ofay was black slang for "white."

54. Roediger and Barrett, "Inbetween Peoples"; Jacobson, *Whiteness of a Different Color*; Guglielmo and Salerno, *Are Italians White?*; Guterl, *Color of Race in America*.

55. Frank Byrd, "Nitelife in Harlem," 16–17, New York, LOC-NSP, A885. For further insight into the racial and sexual politics of slumming and the role of this popular activity in redefining and re-inscribing racial difference, see Heap, *Slumming*, 191–227, especially p. 223, on how "Italians and Jews who visited these districts increasingly positioned themselves as white consumers of a black spectacle."

56. Baxter R. Leach, "Restaurants," 3, reel 3, FWP-NYC-Schomburg.

57. Wilbur Young, "New York City Guide: Hotels, Restaurants, Night Clubs," "Tillie's Chicken Grill," FWP-NYC, Roll 19.

58. This point is central to bell hooks's classic essay, "Eating the Other."

59. Leach, "Restaurant," 3.

60. On the importance of urban black neighborhoods in the creation of modern black identity, see Baldwin, *Chicago's New Negroes*, 9–12; Corbould, *Becoming African Americans*; Gregory, *Southern Diaspora*, 113–52.

61. On the tensions between northern black populations and newly arrived southern migrants regarding food, see Poe, "Origins of Soul Food," 7–10; Grossman, *Land of Hope*, 150–54. For a broader assessment of the relationship between "old" and "new" settlers in the northern metropolis, see Baldwin, *Chicago's New Negroes*, 21–52.

62. Historians have identified the 1930s politicization of the community as the seeds of the postwar civil rights movement. See Sitkoff, *New Deal for Blacks*; Greenberg, *Or Does It Explode?*; Kelley, *Hammer and Hoe*, 212.

63. On black urban food in the interwar period, see Opie, *Hog and Hominy*, 55–100; Poe, "Origins of Soul Food"; Mosley, "Cooking Up Heritage in Harlem."

64. Dorothy West, "Cocktail Party: Personal Experience," January 10, 1939, ALH Online, http://www.loc.gov/item/wpalh001722 (accessed on November 17, 2014); The "crème de la crème" quote is from Byrd, "Nitelife in Harlem,"

65. Poe, "Origins of Soul Food," 25–27.

66. "Negroes of New York," 2, roll 263, FWP-NYC. Though no author is mentioned in the archived draft of "Negroes of New York," it is widely attributed to Roi Ottley, who published it as a book in the late 1960s. Ottley and Weatherby, *Negro in New York*.

67. Ottley, "Cooking." On the use of chicken in racist stereotypes, see Williams-Forson, *Building Houses*, 38–79.

68. Richard Wright, "A Survey of the Amusement Facilities of District #35," Chicago, Ill: Contemporary Culture, LOC-NSP, A875; "The Negro in Manhattan," 12, reel 3, FWP-NYC-Schomburg.

69. Jack Smith, "Negro Folk Expressions Peculiar to Iowa," Iowa: Folklore, LOC-NSP, A881.

70. Roi Ottley, "Speech," May 24, 1938, New York: Contemporary Culture, LOC-NSP, A885. The expression "monkey chaser" was derogatory and unveils the tension within the New York black community. Jack Smith explained: "The noun implies that the Negroes

of the English possession live in close physical and spiritual bondage with the apes and monkeys of their own islands. It means more than this. It means that you can't tell one from the other—and to a West Indian it means a fight" (Smith, "Negro Folk Expressions").

71. Laura Middleton, "Negro Lore, Food, and Drink," "Negro Restaurants in Charleston," South Carolina, LOC-FP, A670.

72. Opie, *Hog and Hominy*, 95. On toting, see Sharpless, *Cooking*, 74–77.

73. FWP, *Louisiana*, 230.

74. FWP, *South Carolina*, 154.

75. Smith, *Sensing the Past*, 90.

76. FWP, *Louisiana*, 231.

77. "Cookery," in FWP, *South Carolina*, 155.

78. All these terms are repeatedly used throughout the FWP research papers, typescripts, and books.

79. Ferris, *Edible South*, 128–31.

80. "The South," 3.

81. FWP, *South Carolina*, 155.

82. Engelhardt, *Mess of Greens*, 51–82. For a more detailed discussion of dietary reform in the late-nineteenth and early-twentieth-century South, see Ferris, *Edible South*, 109–65. On scientific explanations of African Americans dietary choices, see Ferris, *Edible South*, 157–58. See also Smith, *How Race Is Made*: on vernacular explanations for poor nutrition, 88–89; and on class distinctions and tensions in the white southern community, 92–95.

83. For further insight into the FWP interviews with poor whites, see Stephen Fender, "Poor Whites," 141–63; Currell, "Introduction," 8–9.

84. Barbara Berry Darsey, "Alice Fairweather: Squatter Farmer," December 16–20, 1938, ALH Online, http://www.loc.gov/item/wpalh000394 (accessed November 17, 2014).

85. Elvira Burnell, "Anna Alden," February 16, 1939, ALH Online, http://www.loc.gov/item/wpalh000384 (accessed November 17, 2014).

86. "A Florida Squatter Family," December 1938, ALH Online, http://www.loc.gov/item/wpalh000489 (accessed November 17, 2014).

87. The comment about the cohabitation between white and black is from FWP, *Cincinnati*, 191.

88. On New Deal photographic programs in the South, see, Kidd, "Dissonant Encounters," 25–47. Nicholas Natanson notes (*Black Image*, 4) the underrepresentation of blacks in the iconic images of the South in the period.

89. Kirby, *Media-Made Dixie*, 64. See also, Hale, *Making Whiteness*, 134 and 185.

90. Reba Wood, "Cotton Row 'Cue," 3, Georgia: Notes, Essays, Reports, LOC-AE, A831.

91. Ibid., 3.

92. Smith, *How Race Is Made*, 6.

93. On the making of the musical/sonic color line at the same period, see Miller, *Segregating Sound*; Stoever-Ackerman, "Splicing the Sonic Color-Line"; Corbould, "Streets, Sounds, and Identity."

94. Opie, *Hog and Hominy*, 132

95. On whether people become "soulful" by eating soul food or whether foods become "soulful" when eaten by "soul people" as well as the variegated position taken within the African American community on this question, see Witt, *Black Hunger*, 7–17.

96. On the issue of the "historical accuracy" of soul food and its problematic status as an "iconic cuisine," see Mosley, "Cooking," 274–91.

Chapter 4. An American Culinary Heritage?

1. Three versions of the same essay exist. The first one was written by the Texas FWP for *America Eats* and titled "Mexican Quarter Chili Stands," Texas: Notes, Essays, Reports, LOC-AE, A832. Arthur J. Brooks reworked the Texas essay in both versions of the section essay, sometimes word for word; see, Brooks, "America Eats (Southwest Section)," version 1, 16–18 and "America Eats (Southwest Section)," version 2, January 1942, 10–14, LOC-AE, A833. Similar narratives can be found in the archives of the American Guide Series and Folklore Projects; see for instance, Salinas, "Chile Stands," 4, Hispano Lore, Texas: Folklore, LOC-AGF, A444.

2. On the San Antonio's "Chili Queens," see Pilcher, "Who Chased Out the 'Chili Queens'?" and Pilcher, *Planet Taco*, 105–29.

3. "Mexican Quarter Chili Stands," 3–4; Brooks, "America Eats (Southwest Section)," version 1, 17.

4. There is a vast literature on tourism in the Southwest; see, Kropp, *California Vieja*; the essays in Rothman, *Culture of Tourism*; Mullin, *Culture in the Marketplace*; the essays in Wrobel and Long, *Seeing and Being Seen*; Wilson, *Myth of Santa Fe*; Dilworth, *Imagining Indians*; Hyde, *American Vision*.

5. Brooks, "America Eats (Southwest Section)," version 1, 17

6. Gutiérrez, *Walls and Mirrors*, 7 and 13–38.

7. Ngai, *Impossible Subjects*, 67.

8. Some scholars draw analogies between the Southwest kaleidoscopic racial landscape and language; Linda Gordon, in her analysis of Arizona, for instance, states that "race is like a language, structured out of irregularities as well as rules, the inconsistencies as numerous as those of English grammar" (*Great Arizona Orphan Abduction*, 97–105, quote is on p. 97). Others compare it to tectonic plates; for instance, in his study of central Texas's racial hierarchy, Neil Foley considers how whiteness and "Mexicaness . . . shifted over time, slipping over and under one another and creating new ethnoracial terrain" (*White Scourge*, 211, see also 5–13).

9. Almaguer, *Racial Fault Lines*, 3; see also, 1–13, 205–6, 210.

10. Gordon, *Great Arizona Orphan Abduction*, 98.

11. On the history of Mexican American cultural and political identity in the first half of the twentieth century, see, Sanchez, *Becoming Mexican American*.

12. Kropp, *California Vieja*, 9; Foley, *White Scourge*, 8. Writing on whiteness in the southwest, Pablo Mitchell explains that "to claim whiteness . . . Anglos . . . could not simply racialize Indians and Hispanos as nonwhite" but "would have to assert their own whiteness as well, in effect racialize themselves as white" (*Coyote Nation*, 5).

13. Brooks, "America Eats (Southwest Section)," version 2, 2.

14. Analyzing the process of regional sensory commodification and unification is at the core of the project of this chapter; therefore, I will mention geographical indications but will address local specificities only when necessary to the understanding of the FWP records. The *America Eats* project divided the "West," into two regions (not counting the

Middle West): the "Southwest" and the "Far West." Though the focus of this chapter is on the Southwest, I occasionally use primary sources from the other two, especially the files from the "Far West." Following the FWP's geographical filing system, the "Southwest" was composed of the states of Texas, Southern California, New Mexico, Arizona, and Oklahoma. The "Far West" was composed of Colorado, Idaho, Montana, Nevada, Northern California, Oregon, Utah, Washington State and Wyoming.

15. Edward P. Ware, "Some Things the Spanish Americans Eat," 10, subsection of an article entitled "Out-of-doors-cookery," Arizona: Notes, Essays, Reports, LOC-AE, A830.

16. Deutsch, *No Separate Refuge*, 36.

17. Pilcher, "Tex-Mex," 659.

18. Brooks, "America Eats (Southwest Section)," version 1, 30.

19. The term "Tex Mex," coined in the late 1960s, often points to industrialized and commercialized versions of Southwestern cuisine. Robb Walsh, journalist and cookbook author, studied the web of meaning around the notion of Tex-Mex cuisine and showed how, in the wake of the publication of Dianna Kennedy's *The Cuisines of Mexico* in 1972, this adjective was first used in a derogatory way to point to "inauthentic" Mexican foods served in the United States. It was forged as a condescending adjective to describe foods, such as "chili gravy," served in "old-fashioned Mexican restaurants that catered to Anglo taste." The term has only recently been reclaimed as a positive adjective. Robb Walsh's remarks are part of his six-part history of Tex Mex published in the *Houston Press* in 2000. See especially "Pralines and Pushcarts," http://www.houstonpress.com/2000-07-27/dining/pralines-and-pushcarts/full (accessed November 2, 2010); "Combination Plates," http://www.houstonpress.com/2000-08-31/dining/combination-plates/full (accessed November 2, 2010); "Mama's Got a Brand-New Bag," http://www.houstonpress.com/2000-09-28/dining/mama-s-got-a-brand-new-bag/full (accessed November 2, 2010); "The Authenticity Myth," http://www.houstonpress.com/2000-10-26/dining/the-authenticity-myth/full (accessed November 2, 2010); and "The French Connection," http://www.houstonpress.com/2000-11-23/dining/the-french-connection/full/ (accessed November 2, 2010). See also his informative cookbook, *Tex-Mex Cookbook*.

20. Salinas, "Chile Stands," 2.

21. For a masterly overview of the Southwest's culinary history, see Pilcher, *Planet Taco*, especially parts 1 and 2.

22. "New Mexico Cookery," 1, New Mexico: Notes, Essays, Reports, LOC-AE, A831. On the evolution of the field of folklore and the FWP's role in shifting its focus, see chapter 1.

23. FWP, *Colorado*, 335–36; On this process, see also, Wilson, *Myth of Santa Fe*, 146–68.

24. Titles of essays in the *America Eats* New Mexico file, New Mexico: Notes, Essays, Reports, LOC-AE, A831.

25. A. E. Ensign, "Notes on the Folklore of Yavapai," January 7, 1936, 4, Arizona, LOC-AGF, A21.

26. In her work on the cultural relations between the United States and Mexico in the interwar period, historian Helen Delpar studies the appeal of depictions of Mexico as a primitive and "soul-satisfying" society for Americans in the mid-1930s. A similar trend was active in the Southwest since the late 1910s as artists, anthropologists, and archeologists "discovered" the Indian and Spanish pasts and launched a revival embodied in

the promotion of a romantic architectural style mimicking the Pueblo adobes. Delpar, *Enormous Vogue*.

27. Forrest, *Preservation of the Village*, 108–9.

28. "New Mexico Cookery," 1; Carrie L. Hodges, "Cuisine Peculiar to the State," 6–7, New Mexico: Cuisine, LOC-AGF, A286.

29. "New Mexico Cookery," 1; on the "tensions" and "contradictions" of the "New Deal ethic," see Deutsch, *No Separate Refuge*, 187–208; regarding New Mexico in particular, see Forrest, *Preservation of the Village*, 103–27.

30. Claire Hildman and Athelene Watson, "Arizona Cuisine," 3, Arizona: Notes, Essays, Reports, LOC-AE, A830.

31. Ibid.,1–2. A similar mention of the role of boarding schools in modifying food habits appears in a New Mexico description of a 1934 Inter-Tribal Buffalo barbecue given on the Indian school ground near Yellowstone National Park, which, according to its anonymous author, "gave many of the Indians some knowledge of where their children were being educated, acquainting them with the advantages their children were receiving." "New Mexico Cookery," 19. Historian Brenda Child has documented the malnourishment of numerous students as part of her larger work on the boarding schools. The nutritional effects of boarding schools on indigenous populations in the United States is a topic that begs for more historical research, especially in light of food historian Ian Mosby's research on nutritional experiments conducted in residential schools in Canada. See Child, *Boarding School Seasons*, 32–35, and Mosby, "Administering Colonial Science."

32. Ware, "Out-of-doors-cookery," 2–5.

33. See Brooks, "America Eats (Southwest Section)," version 1, 2–6; Peter J. Hudson, "Choctaw Indian Dishes"; "Notes on Various Indian Dishes, Modern and Old (From a Collection of Interviews Obtained by the Oklahoma W.P.A.)"; "Nut Trees Protected by Indians for their Food Values," "Scrambled Eggs and Wild Onions," Oklahoma: Notes, Essays, Reports: A832. Indigenous foodways were also documented in the *America Eats* regional essay on the Midwest. The author, possibly Nelson Algren, used the worn-out cliché of the "noble savages" to describe Indians and their "copper-brown women" through the eyes of the French colonizers: "In October, by the rivers of the wilderness, and among the rushes of the swamps, the French adventurers watched Illiniwek braves harvesting knotted stalks of wild oats." He mixed registers, though, and followed a couple of pages later with a recognition of indigenous agricultural knowledge and the comment that "the Indian taught the white man to exist in the wilderness . . . ; and, in turn, the frontiersmen instructed the Indian in the fastest known methods of getting blind drunk on barrel-whiskey." According to Algren, "in killing, [the white man] surpassed any savages" and "by the time of the War Between the States, the white had modified the Indian's natural diet in more ways that one. In fact, he had just about put a stop to it altogether," leading them to eat "government rations from tins." Algren(?), "A Short History of the American Diet," 1–10, 25–30.

34. Ruíz, *From Out of the Shadows*, 6; Sanchez, *Becoming Mexican-American*, 18.

35. On the life and work of Aurora Lucero White, see Ruiz and Korrol, *Latinas in the United States*, 392; Meléndez, *Spanish-Language Newspapers*, 201–6; Weigle and Fiore, *Santa Fe and Taos*, 56–57.

36. Aurora Lucero White, "Spanish Fiestas in New Mexico," June 10, 1936, 9 New Mexico: Folklore, LOC-AGF, A286.

37. One of the threats Aurora Lucero White identified had to do with alleged attempts
by the "the sister Republic . . . to impose upon us a more recently discovered Indian folk
elements. . . . The Indian (Atzec) folk heritage properly belongs to Mexico; New Mexico
should cling to its Spanish folk tradition," Ibid. For more insights on the fetishization of
Spanish American folklore and its framing in contrast to Mexican migrant culture by
Spanish Americans and Anglos in the Southwest, and in New Mexico in particular, see
Wilson, *Myth of Santa Fe*, 146–68; Meléndez, *Spanish-Language Newspapers*, 203–6. For
further insights on the social, cultural, and political cleavages between Mexican American
and Mexican migrants from in the interwar period, see Gutiérrez, *Walls and Mirrors*,
56–116.

38. The 1929 market crash and the following decade of economic depression consoli-
dated the interwar racial order in the Southwest and deeply affected the Mexican migrant
community: not only did workers lose their jobs, but their importance in the agricultural
and industrial labor force also made them easy scapegoats for unemployment rates and
the lack of sufficient relief funds. The FWP sources rarely mentioned the forced departures
that took place during the early years of the Depression. M. Gleason, a San Francisco
FWP worker, seemed satisfied with a mention that "there were more Mexicans . . . before
the depression than at the present time, during the hard years many of them returned to
their country" ("Mexican Colony," California: Racial Elements, LOC-AGF, A31). Indeed,
the New Deal administration put an end to the repatriation and deportation programs
and promoted a more racially inclusive relief plan—but the legacy of the early Depression loomed large on the racial landscape of the late 1930s in the Southwest. On average,
historians agree that the incentive to leave, deployed by the American government and
relayed by Mexican officials, led to the repatriation of approximately one million people,
of which fifty thousand were deported by force in the first years of the Depression (Balderrama and Rodriguez, *Decade of Betrayal*, especially 63–82). On the "Mexican" category
in the 1930 U.S. Census, see Ngai, *Impossible Subjects*, 56–90.

39. Sanchez, *Becoming Mexican-American*, 10–13.

40. Pilcher, *Que Viva Los Tamales!* 123.

41. Salinas, "Chile Stands," 2. On the history of tacos in the United States, see also
Pilcher, "Was the Taco Invented?"

42. "Mexican Stores in San Francisco," California: Racial Elements, LOC-AGF, A31.

43. "New Mexico Cookery," 17.

44. White, "Spanish Fiestas."

45. A historical account of the creation of Mexican American food can be found in
Pilcher, *Planet Taco*, 130–52.

46. Hodges, "Cuisine Peculiar to the State." FWP workers occasionally used the word
"Mexican-American" but, under their pens, this epithet did not point to an ethnic group
or a hyphenated identity; rather, they used this term to talk about people of the Mexican
race who happened to have American citizenship because of regional history or naturalization. As Linda Gordon explains, "race had another peculiarity in the West, one that
rewrote history: here 'white' usually meant 'American,' and 'American' came to mean
'white.' At that time 'Mexican American' would have seemed an oxymoron to Anglos"
(*Great Arizona Orphan Abduction*, 105).

47. "New Mexico Cookery," 1; Brooks, "America Eats (Southwest Section)," version 1,
14 and throughout. Don Dolan, "Local Cuisine," August, 5th, 1936, Drafts pertaining to

the American Guide Series, Newspaper writers' project, and related research activities prepared by the Los Angeles district office, 1935–1938, box 34, RG 69.

48. "Spanish American Folk Customs," 16, Texas: Food, Celebrations. LOC-FP, A681. That the epithet "Spanish American" used in the title did not re-appear in the body of the essay is another indication of the racialization of all Spanish-speaking populations as simply "Mexican."

49. Brooks, "America Eats (Southwest Section)," version 2, 15–16.

50. "New Mexico Cookery," 2.

51. Ware, "Some Things the Spanish Americans Eat," 9; "New Mexico Cookery," 1; "Point of interests, Mr. Gomez' Cafe, Mexican Foods," November 16, 1936, New Mexico: Cuisine, LOC-AGF, A286.

52. Hodges, "Cuisine Peculiar to the State," 2; "New Mexico Cookery," 2.

53. "New Mexico Cookery," 2. "Native" in this context referred to Spanish-speaking population installed in New Mexico before the American conquest. Though American citizens, in the 1930 census and increasingly in the region's racial vernacular, most would have been considered racially "Mexican."

54. J. Del Castillo, "A Menudo Party," 3, January 14, 1942, Arizona: Notes, Essays, Reports, LOC-AE, A830.

55. Hodges, "Cuisine Peculiar to the State," 2.

56. Brooks, "America Eats (Southwest Section)," version 2, 9–11.

57. White, "Beef Tour," 5.

58. Brooks, "American Eats (Southwest Section)," version 2, 3; Don Dolan, "Local Cuisine."

59. On the dialectic between savagery and civilization in American culture, see Bederman, *Manliness and Civilization*; Jacobson, *Barbarian Virtues*.

60. Bender, *American Abyss*, 53.

61. FWP, *California*, 7; FWP, *San Diego*, 10, 14; FWP, *Santa Barbara*, 103; Brooks, "America Eats (Southwest Section)," version 2, 12.

62. FWP, *Arizona*, 1.

63. Brooks, "America Eats (Southwest Section)," version 2, 28, 12, and 25.

64. Thomas L. Thienes, "Sheriff's Barbecue," 1, California: Notes, Essays, Reports, LOC-AE, A830.

65. Nash, *American West Transformed*.

66. Shaffer, "Playing American," 73. On railroad and tourism in the Southwest, see, Hyde, *American Vision*, 53–146. On tourism in the twentieth century Southwest and automobile tourism in particular, see Kropp, *California Vieja*, 47–102; Shaffer, *See America First*, chap. 4, "A Nation on Wheels," 130–68.

67. Kropp, *California Vieja*, 2; 4–5; 10; see also Wilson, *Myth of Santa Fe*, 8.

68. Long, "Culinary Tourism," 21. On heritage making as a mode of cultural production, see Kirschenblatt-Gimblett, *Destination Culture*.

69. Long looks at the different "strategies of negotiation" at work when a cuisine gets staged as an "authentic" element of culture and cites five of them: framing, translation (or naming), explanation, menu selection, recipes adaptation. FWP workers used all of these rhetorical tools. Long, "Culinary Tourism," 37- 43.

70. Hildman and Watson, "Arizona Cuisine," 4.

71. "Spanish Foods in Colorado," Colorado: Notes, Essays, Reports, LOC-AE, A830. On the tortilla-making process, see also Pilcher, *Que Vivan Los Tamales!* 101.

72. Arizona FWP worker Edward P. Ware describes enchiladas as "blue cornmeal pancakes spread with chopped raw onions and melted cheese, the steak swamped with chile sauce, and two fried eggs on top staring out like drowning yellow eyes"; the dish could also be rolled and "done up jelly-roll style" (Ware, "Some Things the Spanish Americans Eat," 11–12). In New Mexico, enchiladas were "made from tortillas fried in hot, deep fat. Each one is sprinkled with chopped onion and grated cheese, with chile sauce added. Filed two in a stack, usually, a fried or poached egg is placed and top and more chile sauce is added." Tacos, themselves a relatively recent addition to Mexican cuisine, were tortillas "fried and folded in the center" and filled with "boiled ground beef, diced potatoes seasoned in the Spanish way" as well as "various fillings, from mashed beans to chicken, cheese, and shredded lettuce"; they would be served with chile sauce ("New Mexico Cookery," 4–5). On the history of tacos, see Pilcher, *Planet Tacos.*

73. Long, "Culinary Tourism."

74. "Mexican Food Recipes," Texas: Notes, Essays, Reports, LOC-AE, A832.

75. "Revival of Arizona Traditions," 5, Arizona, LOC-AGF, A21.

76. Hoganson, *Consumers' Imperium*, 134–35. On Anglo women's use of the Spanish past in Southern California, see also Kropp, *California Vieja*, 11, 58.

77. "Mexican Quarter Chili Stands," 1.

78. Lucille Hogas, "Caldwell Country," Texas: Celebrations, LOC-FP, A681.

79. "New Mexico Cookery," 4.

80. Theodore Baron was the guidebook photograph editor, but while several other photographs were attributed to him or Horace Bristol, the Olvera Street tortilla maker photograph is not attributed. The same picture appears in the Los Angeles Area Chamber of Commerce collection at the University of Southern California. Baron probably used their resources to illustrate the guidebook. *Women Tortilla Makers in Olvera Street*, Los Angeles Area Chamber of Commerce Collection, 1890–1860, California Historical Society, 1860–1960, http://digitallibrary.usc.edu/cdm/ref/collection/p15799coll65/id/11498 (accessed November 13, 2014).

81. Brooks, "America Eats (Southwest Section)," version 2, 14; FWP, *Texas*, 341; on the use of cigarettes in stereotypical representations of Mexican women, see Pilcher, *Planet Taco*, 110–11.

82. On Horace Bristol photographic work and life, see Conner and Heimerdinger, *Horace Bristol.*

83. FWP, *California*, 5 and 77.

84. Although this photograph is not attributed in the guidebook, it is part of Dorothea Lange's body of work for the Farm Security Administration and was taken near Westley, California, in April 1938. Mexican workers mingled with Dust Bowl refugees in the fields. Available at http://www.loc.gov/pictures/collection/fsa/item/fsa2000001828/PP (accessed November 13, 2014).

85. On Mexican women in the canning industry, see Ruíz, *Cannery Women.*

86. FWP, *Los Angeles*, 153; FWP, *California*, 215.

87. Kropp dedicates an entire chapter to Olvera Street, titled "The Market: Olvera Street and Urban Space" (*California Vieja*, 207–60, quote on p. 233).

88. Ibid., 239.

89. The Los Angeles Public Library photograph collection includes, as part of the Security Pacific National Bank collection, two photographs of the El Sol del Mayo plant that are strikingly similar to the one included in the FWP guidebook, potentially locating the tortilla maker on 110 North Spring Street rather than Olvera Street. These two pictures are not attributed, either, and seem to adopt a more overtly documentary aesthetic than the posed picture included in the guidebook, capturing the women on the job. Cigarettes are central to both images, however. This collection overlaps with the Los Angeles Area Chamber of Commerce collection at the University of Southern California. *Women Making Tortillas*, Security Pacific National Bank Collection, Los Angeles Public Library, http://jpg1.lapl.org/pics23/00031480.jpg (accessed November 13, 2014); *El Sol del Mayo Tortilla Plant*, Security Pacific National Bank Collection, Los Angeles Public Library, http://jpg1.lapl.org/pics23/00031481.jpg (accessed November 13, 2014).

90. FWP, *Texas*, 319.

91. On cowboy food, see "Cow Boy Food," 2, Colorado: Notes, Essays, Reports, LOC-AE, A830. See also "Typical Cow Boy Breakfast," Arizona: Notes, Essays, Reports, LOC-AE, A830; Reynolds, "Farwest," 72–86; "History of Grazing," New Mexico: Notes, Essays, Reports, LOC-AE, A831; Brooks, "America Eats (Southwest Section)," version 2, 28–29; "Popularity of Ham and Eggs," "The Chuck Wagon (including son-of-a-gun stew)," Texas: Notes, Essays, Reports, LOC-AE, A832; "Come and Get It or I'll Throw It Out," " Roundup and Camp Cookery," Wyoming: Notes, Essays, Reports, LOC-AE, A832; FWP, *Arizona*, 56; FWP, *Texas*, 92–99; FWP, *Nevada*, 69, 76.

92. Mary Carter, "Old Timer Dictionary," 2, ALH Online, http://www.loc.gov/item/wpalh001136 (accessed December 2, 2014).

93. On the administrative division of "the West" in New Deal food writing, and *America Eats* in particular, see chapter 1.

94. On "embattled masculinity" in the 1930s, see, Melosh, *Engendering Culture*, 33–43. On the myth of the West and cowboys in particular in the making of western masculinity in popular culture, see Slotkin, *Gunfighter Nation*, 194–277 and 282; Basso and McCall, *Across the Great Divide*; Bederman, *Manliness and Civilization*; 170–87.

95. Brooks, "America Eats (Southwest Section)," version 2, 5.

96. The story of the invention of the son-of-a-gun stew is told in Kelley, "Son of a Bitch," January 21, 1942, Arizona: Notes, Essays, Reports, LOC-AE, A830; see also White, "Beef Tour," 5; Georgia Redfield, "Old-timers Celebration and Barbecue," New Mexico: Annual Events, LOC-AGF, A280; "The Chuck Wagon"; Reynolds, "Farwest," 73.

97. John M. Ockinson, "Prairie Oysters," Oklahoma: Notes, Essays, Reports, LOC-AE, A832

98. "Revival of Arizona Traditions," 2–3; for a historical perspective on interwar fiestas, in particular Santa Fe's fiesta, see Wilson, *Myth of Santa Fe*, 181–231.

99. "The Chuck Wagon," 4.

100. FWP, *Arizona*, 217.

101. "The Sunburnt West of Yesterday" is the title of a section of part 1 of the state guide titled "Arizona's Background," FWP, *Arizona*, 56.

102. Thienes, "Sheriff's Barbecue." The Southwest Essay section contains an altered version of this essay, Brooks, "America Eats (Southwest Section)," version 2, 7–9.

103. On the link between meat, especially red meat, and masculinity in the 1930s and 1940s, see also Bentley, *Eating for Victory*, 91–102.

104. Brooks, "America Eats (Southwest Section)," version 2, 25.

105. Lorin Brown, "Noche Buena (Christmas Eve)," 3, New Mexico: Folklore, LOC-AGF, A286. On Lorin Brown, see Brown, *Hispano Folklife of New Mexico*.

106. Brooks, "America Eats (Southwest Section)," version 2, 25.

107. "Mexican Food Recipes," 1; "Spanish Foods in Colorado."

108. Tamales were the first Mexican food to be popularized among a non-Mexican population. They were adopted and adapted by African Americans in the Mississippi delta, where they entered in culinary contact with the Mexican migratory workforce. This gave birth to a well-documented regional fusion food known as "hot tamale." A Texas FWP worker explains: "The main Mexican foods known in Austin are tortillas, tamales, enchiladas, tacos, chili, and, to a lesser degree, mole. The preparation of these foods belongs specifically to the Mexican folkways, and for a time they were used almost exclusively in this country by the Mexican population, except for tamales sold to some extent." "Spanish American Folk Customs," Texas: Food, Celebrations, LOC-FP, A681. For more details on the history of the "hot tamales," see the oral history project of the Southern Foodways Alliance, http://www.tamaletrail.com (accessed December, 6, 2010); and Gabaccia, *We Are What We Eat*, 106. See also, "Hot Tamales," 1938, Ohio: Food, Celebration, LOC-FP, A661; "Recipes: Hot Tamale Pie," Arkansas: Notes, Essays, Reports, AE-LOC, A830.

109. "Mexican Food Recipes," 3. The Southwest section essay explained: "Tamales, [like chili con carne], have become Anglicized, but without suffering as much in the transition. For strangers to the art of making tamales, the use of the canned products will avoid wear and tear on their patience, for considerable practice is necessary in order to make them properly." Brooks, "America Eats (Southwest Section)," version 2, 14. See also Pilcher, "Rise and Fall of the Chili Queen," 186–88.

110. Hildman and Watson, "Arizona Cuisine," 6.

111. "Mexican Food Recipes,"1.

112. Hodges, "Cuisine Peculiar to the State," 8–10.

113. For more perspective on the Gerbhardt brand and the commercialization of chili powder, see Gabaccia, *We Are What We Eat*, 159–60; Walsh, *Tex-Mex Cookbook*, 68–69; as well as the University of Texas at San Antonio online exhibit on the brand's history, available at http://webapp.lib.utsa.edu/Gebhardt (accessed December 3, 2014).

114. FWP, *Texas*, 340.

115. Reyes Martinez, "Foods of the Southwest," 3, New Mexico: Cuisine, LOC-AGF, A286.

116. "Influence of Nationality Groups: Mexican Chili," Kansas: Notes, Essays, Reports, LOC-AE, A831. Richard Wright reported on the "many chilli parlors, selling chilli at ten cents per bowl," of Chicago's South Side in Wright, "A Survey of the Amusement Facilities of District #35."

For more perspective on the history of chili con carne, see also Gabaccia, *We Are What We Eat*, 159, 109; Walsh, *Tex-Mex Cookbook*, 40–47. For an overview of the "chili migrations" across the United States and the culinary debates that ensued, see Pilcher, *Planet Taco*, 115–21.

117. Martinez, "Foods of the Southwest," 3.

118. Reyes Martinez instructed cooks to use "a quantity of lean pork, cut into one-inch cubes [that] should be boiled in twice the amount of water until tender, adding a small quantity of sage and a little crushed garlic and salt to suit the taste. Take the meat out of the liquid and fry it in pure lard, adding to it the required quantity of chile powder, gauged to taste experience, and two or three table-spoonful of browned flour. Place this mixture back into the liquid to boil down to the consistency of a medium thick soup" ("Foods of the Southwest," 3). Martinez was a talented high school student from Arroyo Hondo while employed by the FWP, testifying to the diversity of FWP employees. Weigle and Fiore, *Santa Fe and Taos*, 56.

119. On the global reach of Mexican and Mexican American food, see Pilcher, *Planet Taco*. On the national marketing of Mexican food in packaged and frozen form, see Gabaccia, *We Are What We Eat*, 165–67.

120. Brooks, "America Eats (Southwest Section)," version 2, 14; "America Eats (Southwest Section)," version 1, 17.

121. Brooks, "America Eats (Southwest Section)," version 2, 13–14.

Chapter 5. A *"Well-Filled Melting Pot"*

1. Diner, *Hungering for America*, 51–55; Poe, "Labour and Leisure," 140; Cinotto, "Leonard Covello," 499.

2. Jacobson, *Whiteness*, 39–135; On housing policies, industrial unions, and ethnicity in the 1930s, see, Roediger, *Working toward Whiteness*, 157–234; see also Cohen, *Making a New Deal*, especially 99–158 on ethnicity and mass culture.

3. For more perspective on the process of "ethnicization," see Conzen et al., "Invention of Ethnicity."

4. Gaurino, "Italian Munitions Worker," December 6, 1938, ALH Online, http://www.loc.gov/item/wpalh000232 (accessed November, 22, 2014).

5. Gaurino, "Italian Munitions Worker."

6. Gabaccia, *We Are What We Eat*, 139.

7. Ngai, *Impossible Subjects* (see especially 91–224 on Asians, Mexicans, and Filipinos).

8. Allen B. Eaton to Eva Bourgeois, December 27, 1941, 3, Correspondence: November–December 1941, LOC-AE, A830.

9. On Chinese immigration, see Lee, *At America's Gate*. On Japanese immigration and the evolution of Japanese American identity, see Kurashige, *Japanese American Celebration and Conflict*. For more perspective on the history of Chinese American food, see Coe, *Chop Suey*. Sukiyaki is the main Japanese dish documented in New Deal food writing: see Madeline Gleason, "Japanese Colony," 4–5, May 29, 1938, Racial Elements, California, LOC-AGS, A31; Henry Reiter, "Japanese," Chicago: Japanese, LOC-SES, A741; Maryse Rutledge and Mary H. Weik, "Eating in New York among Foreign Background," 9, Miscellaneous, FWP-NYC, roll 294 (several versions of this essay exist in the FWP-NYC archive and will be cited accordingly); Weik, "Introduction to New York Restaurants," 2.

10. "Pockets in America," Administrative Material, LOC-SSP, A853. For more perspective on the "cultural gifts movement," see Hoganson, *Consumer's Imperium*, 209–50; Selig, *Americans All*.

11. "The Chinese in New York," 1, New York City Guide: Racial Groups, FWP-NYC, roll 66; Leonard E. Strong, "Arabian Colony in Brooklyn," 2–3, New York City Guide: Racial Groups, FWP-NYC, roll 66; Audrey Buck, "Mexican customs in the Adobe colony at Billings Montana," October 1936, Montana: Celebration, LOC-AGF, A632; "Ybor City, Tampa's Latin Colony," Pockets in America: Florida, LOC-SSP, A853.

12. "The Greek in America, Instruction for Socio-Ethnic Studies," 8, 12, "Reports Pertaining to Ethnic Studies, 1938–39," RG 69, P1–57, entry 20.

13. On the FWP's evolution from a "contribution" to a "participation" school, see Bold, *Writers, Plumbers, and Anarchists,* 143–52.

14. "Brief Description of Proposed Book," 2.

15. "Nationality Groups," in "Notations," 2, Indiana: Notes, Essays, Reports, LOC-AE, A831.

16. Zangwill, quoted in Sarah Wilson, *Melting Pot Modernism,* 3.

17. Ibid., 2–3.

18. Ibid., 15–16.

19. Ibid., 2–3.

20. "Cuisine peculiar to the State, Southeast Missouri, Sikeston District," February, 17, 1936, and "Cuisine peculiar to the State, Northeast," 2, Missouri: Foods, LOC-FP, A628. On the perceived threat of immigrant foodways in the first decades of the century and efforts at changing them, see Hoganson, *Consumers' Imperium,* 211–12; Gabaccia, *We Are What We Eat,* 123–36; Shapiro, *Perfection Salad,* 125–68.

21. Algren (?), "America Eats, a Short History of American Diet," 67.

22. "Note on Population," 3, Arkansas, LOC-AGF, A25.

23. FWP, *San Francisco,* 220–21.

24. On the depiction of Chinese food as unfit for consumption at the turn of the century and early twentieth century, see Gabaccia, *We Are What We Eat,* 103.

25. "The Art of Chinese Cooking," Chicago: Chinese, FWP-SES, A739.

26. "The Chinese in New York," 1, New York City Guide: Racial Groups, FWP-NYC, roll 66.

27. Strong, "Chinatown," 4, New York City Guide: Racial Groups, FWP-NYC, roll 66.

28. "Ethnic Groups," 13, New York: Ethnic Groups, LOC-AGF, A321.

29. Algren (?), "America Eats, a Short History of American Diet," 1.

30. Michael Denning in *The Cultural Front* defines this strand of regionalism by noting that, "whereas conservative regionalists nostalgically evoked past ways of life, radical regionalists paradoxically pointed to the absence of culture, the lack of roots" and attempted at imagining a multiethnic and multiracial "new culture, a new way of life, a revolution" (133–34). Focusing on the culinary politics of the period, Gabaccia further notes that, by the Great Depression, "ethnicity had . . . become a dimension of multiethnic cross-over exchanges," Gabaccia, *We Are What We Eat,* 120.

31. Reynolds, "Far West," 35–38.

32. Denning, *Cultural Front,* 8–9 and 130–32.

33. Reynolds, "Far West," 15–18. The use of the adjective "foreign" is here particularly revealing. As the context makes clear, these foods were not foreign to the "average [ethnic] housewives" anymore; yet their integration within the scope of "American" food was not yet complete. On working-class culture in Butte, see Murphy, *Mining Cultures.*

34. The insistence of western fieldworkers to describe crossover ethnic tastes as key to the cohesion of working-class multiethnic communities can be thought of as a sensory legacy of the labor struggles of the 1930s and the rise of new unions. New Deal policies triggered the development of new multiethnic industrial unions as part of the Congress of Industrial Organizations (CIO). The CIO unions fostered a "culture of unity" that sought, in Lizabeth Cohen's words, "just the right balance between acknowledging ethnic difference and articulating worker unity"; their strategy was to "meet workers on their ethnic, or racial, ground and pull them into a self-consciously common culture that transcended those distinctions." Cohen, *Making a New Deal*, 323–60 (quote is on p. 339). On the CIO culture, see also Denning, *Cultural Front*, 6–8 and 21–38; Kazin, *Populist Persuasion*, 135–64. On women's circumscribed role in the CIO, see Faue, *Community of Suffering and Struggle*.

35. Marjorie Ottaway, "Local and State Cuisine," 1–3, March 18, 1936, Minnesota, St. Paul: Cuisine, LOC-AGF, A189. None of the versions of the essay were integrated in the final guidebook.

36. On ethnicity and local taste, see Shortridge and Shortridge, *Taste of American Place*; Brown and Mussell, *Ethnic and Regional Foodways*.

37. Marjorie Ottaway, "Local and State Cuisine," April 14, 1936, Minnesota: Miscellaneous, Cuisine, LOC-AGF, A193.

38. Reynolds, "Far West," 2–3.

39. Mari Tomasi, "Mrs. John Parioli," interviewed November, 4, 1938, ALH Online, http://www.loc.gov/item/wpalh002699 (accessed November 22, 2014). On generational changes in diet among Italian Americans, see also Poe, "Labour and Leisure," 510–12.

40. Cinotto, "Leonard Covello," 515.

41. Mari Tomasi, "Giacomo Coletti," 1938–39, ALH Online, http://www.loc.gov/item/wpalh002726 (accessed November 22, 2014).

42. Gabaccia, *We Are What We Eat*, 123–31; Levenstein, *Revolution at the Table*, 98–108.

43. Shah, *Contagious Divides*, 204.

44. Emmanuel Kanter, "Earliest Colonization and Original Habitat, etc, of Chinese in New York," 9, New York City Guide: Racial Groups, FWP-NYC, roll 66.

45. FWP, *San Francisco*, 221–22.

46. Conzen et al., "Invention of Ethnicity."

47. Diner, *Hungering for America*, 60.

48. Title of chapter 2 in, FWP, *Italians of New York*, 23–35.

49. Ibid., 1.

50. Harry Zahn, "Italian restaurants and foods in New York," 3, Italians of New York, FWP-NYC, roll 260. Mentions of pizza in New Deal food writing were systematically accompanied by detailed explanations, hinting at the dish's novelty status. Some FWP workers described pizza as "a pie baked with Italian cheese, tomatoes, anchovies, and spices," others as a "very thin crust, open and filled with aleches (anchovies), muzzarelle (cheese) or pomoddoro (tomatoes) . . . vary[ing] from the normal pie size to huge circles or rectangles," or as an "unsweetened pastry filled with tomatoes and cheese, meat or fish." "Italians of Newark, stores," 9, New Jersey: Italians of Newark, LOC-SES, A793; FWP, *New York City Guide*, 118.

51. Diner, *Hungering for America*, 53.

52. Laura Earley, "Italy in the Ozarks," November 1937, Arkansas: Pockets in America, LOC-SSP, A853.

53. Gabaccia, *We Are What We Eat*, 77–84; Cohen, *Making a New Deal*: on ethnic grocery stores in the 1920s, 106–20; on how ethnic stores lost ground during the Depression, 234–38. Tracey Deutsch sees signs of the rise of chain stores in ethnic neighborhoods before the Depression, and she highlights how chain stores appealed to customers "with promises of low prices, trustworthy foods, and more freedom from grocers, and community oversight." The 1940s slowed this trend, however, as war rationing and shortages made personal relations with grocers an asset. Deutsch, "Untangling Alliances," 165. On supermarkets' retail strategies, see Longstreth, *Drive-In*, 122–24.

54. Elita Lenz, "Cosmopolitan market" 4, Feeding the City: Market, FWP-NYC, roll 131.

55. Marie Fisher, "Interesting Communities, Little Europe," Chicago, LOC-SES, A739.

56. "Northeast," unpaginated, Section Essay, LOC-AE, A833; Elizabeth Drury, "Old Cathay, " December 14, 1936, Chicago: Cuisine, Restaurants, LOC-AGF, A499. See also Gabaccia, *We Are What We Eat*, on ethnic food entrepreneurs, 64–92; on cross-ethnic eaters, 92–121.

57. Herman H. Globy (consultant Armand Ismile), "Jerusalem Oriental Café"; Theodora Pikowsky, "Jewish Restaurants"; Andrew Christianson (Consultant Padma Clutter), "Shalimar Tea Garden," Chicago: Cuisine, Restaurants, LOC-AGF, A499.

58. I borrow here Krishnendu Ray's formulation in his study of immigrant restaurateurs in contemporary New York City in "Global Flows," 184–185.

59. On the history of the restaurant as "a veritable icon of standardized payment and obligatory visible exchange," see Spang, *Invention of the Restaurant*, 137–138 and 238; see also Haley, *Turning the Tables*, 107–9.

60. A good case study of such relationship is Samantha Barbas's article on chop suey ("I'll Take Chop Suey"), in which she "examine[s] the history of this cross-cultural interaction, its effects on racial attitudes and food preferences, and ultimately, why restaurants were able to facilitate boundary crossing in a way that other institutions could not" (670).

61. FWP, *New York City*, 24–28.

62. On the habit of going out to eat in the interwar period and the increasing acceptance of ethnic cuisines as American food, see Russek, "Appetites without Prejudice," especially p. 38.

63. On foreign-themed restaurants and nightclubs, see Russek, "Appetites without Prejudice."

64. David B. Eskind, "Dining (with entertainment)," Chicago: Cuisine, Restaurants, LOC-AGF, A499.

65. Maryse Rutledge, "Eating in New York among Foreign Background," 1, New York City Guide: Restaurants, FWP-NYC, roll 19. On the attraction of ethnic restaurants as an alternative to conceited French restaurants at the turn of the century, see Haley, *Turning the Tables*, 92–117.

66. Ethnic entrepreneurs also owned restaurants and establishments such as lunchrooms, soda fountains, dinners, and ice-cream parlors in which they did not serve ethnic food. On the case of Greek restaurant owners, see Gabaccia, *We Are What We Eat*, 115–18. See also the FWP Life Histories interviews with Greek restaurateurs in Vermont, Interview

of Demosthenes P. Corsones, John Chilos (Tsilos), and Nicholas Stregos in Vermont: Greek, Life Histories, LOC- SES, A760.

67. Frederick Clayton, "Outline and Plan of Text," 1; and "The City," 3–4, Feeding the City: Draft FWP-NYC, roll 153.

68. "Memorandum for the New York City Supervisor," Feeding the City: America Eats, FWP-NYC, roll 153.

69. For more perspectives on the history of the Progressive Era cosmopolitan ideal, see Hansen, "True Americanism" (quote is on p. 74).

70. Hoganson, *Consumers' Imperium*, 10; for more perspective on cosmopolitan consumerism, 110–51; and Haley, *Turning the Tables*, 8 and 95.

71. Cocks, *Doing the Town*, 174–203; Heap, *Slumming*, 7.

72. Gerald Fitzgerald, "Spanish Restaurants," 5, New York City Guide: Racial Groups, FWP-NYC, roll 26.

73. "Foreign Restaurants, Spanish Restaurants," Feeding the City: Eating Out, FWP-NYC, roll 144; on foreign enclaves as urban tourist sights, see Blake, *How New York Became American*, 110–38.

74. Weik, "Introduction to New York Restaurants," 2.

75. Shah, *Contagious Divides*, 233–35; Barbas, "I'll Take Chop Suey," 669; Gabaccia, *We Are What We Eat*, 102–5; Russek, "Appetite without Prejudices," 40–41; Catharine Cocks notes that "the members of ethnic minorities found opportunities in the commodification of their cultures that often gave them ways to make a living and to retain some aspects of their own heritage" (*Doing the Town*, 200–202).

76. Harry Zahn, "Chinese Restaurants: Some Aspects," New York City Guide: Racial Groups, FWP-NYC, roll 66.

77. Barbas, "I'll Take Chop Suey," 674; Coe, *Chop Suey*, 155–79.

78. FWP, *San Francisco*, 220.

79. Zahn, "Chinese Restaurants: Some Aspects."

80. Nathan Ausubel, "Chop Suey," New York City Guide, Racial Groups: Arab and Chinese, FWP-NYC, roll 66. On Jews and Chinese cooking in New York, see Miller, "Identity Takeout"; Coe, *Chop Suey*, 198–205.

81. On the evolution of the appeal of ethnic neighborhoods to middle-class tourists and "slummers," from the turn of the century to the 1930s, see Blake, *How New York Became American*, 111–38; Gabaccia, *We Are What We Eat*, 100–102.

82. Rutledge and Weik, "Eating in New York among Foreign Background," 1.

83. Heap, *Slumming*, 83.

84. M. Reise, "Russian Restaurants," Chicago: Russian, LOC-SES, A742; Harry Desteese, "Night Clubs of New York," New York City Guide: Hotels, Restaurants, Night Clubs, FWP-NYC, roll 19. See also, Haley, *Turning the Tables*, 106–7.

85. Wilbur Young, "Connie's Inn," New York City Guide: Hotels, Restaurants, Night Clubs, FWP-NYC, roll 20. On this trend, see also Heap, *Slumming*, 218–19 and 229.

86. Desteese, "Night Clubs of New York." On urban nightlife in the 1930s and the rebirth of nightclubs after the repeal of Prohibition, see Perreti, *Nightclub City*.

87. "Italians," 10, New York City Guide: Racial Groups, FWP-NYC, roll 67.

88. Harry Zahn, "Italian Restaurant and Foods in New York," 3, Italians of New York: Organizations, Clubs, FWP-NYC, roll 260. Zahn and others in the New York City unit

seem to have been building their essays from information provided, maybe in Italian, by FWP worker Giulia Morelli, who is listed in several pieces either as author with another worker as editor or as author with another writer as translator. She is listed as part of the editorial staff of *The Italians of New York* publication.

89. Leonard E. Strong, "Arabian Colony in Brooklyn," 2–3, New York City Guide: Racial Groups, FWP-NYC, roll 66.

90. Elizabeth Smyth, "Typical Hungarian Restaurants," 2–3, New York City Guide: Racial Groups, FWP-NYC, roll 24.

91. Russek, "Appetites without Prejudice," 34–55; Haley, *Turning the Tables*, 106–10.

92. Zahn, "Italian Restaurant," 3. For a contemporary perspective on foodies and authenticity, see Johnston, and Baumann, *Foodie*.

93. On this distinction, see also, Russek, "Appetites without Prejudice," 35–37; Haley, *Turning the Tables*, 106.

94. Diner, *Hungering for America*, 75; Gabaccia, *We Are What We Eat*, 83.

95. "Rumanian Restaurants in New York," New York City Guide: Racial Groups, FWP-NYC, roll 68.

96. "Greek Food and Drink in New York," 1, New York City: Greeks, LOC-SES, A750; Selma Culpepper, "Italian Amusement in New York," 10, Italians of New York: Organizations, Clubs, FWP-NYC, roll 260.

97. Stern, "Russian Restaurants in New York," 2, New York City Guide: Racial Groups, FWP-NYC, roll 26; Gerald Fitzgerald, "Greek Restaurants in New York"; Winthrop, "Greek Sections of New York," New York City Guide: Racial Groups, FWP-NYC, roll 27.

98. Fitzgerald, "Greek Restaurants in New York."

99. FWP, *Italians of New York*, 206. On the role of the Depression in triggering a reevaluation of ethnic food, see Gabaccia, *We Are What We Eat*, 138–39.

100. Krupp, "Restaurants for the Poor (Third Avenue and the Bowery)," Feeding the City: Eating Out, FWP-NYC, roll 144.

101. "For the Very Poor," 10, Feeding the City: Draft, FWP-NYC, roll 153.

102. Mari Tomasi, "Italian Feed," Vermont: Notes, Essays, Reports, LOC-AE, AE831; On Tomasi, see Rosa, "Novels of Mari Tomasi."

103. Mari Tomasi, "Italian Feed," September 21, 1940, ALH Online, http://www.loc.gov/item/wpalh002744 (accessed November 25, 2014); Roaldus Richmond, "Sunday Afternoons at Mrs. Gerbati's," ALH Online, http://www.loc.gov/item/wpalh002667 (accessed November 25, 2014); Tomasi, "Italian Feeds" (America Eats Essay).

104. Mari Tomasi, "Waitress," interviewed in August 1940, ALH Online, http://www.loc.gov/item/wpalh002736 (accessed November 23, 2014).

Conclusion

1. Gabaccia, *We Are What We Eat*, 122–48.

2. See, for instance, *Nature's Metropolis*, William Cronon's masterful study of grain as food and grain as commodity in late-nineteenth-century Chicago (esp. 97–147).

3. On Americanism as consumerism, see McGovern, *Sold American*; Cohen, *Consumers' Republic*.

4. See, for instance, Levenstein in *Paradox of Plenty*, 101–30; Bentley, *Eating for Victory*, 171–79; Gabaccia, *We Are What We Eat*, 149–74.

5. Bentley, *Inventing Baby Food*, 77–79.

6. Deutsch, "Memories."

7. Kurlansky, *Food of a Younger Land*.

8. I am inspired here by Amy Trubek's discussion of the contemporary food movement in her article "Radical Taste"; the quote about the fall is on page 194.

9. "Church Supper," 1, Delaware: Notes, Essays, Reports, AE-LOC, A830.

10. Pollan, *Food Rules*, 7–8.

11. "The South (Section Essay)," 48; Trubek, "Radical Taste," 194. For a critique of the "great-grandmother rule" and a reflection on the history of good/bad, real/fake dichotomies in American food culture, see also Brobow-Strain, "What Would Great Grandma Eat?"

12. Madden and Finch, *Eating in Eden*, 2. For more perspective on food, race, and labor in the contemporary food movement, see Gray, *Labor and the Locavore*. On authenticity, see Johnston and Baumann, *Foodies*.

13. On the ambiguous place of women in contemporary food writing, see Allen and Sachs, "Women and Food Chains," 14; Deutsch, "Memories."

14. Brewer, *From Fireplace to Cookstove*, 95–117.

15. See, for instance, the work of Alkon and Agyeman, *Cultivating Food Justice*; O'Neill, "You Say Tomato, I Say Tomahto," 161–66; Trubek, "Radical Taste"; Deutsch, "Memories"; and Heldke, "Down-Home Global Cooking."

Bibliography

Archival Sources

LIBRARY OF CONGRESS, MANUSCRIPT DIVISION,
FEDERAL WRITERS' PROJECT OF THE WORKS
PROGRESS ADMINISTRATION

"America Eats," abbreviated as LOC-AE.
"Social-Ethnic Studies Project," abbreviated as LOC-SES.
"Negro Studies Project," abbreviated as LOC-NSP.
"Folklore Project," abbreviated as LOC-FP.
"American Guide File," abbreviated as LOC-AGF.
"Special Studies and Projects," abbreviated as LOC-SSP.

NATIONAL ARCHIVES AND RECORDS ADMINISTRATION,
COLLEGE PARK, MARYLAND

Record Group 69, Record of the Works Progress Administration, abbreviated as RG 69.

NEW YORK CITY DEPARTMENT OF RECORDS, MUNICIPAL
ARCHIVE'S COLLECTION

WPA Federal Writers' Project, New York City Unit, 1936–1943, abbreviated as FWP-NYC.

NEW YORK PUBLIC LIBRARY, SCHOMBURG CENTER FOR
RESEARCH IN BLACK CULTURE

WPA Writers Program Collection, abbreviated as WP-NYC-Sch.

Primary Sources

(Compiled, written, and/or prepared by state and federal workers for the Work Projects Administration, known until July 1, 1939, as the Works Progress Administration)

"American Life Histories, Manuscripts from the Federal Writers' Project, 1936–1940," available at http://www.loc.gov/collection/federal-writers-project (accessed November 26, 2014), abbreviated ALH Online.

Arizona: The Grand Canyon State. New York: Hastings House, 1956 [1940].

California: A Guide to the Golden State. New York: Hastings House, 1939.

Cincinnati: A Guide to the Queen City and Its Neighbors. Cincinnati: Wiesen-Hart, 1943.

Colorado: A Guide to the Highest State. New York: Hastings House, 1941.

Delaware: A Guide to the First State. New York: Viking, 1938.

The Italians of New York. New York: Random House, 1938.

Los Angeles: A Guide to the City and Its Environs. New York: Hastings House, 1941.

Louisiana: A Guide to the State. New York: Hastings House, 1941.

Missouri: A Guide to the "Show Me" State. New York: Duell, Sloan, and Peace, 1941.

Nevada: A Guide to the Silver State. Portland, Ore.: Binfords and Mort, 1940.

New Orleans City Guide. Boston: Houghton Mifflin, 1938.

New York City Guide: A Comprehensive Guide to the Five Boroughs of the Metropolis. New York: Random House, 1939.

North Carolina: A Guide to the Old North State. Chapel Hill: University of North Carolina Press, 1939.

San Diego: A California City. San Diego: San Diego Historical Society, 1937.

San Francisco: The Bay and Its Cities. New York: Hastings House, 1940.

Santa Barbara: A Guide to the Channel City and Its Environs. New York: Hastings House, 1941.

South Carolina: A Guide to the Palmetto State. New York: Oxford University Press, 1941.

Texas: A Guide to the Lone Star State. New York: Hastings House, 1940.

U.S. One: Maine to Florida. New York: Modern Age, 1938.

Secondary Sources

Ahmed, Sara. "Affective Economies." *Social Text* 79 (Summer 2004): 117–39.

———. *The Cultural Politics of Emotion.* New York: Routledge, 2004.

Algren, Nelson, and David E. Schoonover. *America Eats.* Iowa Szathmáry Culinary Arts Series. Iowa City: University of Iowa Press, 1992.

Alkon, Alison Hope, and Julian Agyeman. *Cultivating Food Justice: Race, Class, and Sustainability.* Cambridge, Mass.: MIT Press, 2011.

Allen, Patricia, and Carolyn Sachs. "Women and Food Chains: The Gendered Politics of Food." *International Journal of Sociology of Agriculture and Food* 15, no. 1 (2007): 1–23.

Almaguer, Tomás. *Racial Fault Lines: The Historical Origins of White Supremacy in California.* Berkeley: University of California Press, 1994.

Anderson, Benedict R. *Imagined Communities: Reflections on the Origin and Spread of Nationalism.* London: Verso, 1983.

Appadurai, Arjun. "How to Make a National Cuisine: Cookbooks in Contemporary India." *Comparative Studies in Society and History* 30, no. 1 (January 1988): 3–24.

———. "Introduction." In *The Social Life of Things: Commodities in Cultural Perspective*, edited by Arjun Appadurai, Arjun, 3–63. Cambridge: Cambridge University Press, 1988.

Avakian, Arlene Voski, and Barbara Haber, eds. *From Betty Crocker to Feminist Food Studies: Critical Perspectives on Women and Food*. Amherst: University of Massachusetts Press, 2005.

Ayers, Edward L., Patricia Nelson Limerick, Stephen Nissenbaum, and Peter S. Onuf, eds. *All Over the Map: Rethinking American Regions*. Baltimore, Md.: Johns Hopkins University Press, 1996.

Balderrama, Francisco E., and Raymond Rodriguez. *Decade of Betrayal: Mexican Repatriation in the 1930s*. Albuquerque: University of New Mexico Press, 2006.

Baldwin, Davarian L. *Chicago's New Negroes: Modernity, the Great Migration, and Black Urban Life*. Chapel Hill: University of North Carolina Press, 2007.

Barbas, Samantha. "'I'll Take Chop Suey': Restaurant as Agents of Culinary and Cultural Change." *Journal of Popular Culture* 36, no. 4 (May 2003): 669–86.

Barrett, James R., and David Roediger. "Inbetween Peoples: Race, Nationality and the 'New Immigrant' Working Class." *Journal of American Ethnic History* 16, no. 3 (Spring 1997): 3–44.

Basso, Matthew, Laura McCall, and Dee Garceau. *Across the Great Divide: Cultures of Manhood in the American West*. New York: Routledge, 2001.

Becker, Jane S. *Selling Tradition: Appalachia and the Construction of an American Folk, 1930–1940*. Chapel Hill: University of North Carolina Press, 1998.

Becker, Jane S., and Barbara Franco, eds. *Folk Roots, New Roots: Folklore in American Life*. Lexington, Mass.: Museum of Our National Heritage, 1988.

Bederman, Gail. *Manliness and Civilization: A Cultural History of Gender and Race in the United States, 1880–1917*. Women in Culture and Society. Chicago: University of Chicago Press, 1995.

Belasco, Warren James, and Philip Scranton, eds. *Food Nations: Selling Taste in Consumer Societies*. New York: Routledge, 2001.

Bender, Daniel E. *American Abyss: Savagery and Civilization in the Age of Industry*. Ithaca, N.Y.: Cornell University Press, 2009.

Bentley, Amy. *Eating for Victory: Food Rationing and the Politics of Domesticity*. Urbana: University of Illinois Press, 1998.

———. *Inventing Baby Food: Taste, Health, and the Industrialization of the American Diet*. California Studies in Food Culture. Berkeley: University of California Press, 2014.

Biltekoff, Charlotte. *Eating Right in America: The Cultural Politics of Food and Health*. Durham, N.C.: Duke University Press, 2013.

Blake, Angela M. *How New York Became American, 1890–1924*. Baltimore, Md.: Johns Hopkins University Press, 2006.

Blight, David W. *Race and Reunion: The Civil War in American Memory*. Cambridge, Mass.: Harvard University Press, 2001.

Bobrow-Strain, Aaron. "What Would Great Grandma Eat?" *Chronicle of Higher Education*, February 26, 2012. Available at http://chronicle.com/article/What-Would-Great -Grandma-Eat-/130890 (accessed May 20, 2015).

———. *White Bread: A Social History of the Store-Bought Loaf*. Boston: Beacon, 2012.

Bold, Christine. *The WPA Guides: Mapping America*. Jackson: University Press of Mississippi, 1999.

———. *Writers, Plumbers, and Anarchists: the WPA Writers' Project in Massachusetts*. Amherst: University of Massachusetts Press, 2006.

Bourdieu, Pierre. *Distinction: A Social Critique of the Judgement of Taste*. Cambridge, Mass.: Harvard University Press, 1984.

Bower, Anne, ed. *Recipes for Reading: Community Cookbooks, Stories, Histories*. Amherst: University of Massachusetts Press, 1997.

Boym, Svetlana. *The Future of Nostalgia*. New York: Basic, 2001.

Brewer, Priscilla J. *From Fireplace to Cookstove: Technology and the Domestic Ideal in America*. Syracuse, N.Y.: Syracuse University Press, 2000.

Brinkley, Alan. *Voices of Protest: Huey Long, Father Coughlin, and the Great Depression*. New York: Vintage, 1983.

Bronner, Simon J. "In Search of American Tradition." In *Folk Nation: Folklore in the Creation of American Tradition*, edited by Simon J. Bronner. Wilmington, Del.: Scholarly Resources, 2002.

Brown, Jayna. *Babylon Girls: Black Women Performers and the Shaping of the Modern*. Durham, N.C.: Duke University Press, 2008.

Brown, Linda Keller, and Kay Mussell. *Ethnic and Regional Foodways in the United States: The Performance of Group Identity*. Knoxville: University of Tennessee Press, 1984.

Brown, Lorin W. *Hispano Folklife of New Mexico: The Lorin W. Brown Federal Writers' Project Manuscripts*. Albuquerque: University of New Mexico Press, 1978.

Camp, John Charles. "America Eats: Toward a Social Definition of American Foodways." PhD diss., University of Pennsylvania, 1978.

Child, Brenda J. *Boarding School Seasons: American Indian Families, 1900–1940*. North American Indian Prose Award Series. Lincoln: University of Nebraska Press, 1998.

Cinotto, Simone. "Leonard Covello, the Covello Papers, and the History of Eating Habits among Italian Immigrants in New York." *Journal of American History* 91, no. 2 (2004): 497–521.

Classen, Constance. *The Deepest Sense: A Cultural History of Touch*. Studies in Sensory History. Urbana: University of Illinois Press, 2012.

———. *Worlds of Sense: Exploring the Senses in History and across Cultures*. London: Routledge, 1993.

Cocks, Catherine. *Doing the Town: The Rise of Urban Tourism in the United States, 1850–1915*. Berkeley: University of California Press, 2001.

Coe, Andrew. *Chop Suey: A Cultural History of Chinese Food in the United States*. New York: Oxford University Press, 2009.

Cohen, Lizabeth. *A Consumer's Republic: The Politics of Mass Consumption in Postwar America*. New York: Knopf, 2003.

———. *Making a New Deal: Industrial Workers in Chicago, 1919–1939*. Cambridge: Cambridge University Press, 1990.

Conner, Ken, and Debra Heimerdinger. *Horace Bristol: An American View*. San Francisco: Chronicle, 1996.

Conzen, Kathleen Neils, Ewa Morawska, David A. Gerber, George E. Pozzetta, and Rudolph J. Vecoli. "The Invention of Ethnicity: A Perspective from the U.S.A." *Journal of American Ethnic History* 12, no. 1 (Fall 1992): 3–41.

Corbin, Alain. *The Foul and the Fragrant: Odor and the French Social Imagination.* Cambridge, Mass.: Harvard University Press, [1982] 1986.

———. *Time, Desire and Horror: Towards a History of the Senses.* Cambridge: Polity, 1995.

———. *Village Bells: Sound and Meaning in the 19th-Century French Countryside.* Columbia University Press, 1998.

Corbould, Clare. *Becoming African Americans: Black Public Life in Harlem, 1919–1939.* Cambridge, Mass.: Harvard University Press, 2009.

———. "Streets, Sounds and Identity in Interwar Harlem." *Journal of Social History* 40, no. 4 (Summer 2007): 859–94.

Cronon, William. *Nature's Metropolis: Chicago and the Great West.* New York: Norton, 1991.

Crosby, Alfred W. *The Columbian Exchange: Biological and Cultural Consequences of 1492.* Westport, Conn.: Greenwood, 1972.

Csergo, Julia. "The Emergence of Regional Cuisine." In Jean-Louis Flandrin and Massimo Montanari, *Food: A Culinary History from Antiquity to the Present,* 500–515. New York: Columbia University Press, 1999.

Currell, Susan. "Introduction." In *Popular Eugenics: National Efficiency and American Mass Culture in the 1930s,* edited by Susan Currell and Christina Cogdell. Athens: Ohio University Press, 2006.

Daniel, Pete, Merry A. Foresta, Maren Stange, and Sally Stein. *Official Images: New Deal Photography.* Washington, D.C.: Smithsonian Institution Press, 1987.

Delpar, Helen. *The Enormous Vogue of Things Mexican: Cultural Relations between the United States and Mexico, 1920–1935.* Tuscaloosa: University of Alabama Press, 1992.

Denning, Michael. *The Cultural Front: The Laboring of American Culture in the Twentieth Century.* New York: Verso, 1998.

———. *Culture in the Age of Three Worlds.* New York: Verso, 2004

DePastino, Todd. *Citizen Hobo: How a Century of Homelessness Shaped America.* Chicago: University of Chicago Press, 2003.

Deutsch, Sarah. *No Separate Refuge: Culture, Class, and Gender on an Anglo-Hispanic Frontier in the American Southwest, 1880–1940.* New York: Oxford University

Deutsch, Tracey. *Building a Housewife's Paradise: Gender, Politics, and American Grocery Stores in the Twentieth Century.* Chapel Hill: University of North Carolina Press, 2010.

———. "Memories of Mothers in the Kitchen: Local Foods, History, and Women's Work." *Radical History Review* 2011, no. 110 (Spring 2011): 167–77.

———. "Untangling Alliances: Social Tensions Surrounding Independent Grocery Stores and the Rise of Mass Retailing." In Belasco and Scranton, *Food Nations,* 156–74.

Dilworth, Leah. *Imagining Indians in the Southwest: Persistent Visions of a Primitive Past.* Washington, D.C.: Smithsonian Institution Press, 1996.

Diner, Hasia R. *Hungering for America: Italian, Irish, and Jewish Foodways in the Age of Migration.* Cambridge, Mass.: Harvard University Press, 2001.

Dorman, Robert L. "Revolt of the Provinces: The Regionalist Movement in America 1920–1945." In *The New Regionalism,* edited by Charles Reagan Wilson. Jackson: University Press of Mississippi, 1998.

———. *Revolt of the Provinces: The Regionalist Movement in America, 1920–1945.* Chapel Hill: University of North Carolina Press, 2003.

Edge, John T., Charles Reagan Wilson, James G. Thomas, Ann J. Abadie. *The New Encyclopedia of Southern Culture: Foodways*. Vol. 7. Chapel Hill: University of North Carolina Press, 2007.

Edmonds, Michael. "The Federal Writers' Project in Wisconsin, 1935–1942." *Wisconsin Magazine of History* 94, no. 3 (Spring 2011): 42–53.

Elliot, Nils Lindahl. "See It, Sense It, Save It: Economies of Multisensuality in Contemporary Zoos." *Senses and Society* 1, no. 2 (2006): 203–23.

Engelhardt, Elizabeth S. D. *A Mess of Greens: Southern Gender and Southern Food*. Athens: University of Georgia Press, 2011.

Faue, Elizabeth. *Community of Suffering and Struggle: Women, Men, and the Labor Movement in Minneapolis, 1915–1945*. Chapel Hill: University of North Carolina Press, 1991.

Fender, Stephen. "Poor Whites and the FWP: The Rhetoric of Eugenics in the Southern Life Histories." In *Popular Eugenics: National Efficiency and American Mass Culture in the 1930s*, edited by Susan Currell and Christina Cogdell, 140–63. Athens: Ohio University Press, 2006.

Ferguson, Karen. *Black Politics in New Deal Atlanta*. Chapel Hill: University of North Carolina Press, 2002.

Ferguson, Priscilla Parkhurst. "The Senses of Taste." *American Historical Review* 116, no. 2 (2011): 371–84.

Ferris, Marcie Cohen. *The Edible South: The Power of Food and the Making of an American Region*. Chapel Hill: University of North Carolina Press, 2014.

Fischer, David Hackett. *Albion's Seed: Four British Folkways in America*. Oxford: Oxford University Press, 1991.

Fitzgerald, Gerard J., and Gabriella M. Petrick. "In Good Taste: Rethinking American History with Our Palates." *Journal of American History* 95, no. 2 (2008): 392–404.

Fleischhauer, Carl, Beverly W. Brannan, Lawrence W. Levine, and Alan Trachtenberg. *Documenting America, 1935–1943*. Berkeley: University of California Press in association with the Library of Congress, 1988.

Foley, Neil. *The White Scourge: Mexicans, Blacks, and Poor Whites in Texas Cotton Culture*. Berkeley: University of California Press, 1997.

Forrest, Suzanne. *The Preservation of the Village: New Mexico's Hispanics and the New Deal*. Albuquerque: University of New Mexico Press, 1998.

Freidberg, Susanne. *Fresh: A Perishable History*. Cambridge, Mass.: Belknap, 2010.

Gabaccia, Donna R. *We Are What We Eat: Ethnic Food and the Making of Americans*. Cambridge, Mass.: Harvard University Press, 1998.

Gabaccia, Donna R., and Jeffrey M. Pilcher. "'Chili Queens' and Checkered Tablecloths: Public Dining Cultures of Italians in New York City and Mexicans in San Antonio, Texas, 1870s–1940s." *Radical History Review* 2011, no. 110 (n.d.): 109–26.

Gerstle, Gary. *American Crucible: Race and Nation in the Twentieth Century*. Princeton, N.J.: Princeton University Press, 2002.

Gerstle, Gary, and Steve Fraser. *The Rise and Fall of the New Deal Order*. Princeton, N.J.: Princeton University Press, 1989.

Gilmore, Glenda Elizabeth. *Gender and Jim Crow: Women and the Politics of White Supremacy in North Carolina, 1896–1920*. Chapel Hill: University of North Carolina Press, 1996.

Gordon, Linda. *Dorothea Lange: A Life Beyond Limits*. New York: Norton, 2010.

———. *The Great Arizona Orphan Abduction.* Cambridge, Mass.: Harvard University Press, 1999.

Gray, Margaret. *Labor and the Locavore: The Making of a Comprehensive Food Ethic.* Berkeley: University of California Press, 2014.

Greenberg, Cheryl Lynn. *"Or Does It Explode?" Black Harlem in the Great Depression.* New York: Oxford University Press, 1997.

Gregory, James N. *American Exodus: The Dust Bowl Migration and Okie Culture in California.* New York: Oxford University Press, 1989.

———. *The Southern Diaspora: How the Great Migrations of Black and White Southerners Transformed America.* Chapel Hill: University of North Carolina Press, 2005.

Gross, Andrew S. "The American Guide Series: Patriotism as Brand-Name Identification." *Arizona Quarterly* 62, no. 1 (Spring 2006): 85–11.

Grossman, James R. *Land of Hope: Chicago, Black Southerners, and the Great Migration.* Chicago: University of Chicago Press, 1991.

Guglielmo, Jennifer, and Salvatore Salerno, eds. *Are Italians White? How Race Is Made in America.* New York: Routledge, 2003.

Guglielmo, Thomas A. *White on Arrival: Italians, Race, Color, and Power in Chicago, 1890–1945.* Oxford: Oxford University Press, 2004.

Guterl, Matthew Pratt. *The Color of Race in America, 1900–1940.* Cambridge, Mass.: Harvard University Press, 2001.

Gutiérrez, David G. *Walls and Mirrors: Mexican Americans, Mexican Immigrants, and the Politics of Ethnicity.* Berkeley: University of California Press, 1995.

Hale, Grace Elizabeth. *Making Whiteness: The Culture of Segregation in the South, 1890–1940.* New York: Vintage, 1998.

Haley, Andrew P. *Turning the Tables: Restaurants and the Rise of the American Middle Class, 1880–1920.* Chapel Hill: University of North Carolina Press, 2011.

Hansen, Jonathan. "True Americanism: Progressive Era Intellectuals and the Problem of Liberal Nationalism." In *Americanism: New Perspectives on the History of an Ideal,* edited by Michael Kazin and Joseph A. McCartin, 73–89. Chapel Hill: University of North Carolina Press, 2006.

Harris, Jonathan. *Federal Art and National Culture: The Politics of Identity in New Deal America.* Cambridge Studies in American Visual Culture. New York: Cambridge University Press, 1995.

Heap, Chad C. *Slumming: Sexual and Racial Encounters in American Nightlife, 1885–1940.* Historical Studies in Urban America. Chicago: University of Chicago Press, 2009.

Heldke, Lisa M. "Down-Home Global Cooking: A Third Option between Cosmopolitanism and Localism." In *The Philosophy of Food,* edited by David M. Kaplan, 33–51. Berkeley: University of California Press, 2012.

Hennion, Antoine. "Pragmatics of Taste." In *The Blackwell Companion to the Sociology of Culture,* edited by Mark D. Jacobs and Nancy Weiss Hanrahan, 131–44. Oxford: Blackwell, 2004.

Hernández-Ehrisman, Laura. *Inventing the Fiesta City: Heritage and Carnival in San Antonio.* Albuquerque: University of New Mexico Press, 2008.

Highmore, Ben. "Bitter After Taste: Affect, Food, and Social Aesthetics." in *The Affect Theory Reader,* edited by Melissa Gregg and Gregory J. Seigworth, 118–38. Durham, N.C.: Duke University Press, 2010.

Hirsch, Jerrold. "Before Columbia: The FWP and American Oral History Research." *Oral History Review* 34, no. 2 (2007): 1–16.

———. "Cultural Pluralism and Applied Folklore: The New Deal Precedent." In *The Conservation of Culture*, edited by Burt Feintuch. Lexington, Ky.: Publication of the American Folklore Society, 1988.

———. "Folklore in the Making: B. A. Botkin." *Journal of American Folklore.* 100 (1987): 3–38.

———. *Portrait of America: A Cultural History of the Federal Writers' Project.* Chapel Hill: University of North Carolina Press, 2003.

Hobsbawm, Eric J., and Terence O. Ranger. *The Invention of Tradition.* Cambridge: Cambridge University Press, 1983.

Hoganson, Kristin L. *Consumers' Imperium: The Global Production of American Domesticity, 1865–1920.* Chapel Hill: University of North Carolina Press, 2007.

hooks, bell. "Eating the Other: Desire and Resistance." In *Black Looks: Race and Representation*, 21–40. Boston: South End, 1992.

Horowitz, Roger. *Putting Meat on the American Table: Taste, Technology, Transformation.* Baltimore, Md.: Johns Hopkins University Press, 2006.

Howes, David. "Can These Dry Bones Live? An Anthropological Approach to the History of the Senses." *Journal of American History* 95, no. 2 (September 2008): 442–51.

———. "The Expanding Field of Sensory Studies." Available at http://www.sensory studies.org/sensorial-investigations/the-expanding-field-of-sensory-studies (accessed September 10, 2014).

———. *Sensual Relations: Engaging the Senses in Culture and Social Theory.* Ann Arbor: University of Michigan Press, 2003.

———, ed. *The Varieties of Sensory Experience.* Toronto: University of Toronto Press, 1991.

Howes, David, and Constance Classen. *Ways of Sensing: Understanding the Senses in Society.* New York: Routledge, 2013.

Hyde, Anne Farrar. *An American Vision: Far Western Landscape and National Culture, 1820–1920.* New York: New York University Press, 1990.

Iacovetta, Franca. "Immigrant Gifts, Canadian Treasures, and Spectacles of Pluralism: The International Institute of Toronto in North American Context, 1950s–1970s." *Journal of American Ethnic History* 31, no. 1 (Fall 2011): 34–73.

Jacobson, Matthew Frye. *Barbarian Virtues: The United States Encounters Foreign Peoples at Home and Abroad, 1876–1917.* New York: Hill and Wang, 2000.

———. *Roots Too: White Ethnic Revival in Post–Civil Rights America.* Cambridge, Mass.: Harvard University Press, 2008.

———. *Whiteness of a Different Color: European Immigrants and the Alchemy of Race.* Cambridge, Mass.: Harvard University Press, 1999.

Johnston, Josée, and Shyon Baumann. *Foodies: Democracy and Distinction in the Gourmet Foodscape.* Cultural Spaces Series. New York: Routledge, 2009.

Jütte, Robert. *A History of the Senses: From Antiquity to Cyberspace.* Cambridge: Polity, 2005.

Kammen, Michael. *Mystic Chords of Memory: The Transformation of Tradition in American Culture.* New York: Knopf, 1991.

Kaplan, Amy. "Manifest Domesticity." *American Literature* 70, no. 3 (September 1998): 581–606.

Kazin, Michael. *The Populist Persuasion: An American History.* Ithaca, N.Y.: Cornell University Press, 1998.

Kelley, Robin D. G. *Hammer and Hoe: Alabama Communists during the Great Depression.* Chapel Hill: University of North Carolina Press, 1990.

Kennedy, Stetson. "Florida Memory—Zora Neale Hurston, the WPA in Florida, and the Cross City Turpentine Camp." *Florida Memory.* Accessed November 20, 2014. http://floridamemory.com/onlineclassroom/zora_hurston/documents/stetsonkennedy.

———. *The Klan Unmasked.* Originally titled *I Rode with the Ku Klux Klan* (London: Arco, 1954). Tuscaloosa: University of Alabama Press.

———. *Southern Exposure.* Garden City, N.Y.: Doubleday, 1946

Kessler-Harris, Alice. "In the Nation's Image: The Gendered Limits of Social Citizenship in the Depression Era." *Journal of American History* 86, no. 3 (1999): 1251–79.

Kidd, Stuart. "Dissonant Encounters: FSA Photographs and the Southern Underclass 1935–1943." In *Reading Southern Poverty between the Wars, 1918–1939,* edited by Richard Godden and Martin Crawford. Athens: University of Georgia Press, 2006.

Kimmel, Michael S. *Manhood in America: A Cultural History.* New York: Oxford University Press, 2006.

Kirby, Jack Temple. *Media-Made Dixie: The South in the American Imagination.* Athens: University of Georgia Press, 1986.

Kirshenblatt-Gimblett, Barbara. *Destination Culture: Tourism, Museums, and Heritage.* Berkeley: University of California Press, 1998.

Korsmeyer, Carolyn. *Savoring Disgust: The Foul and the Fair in Aesthetics.* New York: Oxford University Press, 2011.

Kropp, Phoebe S. *California Vieja: Culture and Memory in a Modern American Place.* Berkeley: University of California Press, 2006.

Kurashige, Lon. *Japanese American Celebration and Conflict: A History of Ethnic Identity and Festival, 1934–1990.* American Crossroads Series. Berkeley: University of California Press, 2002.

Kurlansky, Mark, and United States Works Progress Administration. *The Food of a Younger Land: A Portrait of American Food before the National Highway System, before Chain Restaurants, and before Frozen Food, When the Nation's Food Was Seasonal, Regional, and Traditional—from the Lost WPA Files.* New York: Riverhead, 2009.

Lee, Erika. *At America's Gates: Chinese Immigration during the Exclusion Era, 1882–1943.* Chapel Hill: University of North Carolina Press, 2003.

Le Sueur, Meridel. "Women on the Breadlines." In *Harvest Song: Collected Essays and Stories,* 166–71. Albuquerque: West End, 1990.

Levenstein, Harvey A. *Paradox of Plenty: A Social History of Eating in Modern America.* Oxford: Oxford University Press, 1994.

———. *Revolution at the Table: The Transformation of the American Diet.* Oxford: Oxford University Press, 1988.

Lewis, David L. *When Harlem Was in Vogue.* New York: Random House, 1981.

Lipsitz, George. *Rainbow at Midnight: Labor and Culture in the 1940s.* Urbana: University of Illinois Press, 1994.

Long, Lucy M. "Culinary Tourism: A Folkloristic Perspective on Eating and Otherness." In *Culinary Tourism,* edited by Lucy M. Long, 20–50. Lexington: University Press of Kentucky, 2004

Longstreth, Richard W. *The Drive-In, the Supermarket, and the Transformation of Commercial Space in Los Angeles, 1914–1941.* Cambridge, Mass.: MIT Press, 1999.

Lott, Eric. *Love and Theft: Blackface Minstrelsy and the American Working Class*. Race and American Culture Series. Oxford: Oxford University Press, 1995.

Macbeth, Helen M., and Jeremy MacClancy. *Researching Food Habits: Methods and Problems*. Anthropology of Food and Nutrition Series. Oxford: Berghahn, 2004.

Madden, Etta M., and Martha L. Finch. *Eating in Eden: Food and American Utopias*. Lincoln: University of Nebraska Press, 2006.

Mangione, Jerre. *The Dream and the Deal: The Federal Writers' Project, 1935–1943*. Boston: Little, Brown, 1972.

Manring, Maurice M. *Slave in a Box: The Strange Career of Aunt Jemima*. American South Series. Charlottesville: University Press of Virginia, 1998.

Marling, Karal Ann. *Wall-to-Wall America: A Cultural History of Post-Office Murals in the Great Depression*. Minneapolis: University of Minnesota Press, 1982.

May, Elaine Tyler. "Cold War–Warm Hearth: Politics and the Family in Postwar America." In Gerstle and Fraser, *Rise and Fall of the New Deal Order*, 153–84.

———. *Homeward Bound: American Families in the Cold War Era*. New York: Basic, 2008.

McClintock, Anne. *Imperial Leather: Race, Gender, and Sexuality in the Colonial Contest*. New York: Routledge, 1995.

McDearma, Karen M., and Nfrances Abbott. "Chitterlings." In *The New Encyclopedia of Southern Culture*, vol. 7: Foodways, edited by John T. Edge, 143–45. Chapel Hill: University of North Carolina Press, 2007.

McElya, Micki. *Clinging to Mammy: The Faithful Slave in Twentieth-Century America*. Cambridge, Mass.: Harvard University Press, 2007.

McGovern, Charles. *Sold American: Consumption and Citizenship, 1890–1945*. Chapel Hill: University of North Carolina Press, 2006.

McWilliams, James E. *A Revolution in Eating: How the Quest for Food Shaped America*. Arts and Traditions of the Table: Perspectives on Culinary History. New York: Columbia University Press, 2005.

Meléndez, Anthony Gabriel. *Spanish-Language Newspapers in New Mexico, 1834–1958*. Tucson: University of Arizona Press, 2005.

Melosh, Barbara. *Engendering Culture: Manhood and Womanhood in New Deal Public Art and Federal Theater*. Washington, D.C.: Smithsonian Institution Press, 1991.

Mendelson, Anne. "Cookbooks and Manuscripts, from World War I to World War II." In *The Oxford Encyclopedia of Food and Drink in America*. New York: Oxford University Press, 2004.

Miller, Hanna. "Identity Takeout: How American Jews Made Chinese Food Their Ethnic Cuisine." *Journal of Popular Culture* 39, no. 3 (June 2006).

Miller, Karl Hagstrom. *Segregating Sound: Inventing Folk and Pop Music in the Age of Jim Crow*. Refiguring American Music Series. Durham, N.C.: Duke University Press, 2010.

Mintz, Sydney "Eating Communities: The Mixed Appeals of Sodality." In *Eating Culture: The Poetics and Politics of Food*, edited by Tobias Döring, Markus Heide, Susanne Muehleisen. American Studies Monograph Series, vol. 106. Heidelberg: Universistatverlag, Winter 2003.

Mitchell, Pablo. *Coyote Nation: Sexuality, Race, and Conquest in Modernizing New Mexico, 1880–1920*. Chicago: University of Chicago Press, 2005.

Mitchell, Timothy. "Economy." In *Keywords for American Cultural Studies*, edited by Bruce Burgett and Glenn Hendler. New York: NYU Press, 2007.

———. "Fixing the Economy." *Cultural Studies* 12, no. 1 (January 1, 1998): 82–101.

———. "Rethinking Economy." *Geoforum* 39, no. 3 (2008): 1116–21.

Montanari, Massimo. "Regional versus National Cuisine in Italy." Paper presented at the annual meeting of the American Historical Association, New Orleans, Louisiana, January 3–6, 2013.

Mosby, Ian. "Administering Colonial Science: Nutrition Research and Human Biomedical Experimentation in Aboriginal Communities and Residential Schools, 1942–1952." *Histoire sociale/Social History* 46, no. 1 (2013): 145–72.

———. *Food Will Win the War: The Politics, Culture, and Science of Food on Canada's Home Front.* Vancouver: University of British Columbia Press, 2014.

Mosley, Damian. "Cooking Up Heritage in Harlem." In *Gastropolis: Food and New York City,* edited by Annie Hauck-Lawson and Jonathan Deutsch, 274–92. New York: Columbia University Press, 2009.

Mullin, Molly H. *Culture in the Marketplace: Gender, Art, and Value in the American Southwest.* Durham, N.C.: Duke University Press, 2001.

Murphy, Mary. *Mining Cultures: Men, Women, and Leisure in Butte, 1914–41.* Women in American History Series. Urbana: University of Illinois Press, 1997.

Nash, Gerald D. *The American West Transformed: The Impact of the Second World War.* Bloomington: Indiana University Press, 1985.

Natanson, Nicholas. *The Black Image in the New Deal: The Politics of FSA Photography.* Knoxville: University of Tennessee Press, 1992.

Nestle, Marion. *Food Politics: How the Food Industry Influences Nutrition and Health.* Berkeley: University of California Press, 2007.

Neuhaus, Jessamyn. *Manly Meals and Mom's Home Cooking: Cookbooks and Gender in Modern America.* Baltimore, Md.: Johns Hopkins University Press, 2003.

Ngai, Mae M. *Impossible Subjects: Illegal Aliens and the Making of Modern America.* Politics and Society in Twentieth-Century America Series. Princeton, N.J.: Princeton University Press, 2004.

Nora, Pierre, and Lawrence D. Kritzman. *Realms of Memory: Rethinking the French Past.* New York: Columbia University Press, 1996.

O'Neill, Rebecca. "'You Say Tomato, I Say Tomahto': Applying the Tools of Food History to the Food Movement Dialogue." *Radical History Review* 2011, no. 110 (March 20, 2011): 161–66.

Ong, Walter J. *Interfaces of the Word: Studies in the Evolution of Consciousness and Culture. 1977.* Reprint, Ithaca, N.Y.: Cornell University Press, 2012.

Opie, Frederick Douglass. *Hog and Hominy: Soul Food from Africa to America.* Arts and Traditions of the Table: Perspectives on Culinary History Series. New York: Columbia University Press, 2008.

Orvell, Miles. *The Real Thing: Imitation and Authenticity in American Culture, 1880–1940.* Cultural Studies of the United States Series. Chapel Hill: University of North Carolina Press, 1989.

Ottley, Roi. *New World A-Coming: Inside Black America.* Boston: Houghton Mifflin, 1943.

Ottley, Roi, and W. J. Weatherby. *The Negro in New York: An Informal Social History, 1626–1940.* New York: Praeger, 1969.

Peiss, Kathy. *Hope in a Jar: The Making of America's Beauty Culture.* New York: Metropolitan, 1998.

Perdue, Charles L., Thomas E. Barden, and Robert K. Phillips. *Weevils in the Wheat: Interviews with Virginia Ex-Slaves.* Charlottesville: University Press of Virginia, 1976.

Peretti, Burton W. *Nightclub City: Politics and Amusement in Manhattan.* Philadelphia: University of Pennsylvania Press, 2007.

Petrick, Gabriella M. "The Arbiters of Taste: Producers, Consumers, and the Industrialization of Taste in America, 1900–1960." Ph.D. diss., University of Delaware, 2007.

Pilcher, Jeffrey M. *Planet Taco: A Global History of Mexican Food.* New York: Oxford University Press, 2012.

———. *Que vivan los tamales! Food and the Making of Mexican Identity.* Dialogos Series. Albuquerque: University of New Mexico Press, 1998.

———. "Tasting the Patria (Chica): Regional and National Culinary Identities in Latin America." Paper presented at the annual meeting of the American Historical Association, New Orleans, Louisiana, January 3–6, 2013.

———. "Tex-Mex, Cal-Mex, New Mex, or Whose Mex? Notes on the Historical Geography of Southwestern Cuisine." *Journal of the Southwest* 43, no. 4 (2001): 659–79.

———. "Was the Taco Invented in Southern California?" *Gastronomica* 8, no. 1 (Winter 2008).

———. "Who Chased Out the 'Chili Queens'? Gender, Race, and Urban Reform in San Antonio, Texas, 1880–1943." *Food and Foodways* 16, no. 3 (2008): 173–200.

Poe, Tracy N. "The Labour and Leisure of Food Production as a Mode of Ethnic Identity Building among Italians in Chicago, 1890–1940." *Rethinking History* 5, no. 1 (2001): 131–48.

———. "The Origins of Soul Food in Black Urban Identity: Chicago, 1915–1947." *American Studies International* 37, no. 1 (1999): 4–34.

Pollan, Michael. *Food Rules: An Eater's Manual.* New York: Penguin, 2009.

Poppendieck, Janet. *Breadlines Knee-Deep in Wheat: Food Assistance in the Great Depression.* California Studies in Food and Culture Series. New Brunswick, N.J.: Rutgers University Press, 1986.

Powell, Lawrence N. "Lyle Saxon and the WPA Guide to New Orleans." *Southern Spaces,* July 29, 2009. Available at http://southernspaces.org/2009/lyle-saxon-and-wpa-guide-new-orleans (accessed February 25, 2014).

Probyn, Elspeth. *Carnal Appetites: FoodSexIdentities.* London: Routledge, 2000.

———. "In the Interests of Taste and Place: Economies of Attachement." In *The Global and the Intimate: Feminism in Our Time,* edited by Geraldine Pratt and Victoria Rosner. New York: Columbia University Press, 2012. 57—84.

Rabinowitz, Paula. *Labor and Desire: Women's Revolutionary Fiction in Depression America.* Chapel Hill: University of North Carolina Press, 1991.

Ray, Krishnendu. "Global Flows, Local Bodies: Dreams of Pakistani Grill in Manhattan." In *Curried Cultures: Globalization, Food, and South Asia,* edited by Krishnendu Ray and Tulasi Srinivas, 175–95. Berkeley: University of California Press, 2012.

Rodgers, Daniel T. *Atlantic Crossings: Social Politics in a Progressive Age.* Cambridge: Belknap/Harvard University Press, 2000.

Roediger, David R. *The Wages of Whiteness: Race and the Making of the American Working Class.* New York: Verso, 1991.

———. *Working toward Whiteness: How America's Immigrants Became White; The Strange Journey from Ellis Island to the Suburbs.* New York: Basic, 2005.

Rosa, Alfred F. "The Novels of Mari Tomasi." *Italian Americana* 2, no. 1 (1975): 66.

Rosaldo, Renato. "Imperialist Nostalgia," *Representation* 26 (Spring 1989): 108.

Rothman, Hal, ed. *The Culture of Tourism, the Tourism of Culture: Selling the Past to the Present in the American Southwest.* Albuquerque: University of New Mexico Press, 2003.

Ruíz, Vicki. *Cannery Women, Cannery Lives: Mexican Women, Unionization, and the California Food Processing Industry, 1930–1950.* Albuquerque: University of New Mexico Press, 1987.

———. *From Out of the Shadows: Mexican Women in Twentieth-Century America.* New York: Oxford University Press, 1998.

Ruíz, Vicki L., and Virginia Sánchez Korrol. *Latinas in the United States: A Historical Encyclopedia.* 3 vols. Bloomington: Indiana University Press, 2006.

Russek, Audrey. "Appetites without Prejudice: U.S. Foreign Restaurants and the Globalization of American Food between the Wars." *Food and Foodways* 19, no. 1–2 (2011): 34–55.

Sanchez, George J. *Becoming Mexican American: Ethnicity, Culture, and Identity in Chicano Los Angeles, 1900–1945.* New York: Oxford University Press, 1993.

Schindler-Carter, Petra. *Vintage Snapshots: The Fabrication of a Nation in the W.P.A. American Guide Series.* New York: Lang, 1999.

Selig, Diana. *Americans All: The Cultural Gifts Movement.* Cambridge, Mass.: Harvard University Press, 2008.

Shaffer, Marguerite S. "Playing American: The Southwestern Scrapbooks of Mildred E. Baker." In Rothman, *Culture of Tourism,* 72–100.

———. *See America First: Tourism and National Identity, 1880–1940.* Washington, D.C.: Smithsonian Books, 2001.

Shah, Nayan. *Contagious Divides: Epidemics and Race in San Francisco's Chinatown.* American Crossroads Series. Berkeley: University of California Press, 2001.

Shapiro, Laura. *Perfection Salad: Women and Cooking at the Turn of the Century.* New York: Farrar, Straus, and Giroux, 1986.

Sharpless, Rebecca. *Cooking in Other Women's Kitchens: Domestic Workers in the South, 1865–1960.* John Hope Franklin Series in African American History and Culture. Chapel Hill: University of North Carolina Press, 2010.

Shortridge, Barbara Gimla, and James R. Shortridge. *The Taste of American Place: A Reader on Regional and Ethnic Foods.* Oxford: Rowman and Littlefield, 1998.

Silber, Nina. *The Romance of Reunion: Northerners and the South, 1865–1900.* Chapel Hill: University of North Carolina Press, 1993.

Sitkoff, Harvard. *A New Deal for Blacks: The Emergence of Civil Rights as a National Issue; The Depression Decade.* New York: Oxford University Press, 2009.

Sklaroff, Lauren Rebecca. *Black Culture and the New Deal: The Quest for Civil Rights in the Roosevelt Era.* Chapel Hill: University of North Carolina Press, 2009.

Slotkin, Richard. *Gunfighter Nation: The Myth of the Frontier in Twentieth-Century America.* Norman: University of Oklahoma Press, 1992.

Smith, Mark M. *How Race Is Made: Slavery, Segregation, and the Senses.* Chapel Hill: University of North Carolina, 2008.

———. "Producing Sense, Consuming Sense, Making Sense: Perils and Prospects for Sensory History." *Journal of Social History* 40, no. 4 (Summer 2007): 841–58.

———. *Sensing the Past: Seeing, Hearing, Smelling, Tasting, and Touching in History.* Berkeley: University of California Press, 2007.

Spang, Rebecca L. *The Invention of the Restaurant: Paris and Modern Gastronomic Culture.* Harvard Historical Studies. Cambridge, Mass.: Harvard University Press, 2000.

Spencer, Charles. *Edisto Island, 1861 to 2006: Ruin, Recovery and Rebirth.* Charleston, S.C.: History Press, 2008.

Stanonis, Anthony J. *Dixie Emporium: Tourism, Foodways, and Consumer Culture in the American South.* Athens: University of Georgia Press, 2008.

Stoever-Ackerman, Jennifer. "Splicing the Sonic Color-Line: Tony Schwartz Remixes Postwar Nueva York." *Social Text* 28, no. 1 102 (Spring 2010): 59–85.

Stoler, Ann Laura. *Along the Archival Grain: Epistemic Anxieties and Colonial Common Sense.* Princeton, N.J.: Princeton University Press, 2009.

———. *Carnal Knowledge and Imperial Power: Race and the Intimate in Colonial Rule.* Berkeley: University of California Press, 2002.

———, ed., *Haunted by Empire: Geographies of Intimacy in North American History.* American Encounters/Global Interaction Series. Durham, N.C.: Duke University Press, 2006.

Stott, William. *Documentary Expression and Thirties America.* New York: Oxford University Press, 1973.

Strasser, Susan. *Satisfaction Guaranteed: The Making of the American Mass Market.* Washington, D.C.: Smithsonian Books, 2004.

Sugrue, Thomas J. *The Origins of the Urban Crisis: Race and Inequality in Postwar Detroit.* Princeton, N.J.: Princeton University Press, 1996.

Susman, Warren. *Culture as History: The Transformation of American Culture in the Twentieth Century.* New York: Pantheon, 1984.

Sutton, David E. *Remembrance of Repasts: An Anthropology of Food and Memory.* Materializing Culture Series. New York: Berg, 2001.

Swislocki, Mark. *Culinary Nostalgia: Regional Food Culture and the Urban Experience in Shanghai.* Stanford, Calif.: Stanford University Press, 2009.

Szalay, Michael. *New Deal Modernism: American Literature and the Invention of the Welfare State.* Post-Contemporary Interventions Series. Durham, N.C.: Duke University Press, 2000.

Theophano, Janet. *Eat My Words: Reading Women's Lives through the Cookbooks They Wrote.* New York: Palgrave, 2002.

Titus, Mary. "'Groaning Tables' and 'Spit in the Kettles': Food and Race in the Nineteenth-Century South." *Southern Quarterly* 44 (Spring 1992): 13–21

Tompkins, Kyla Wazana. *Racial Indigestion: Eating Bodies in the 19th Century.* American and the Long 19th Century Series. New York: New York University Press, 2012.

Trachtenberg, Alan. *Reading American Photographs: Images as History, Mathew Brady to Walker Evans.* New York: Hill and Wang, 1989.

Trubek, Amy B. "Radical Taste: What Is Our Future?" *Radical History Review* 2011, no. 110 (Spring 2011): 192–96.

Veit, Helen Zoe. *Modern Food, Moral Food: Self-Control, Science, and the Rise of Modern American Eating in the Early Twentieth Century.* Chapel Hill: University of North Carolina Press, 2013.

Walsh, Robb. "The Authenticity Myth." *Houston Press*, October 26, 2000. Available at http://www.houstonpress.com/2000-10-26/dining/the-authenticity-myth/full (accessed November 2, 2010).

———. "Combination Plates." *Houston Press*, August 31, 2000. Available at http://www .houstonpress.com/2000-08-31/dining/combination-plates/full (accessed November 2, 2010).

———. "The French Connection." *Houston Press*, November 23, 2000. Available at http:// www.houstonpress.com/2000-11-23/dining/the-french-connection/full (accessed November 2, 2010).

———. "Mama's Got a Brand-new Bag." *Houston Press*, September 28, 2000. Available at http://www.houstonpress.com/2000-09-28/dining/mama-s-got-a-brand-new-bag/full (accessed November 2, 2010).

———. "Pralines and Pushcarts," *Houston Press*, July 27, 2000. Available at http://www .houstonpress.com/2000-07-27/dining/pralines-and-pushcarts/full (accessed November 2, 2010).

———. *Tex-Mex Cookbook: A History in Recipes and Photos*. New York: Broadway, 2004.

Ware, Susan. *Holding Their Own: American Women in the 1930s*. American Women in the Twentieth Century. Boston: Twayne, 1982.

Warnes, Andrew. *Savage Barbecue: Race, Culture, and the Invention of America's First Food*. Athens: University of Georgia Press, 2008.

Wayne, Beatrice. "Migrant Women's Modernity: Food, Culture, and Women in Interwar Harlem." Paper delivered at the annual meeting of the American Historical Association, Chicago, Illinois, January 5–9, 2012.

Weigle, Marta, and Fiore, Kyle. *Santa Fe and Taos: The Writer's Era, 1916–1941*. Santa Fe, N.M.: Sunstone, 2008.

Whisnant, David E. *All That Is Native and Fine: The Politics of Culture in an American Region*. Chapel Hill: University of North Carolina Press, 1983.

White, Ann Folino. *Plowed Under: Food Policy Protests and Performance in New Deal America*. Bloomington: Indiana University Press, 2014.

Williams, Raymond. *Keywords: A Vocabulary of Culture and Society*. New York: Oxford University Press, 1985.

Williams-Forson, Psyche A. *Building Houses Out of Chicken Legs: Black Women, Food, and Power*. Chapel Hill: University of North Carolina Press, 2006.

Wilson, Chris. *The Myth of Santa Fe: Creating a Modern Regional Tradition*. Albuquerque: University of New Mexico Press, 1997.

Wilson, Sarah. *Melting-Pot Modernism*. Ithaca, N.Y.: Cornell University Press, 2010.

Witt, Doris. *Black Hunger: Food and the Politics of U.S. Identity*. Race and American Culture Series. New York: Oxford University Press, 1999.

Woodward, C. Vann. *Origins of the New South: 1877–1913*. Baton Rouge: Louisiana State University Press, 1951.

———. *The Strange Career of Jim Crow*. New York: Oxford University Press, 1966.

Wright, Richard. *Native Son*. New York: Harper Perennial Modern Classic, 2005.

Wrobel, David M., and Long, Patrick T., eds. *Seeing and Being Seen: Tourism in the American West*. Lawrence: University Press of Kansas, 2001.

Yoder, Don. "Folk Cookery." In *Folklore and Folklife: An Introduction*, edited by Richard Mercer Dorson, 326–350. Chicago: University of Chicago Press, 1972.

Index

CAMILLE BÉGIN is a Social Sciences and Humanities Research Council postdoctoral fellow at the Centre for Sensory Studies at Concordia University in Montreal.

Studies in Sensory History

The University of Illinois Press
is a founding member of the
Association of American University Presses.

Composed in 10.5/13 Adobe Minion Pro
at the University of Illinois Press
Manufactured by Sheridan Books, Inc.

University of Illinois Press
1325 South Oak Street
Champaign, IL 61820-6903
www.press.uillinois.edu